# PRAISE FOR DAVID L

"Sanity is a great attribute, and this book, ι
are sympathy, calm reflection, objectivity or pι
ated by the war, but *Vietnam, Now* has those qualities too. . . . There are stories in this
book that you will not forget." — *Washington Post*

"What comes through in these pages is the work of an older and wiser reporter, as well
as a master storyteller, with a keen eye for detail. [Lamb] offers a vibrant and at times
poignant portrait of a country in the midst of change and a people—the young for the
most part—yearning to breathe free." — *Baltimore Sun*

"*Vietnam, Now* offers a tantalizing glimpse of this new kind of relationship between
East and West." — *Los Angeles Times*

"David Lamb is a master at making nations far away from the United States accessible
to stay-at-home readers. As a widely traveled *Los Angeles Times* reporter, Lamb managed
to capture the essences of non-American cultures in *The Africans* and *The Arabs*. Now he
has done the same for Vietnam." — *St. Louis Post-Dispatch*

"An impressive recounting of the complexities of life today in the country whose name
has too long been associated only with war in the minds of many Americans." —*Seattle
Post-Intelligencer*

"Fascinating . . . [Lamb] skillfully intertwines stories of the past from all sides of the
conflict with a vision of the future." — *Rocky Mountain News*

"Such a book offers chances to set history straight; the author does so." — *Associated Press*

"A serious, comprehensive, contemporary look at the country about which it seems we
cannot speak without some reference to war. . . . Worthy to be placed in the Vietnam
canon." — *The Asian Reporter*

"Part memoir, part historical narrative, part travelogue, part journalism, Lamb's worthy
effort is a personality-driven look at Vietnam today." — *Publishers Weekly*

"A truly magnificent book and the first ever to accurately capture Vietnam as it is today. . . . A must read not just for Vietnam watchers, but also for all those still searching for
personal reconciliation or seeking an understanding of our conflict there in the '60s and
'70s." — Ambassador Peter Peterson

"Americans discovered Vietnam during the tragic war there more than a generation
ago. Now David Lamb rediscovers the country in a vivid, perceptive, elucidating narrative
that is bound to rank among the major books on the subject." — Stanley Karnow

ALSO BY DAVID LAMB

*The Africans*
*The Arabs*
*Stolen Season*
*A Sense of Place*
*Over the Hills*

# VIETNAM, NOW

## NOW

{ *A Reporter Returns*

DAVID LAMB

**PublicAffairs**
*New York*

Published in the United States by PublicAffairs™,
a member of the Perseus Books Group.

Printed in the United States of America.

*Book design by Jane Raese*

Library of Congress Cataloging-in-Publication data
Lamb, David, 1940–
p.   cm.
ISBN 1-58648-183-5
1. Vietnam—Description and travel. 2. Vietnam—History—1975–. I. Title.
DS556.39 .L35 2002
959.704′4—DC21
2001059155

10 9 8 7 6 5 4 3 2 1

FOR SANDY

*With whom I shared the adventure side by side,*
*as I have so many others*

# CONTENTS

Introduction   1

1}   Hanoi: City on the Bend in the River   7

2}   One Family   25

3}   The Making of Vietnam   39

4}   Saigon: From Wartime Turmoil to Peacetime Prosperity   57

5}   Reflections on the Fall of Saigon   73

6}   In Search of a Peace Dividend   93

7}   The Ups and Downs of *Doi Moi*   111

8}   Who Runs Vietnam?   129

9}   Awaiting the Passing of the Torch   151

10}   The Painful Art of Reconciliation   171

11} The Missing   191

12} The Viet Kieu: Strong Brains, Deep Pockets   211

13} The Road South   233

14} Closure   253


*Acknowledgments*   271

*Photo Credits*   273

# INTRODUCTION

VIETNAM WAS NEVER PART OF THE GAME PLAN. It is one of those places that just crept into my life, like a stranger come to call, and I had no aim of ever making it more than a stop in the road. But Vietnam's seasons drifted into years, nearly six of them in all, and one day when a bartender in Thailand saw me with a plane ticket in hand and asked where I was headed, I replied, "Home." "You mean the United States?" he asked. "No," I said. "Hanoi." That was the moment, I think, I realized Indochina had captured the soul of another unwary suspect. Vietnam was no longer just my mail drop. It was where I thought of home as being, and it seemed odd that I could feel so at peace in a land I once disliked so intensely.

The Vietnam I experienced was really two different countries, and neither had much to do with the other. The first was the Vietnam of the American War, as the Vietnamese call it, which I covered for United Press International in the late 1960s. It was the Vietnam of body counts and illusionary lights at the end of the tunnel. It was a Vietnam that, I now realize, I understood shamefully little about, being largely ignorant of the country's history, culture, and people. I encountered Vietnamese people but I did not make Vietnamese friends. I joined homesick GIs singing "Danny Boy" and "I Left My Heart in San Francisco" over beers in lonely outposts cut from the jungle, but I never read a line of Vietnamese poetry or knew what songs the Vietnamese sang when they were melancholy. I left that Vietnam—and the war—without a shred of remorse and cared not if I ever saw the wretched country again. I got on with my life.

The other Vietnam is the one that wove the spell and teased me with the ghosts of a bygone Indochina, the one that will forever stir memories of quiet nights dripping with humidity, of golden rice paddies stretching to the mountains, and of an industrious people who have survived, and in some cases even prospered, against all odds. This is the postwar Vietnam, where for the first time in more than 100 years a generation has grown into adulthood not knowing foreign domination or the sound of battle. It is a country that, for me, was born in 1997, when I moved to Hanoi—the "enemy capital" as we used to call it—to open the *Los Angeles Times*'s first peacetime bureau in Vietnam. I stayed four years, far longer than I had intended, and during all that time I found that nothing was quite as I had expected it to be.

Like most Americans, I let Vietnam fade from my radar screen after the Saigon government fell to Hanoi's communist troops in April 1975. Vietnam was a war, not a country, and somehow it was comforting to just let the place be, to retain little of it in the mind's eye except that black-and-white image of a CH-46 chopper lifting off from the roof of the U.S. Embassy, the U.S. ambassador—who had insisted to the eleventh hour and beyond that South Vietnam could be saved from communism—seat-belted and staring straight ahead, the U.S. flag folded and in his lap, while U.S. Marines fired tear gas to cover the retreat and hold a riotous mob of former allies at bay in the streets below.

So my return to Vietnam was not so much the rediscovery of a country as the discovery of a new landscape. Many of my new friends were former North Vietnamese soldiers. Some of the people who welcomed me into their homes had lost two or three sons fighting the Americans—and often, before that, a relative or two fighting the French. Not once was I received with anything less than graciousness. I met writers and teachers and students and laborers and entrepreneurs, and almost everyone—except the Old Guard who was scared stiff by the thought of losing its iron-tight grip on power—knew Vietnam was adrift, a communist state floundering in a noncommunist world. Still, exciting changes were transforming the country. Everywhere I went, from Sapa on the Chinese border to Dien Bien Phu on Laos's doorstep to Can Tho in the clutches of the Mekong Delta, the energy and optimism of the postwar generation were palpable.

What I have written in the pages that follow I believe to be true because it is what I saw and heard and felt. But I have my biases, and—being neither a historian nor an academic—I make no apologies. In returning to Vietnam it was not my intent to spend a lot of time rehashing the war. The history, the polemics, and the U.S. role have been ably assessed and reassessed by many others. I was more interested in what had happened to Vietnam and the Vietnamese people in the years since the shooting stopped. And I still am today, though I quickly learned you cannot write about Vietnam without talking about the war any more than you can write about Saudi Arabia without talking about oil. A thousand years of conflict—against China, France, Japan, the United States, Cambodia, and among one another—is what made the Vietnamese who they are. It is what shaped their character and steeled their spirit. And the war, of course, is why Vietnam still exerts a hold on the soul of America. Just when we think we've buried all those damn memories, up they pop again, as though that brief chapter of our history was always there, lurking just below the surface. In the end, the war played a larger role in my discovery of Vietnam than I thought it would, as did the question of reconciliation, between North and South Vietnam and between the peoples of Vietnam and the United States.

Vietnam, with a population of 80 million, is the world's thirteenth most populous country. Sixty percent of the Vietnamese were born after the last Americans went home in 1975. In spite of—rather than because of—communism, their standard of living has risen dramatically in the past decade, but given Vietnam's great natural resources and its clever, persevering workforce, I know of no other country where the gap between potential and performance is so great. Vietnam remains one of the world's poorest countries. The majority of its people get by on the equivalent of a dollar a day. Most of them—living in the countryside, home to 80 percent of the population—have never been in a bank, seen an escalator, or had access to a flush toilet. It was surprising they didn't complain more. Perhaps the silence of stoicism was the offspring of long struggle and suffering.

The Vietnamese taught me many things: about patience, the value of forgiveness, the strength of community, and family. General William Westmoreland was asked in 1966 about the enormous losses North Vietnam was enduring: "Oh yes," he replied, "but you must understand that they are Asians, and they don't really think about death the way we do. They accept it very fatalistically." That is not what I found to be true at all. But his response did strike a universal chord of truth: Understanding no culture but one's own leads down a dangerous path. As far as I could tell, America's military leadership never had the vaguest idea who the Vietnamese of the North were, what motivated them, or what the limits of their endurance were. We said "so what?"—the Vietnamese were inconsequential except for the niche they had claimed in our wartime history.

A reader of the *Times* wrote after I'd been in Hanoi awhile and asked me to suggest some books on Vietnam worth reading. I offered three—books about the society and culture and history written from the Vietnamese perspective. She went to a university bookshop in New York City and was surprised not to find a single book on Vietnam in any of the

likely sections. She asked the clerk why the store didn't carry Vietnam titles. "Oh, we do, lots of them," the clerk replied. "They're under American history."

We claimed the history and the pain of the war as ours exclusively. The
Vietnam Veterans Memorial wall in Washington became the symbol of
all we had lost. We return to it time and again, to reflect, to mourn, to
heal. The names chiseled into the black granite were the story of the war.
But surely there was more to it than that. Surely one question remained
to be asked: What happened on the other side of the wall?

# HANOI

*City on the Bend in the River*

HANOI IS A GREAT NAME TO DROP AT COCKTAIL PARTIES. I couldn't resist doing it on my occasional trips back to the United States. I'd just let it slip out casually: *I was biking to work in Hanoi the other day and. . . .* The reaction was always the same. The conversation would stop and people would cock their heads and raise their eyebrows. You could hear them thinking, Hanoi? Hanoi? *That* Hanoi? I might as well have said I lived on Mars. They'd say they were surprised that Americans lived in Hanoi. They'd ask if the city had been rebuilt after the war, and they'd wonder aloud what it was like to live in a place where Americans surely were hated. Even my editors at the *Los Angeles Times* were decent enough to compensate me for perceived hardship, with two week-long R&R's a year in Bangkok to tend to medical needs and find a bookstore that offered more than an account of France's defeat at Dien Bien Phu or the writings of Ho Chi Minh. I enjoyed being an object of curiosity. It made me feel unordinary. Back in Washington, I knew I'd be just another working stiff riding the subway to work and worrying about my mortgage.

But in Hanoi I'd stumbled into a life that was beyond the grasp of friends and strangers alike, and there is something to be said for being a big frog in small pond. So for four years I more or less kept my secret. Yes, I'd say, Hanoi is difficult. Not a shopping mall or a supermarket in the entire city. Chaotic, noisy two-wheel traffic jams that will drive you batty. If you need a root canal, it's best to catch one of the daily flights to Singapore or Bangkok. But the truth is that life was good without stores that sell forty brands of toothpaste. What I discovered was a magical city, steeped in beauty and seductive charm, the last capital left possessing the romance of a bygone Indochina. Were Graham Greene alive today to explore the niches of remembered places, I have no doubt that Hanoi is where he would head in a heartbeat.

There were many moments in those first weeks in Hanoi when my past and present, separated by a generation, mingled as one. What I saw and learned, initially at least, was situated in the context of what I had experienced in the war and what I perceived Hanoi to be. Everything seemed out of place. I felt disconnected awakening some mornings and realizing I lived in a city whose bombing I had once cheered, believing its destruction was the road to peace. I was reticent to ask Vietnamese what their lives had been like during the war and its aftermath, until I discovered they had the same curiosity about me; they wondered what had brought me to wartime Vietnam in the first place.

I was twenty-eight years old and working the graveyard shift in San Francisco for United Press International in 1968, expending a lot of energy covering antiwar demonstrations. I more or less supported the U.S. intervention in Vietnam, not because of any deeply held political convictions but because I thought that whenever and wherever America went to war, the honorable thing was to jump on the bandwagon. My military obligations had been fulfilled—two years in the peacetime army in Okinawa—so I was off the hook on Vietnam, at least as a soldier. But I couldn't imagine why any journalist wouldn't want to go there. I had quit my job at the *Oakland Tribune* and joined UPI across the bay because the wire services offered a better shot at getting to Vietnam. When I told my older brother Ernie in Boston that I'd asked UPI to send me to Vietnam, he said: "You dumb shit! They'll do it." Months went by with no encouragement and no word from UPI's foreign desk in New York. Then one morning the San Francisco bureau chief called me at home. He said, "I've got a telex for you from Cactus Jack, the foreign editor. It says, 'Tell Lamb his number is up for Vietnam. We want him there in two weeks. Ask him to write a 200-word bio so when he wins a prize, we can give him his due.'" I was savvy enough to realize he was asking me to write my own obituary.

My pay in wartime Vietnam was $135 per week, no days off, no overtime, no hazardous-duty pay. For most of my two years covering the war, I worked out of Danang, where the U.S. Marine Corps had taken over an old French riverside brothel and turned it into a press camp, with a dozen austere rooms, flush toilets, a bar, a restaurant, and a colonel who could put the American spin on the vicissitudes of war. Like most of the wire guys, I was a grunt reporter, not one of the stars. My job was to get into the field, find out what was happening, and call Bert Oakley in Saigon to pass on news for his daily lead. "Don't forget who told you this," I'd say to Oakley, hoping he'd give me a byline.

Covering the war made me happy in an unhappy sort of way. I hated everything about it yet loved the exhilarating adrenaline rush that engulfed me. I thought a lot about death and dying. I felt fulfilled and empty at the same time, lonely even though sharing the life and death of war is intensely intimate. I really didn't think much about the rightness or wrongness of the war, and I never agreed with U.S. troop commander

General Creighton Abrams's dismissive assessment of reporters: "They're all a bunch of shits," he said. The relative handful of war correspondents I knew—5,000 reporters and photographers from sixty countries covered the decade-long war at various times—were honorable, spirited men and women whose company I enjoyed. They accepted risk, liked adventure, and had no agenda other than to report accurately. General William Westmoreland referred to Vietnam in his memoirs as "the first war in history lost in the columns of the *New York Times*." But reporters didn't lose the war any more than they won the 1968 presidential election. We were only messengers.

My return to Vietnam in 1997 came twenty-nine years to the week of my first landing at Saigon's Tan Son Nhut Airport. Back then a sign in the terminal had warned: "In case of mortar attack don't panic, don't run. Lay on the floor and cover your head with your hands." Now the walls of Hanoi's Noi Bai Airport were covered with posters advertising a new casino and serviced lakeside luxury apartments. A Hong Kong research company had ranked Vietnam as the most economically secure (low-crime) and politically stable of the fourteen Asian countries it had studied.

As before, this time I arrived during the heat of summer. Puddles of rainwater sizzled on the tarmac. I recognized, from long ago, the sweet fragrance that drifted out of the rice paddies. A pig the size of a Volkswagen ambled across the runway. My wife, Sandy, and I went to claim our two cats that had traveled with us, and a passenger confided in a hushed voice, "They eat cats here, you know." The customs man seemed bored. He sat at an empty desk with no phone or paperwork and was in no hurry to release our jet-lagged cats. He wanted to know what we intended to do with them. Sandy said we were just going to let them hang out in the apartment and keep us company. The man looked puzzled. We negotiated at length. Some money changed hands. An hour later, baggage and pets in hand, we were crammed into an old taxi. We bumped along the road that leads from Noi Bai Airport, creeping through villages clogged with bicycles and past fields where peasants stood knee-deep in muck, tossing buckets of water onto their crops. Forty-five minutes ahead lay Hanoi, where we had no office, no home, no telephone, and no friends. Together we stood at the threshold of a new life.

{{{    }}}

EVERY YEAR A MAGAZINE called *Asiaweek* rates the livability of Asia's top forty cities; Hanoi tied for seventeenth place, but I think it deserves a better ranking. One criterion the publication uses is TV sets per 1,000 residents. Hanoi ranks number two in all of Asia on that score, with 765 (three times more than Tokyo). I'm not sure the saturation of television has much to do with quality of life, but it does indicate how dramatically living standards in Vietnam have risen in recent years—and that most Vietnamese don't have a lot of free-time diversions other than to turn up their TVs full blast and sit mesmerized by a soccer game or romantic soap opera. In another *Asiaweek* category, hospital beds per 1,000 people, Hanoi ranks near the bottom with 1.6. The magazine left blank the ranking for vehicles per kilometer of city road because, I presume, it doesn't count motor scooters as vehicles and Hanoi's narrow streets are still relatively empty of cars. Many of the motorcycles are smuggled in from China, anyway, and there wouldn't be any accurate way to count them.

If *Asiaweek* had a category for likability of people—surely a legitimate measure of a city's livability—Hanoi would have topped the survey hands down. Within a week of our arrival, Sandy and I had been invited to dine at the home of a former North Vietnamese soldier, taken by a journalist to a sidewalk stall for a fifty-cent bowl of *pho*, a noodle soup the Vietnamese eat as regularly as Americans do hamburgers, and befriended by a miniplatoon of college students who wanted to practice English and learn more about the world. During my first peacetime encounters with the Vietnamese, what struck me was the smile. Faces aglow, their smiles seemed natural and spontaneous, not a forced, mechanical flash of politeness but rather an expression straight from the heart. A European businessman told me he had rejected a posting in China for one in Vietnam because "in China people are distant and somber. They frown all the time. In Vietnam, I walk out my door in the morning, and people are smiling. They make you feel welcome. They're approachable. They act as though life's pretty good. That's a big plus at the end of the day."

Sandy and I found an apartment overlooking Truc Bach (White Bamboo), the smallest of Hanoi's eleven lakes, in a neighborhood called Ngu Xa. The neighborhood felt like a village, built on a small peninsula that jutted into the water. Starting in the sixteenth century, bronze casters from five villages northeast of Hanoi started making their way to Ngu Xa, and for the next 300 years the finest bells, Buddha statues, and incense urns adorning the pagodas and royal palaces were made in the alleyways outside my doorstep. "Even fireflies have to enjoy the kindling fire of the bronze-casting furnaces," the poet Nguyen Huy Lyong wrote in 1801 in a salute to Ngu Xa's bustling activity.

Over the years the lanes became streets that crisscrossed like rows on a checkerboard, and most of the bronze-casting families turned their attention to working in silver and making aluminum pots and pans and plaster busts of Ho Chi Minh. But Ngu Xa never lost its Vietnamese flavor or became, even during French colonial times, home to more than a handful of foreigners. Only a few families still cast bronze Buddhas in Ngu Xa today, and the *tap, tap, tap* of their tools is a reassuring sound, reminding me that much remains as it was even though Hanoi is gripped by great change.

Although the banks of the Red River have been inhabited for thousands of years, Hanoi's history dates back only to 1010, when the emperor Ly Thai To moved the capital sixty miles from Hoa Lu to a site not far from our apartment. He named the town Thang Long (Soaring Dragon) and ordered the building of dikes and artificial hills to protect his dynasty from invading Chinese. The dikes held the floods at bay but not the Mongols, who sacked the city in the late thirteenth century. Emperor Le

Loi pushed the Chinese out in 1428 and renamed the capital Dong Kinh, which the French later corrupted to Tonkin.

Western traders—Dutch, Portuguese, French—began arriving in the early seventeenth century, and hot on their heels came Jesuit missionaries followed by the Paris Foreign Missions. The town fell into decline and the imperial court was moved to Hue. In 1831, Emperor Tu Duc renamed the old capital Hanoi, or "City on the Bend in the River"—*ha* means "river" and *noi* means "inside"—and set about restoring some of the old splendors. His timing was bad, for France was looking for alternate trade routes to ship goods from China to the Mekong, and Hanoi's location on the right bank of the Red River—at a wide, sweeping bend—offered strategic control of the entire northern delta. Paris sent Francis Garnier and a small expeditionary force to Hanoi in 1873 to reconnoiter. They did their evaluations and then—offering the unlikely explanation that they feared attack—destroyed the Hanoi Citadel. Tu Duc, stunned at how much Garnier had accomplished with so few men, acceded to French demands. Nine years later Hanoi became the capital of France's new protectorate, Tonkin. Vietnam would remain under foreign domination for nine decades, that is, until the Americans fled Saigon in 1975.

The expatriate community I found in Hanoi numbered only a few thousand, small for a capital with 3 million residents. But unlike other places in the developing world I'd lived, I didn't hear much complaining. The Westerners lived in Vietnam by choice. Their lives were more exotic and unpredictable—and, I suspect, interesting—than they would have been back in New York or Sydney. In Cairo and Nairobi, where I once lived, longtime expats used to lament the state of decay and yearn for a past era. "You should have seen the place back *then*," they'd say wistfully. In Hanoi, foreign residents talked about the present as being the good days. They had encountered Hanoi at the perfect moment—after the long, dark years of isolation that followed the Vietnam War and before the city succumbed to the inevitable rush of bulldozed development that had already stripped other Southeast Asia capitals of their charm.

The first change that Hanoi wrought in me was making life simpler. Back in the States, my key chain bulged with a dozen keys to double-bolted house doors, two cars, alarm systems, padlocked windows, a bike lock, a security door to the office. Now it held only two, one to our apartment, the other to the *Times* bureau. I didn't make notes at night on what I had to do the next day, and my office answering machine didn't blink with a score of voicemails if I left for a few hours. I owned a bicycle but no car. And I could safely walk any street at any hour of the day or night. Because civilians didn't own guns and the military didn't abuse guns, the crime rate was negligible, even by the standard of the tamest U.S. city. That, too, made life simpler, giving me an unfamiliar sense of freedom and well-being.

I had never lived in a communist country before, and although everything was new, nothing felt so alien as to be unsettling. There were no soldiers on the streets and few policemen. No one paid much attention to the red banners with slogans that the Communist Party occasionally hung across a street, and the man from the People's Committee who used to wander my neighborhood, keeping an eye on foreigners, never caused me any trouble.

Busts of Ho Chi Minh—"Uncle Ho," as the Vietnamese call him—were everywhere, in shops and homes and offices, and every day thousands of Vietnamese lined up outside his mausoleum in Hanoi's Ba Dinh Square, the place where he had declared Vietnam's short-lived independence in 1945. Inside they would file solemnly past the open coffin containing the eerie corpse of Ho, waxen-looking, not a hair of his stringy beard out of place. They carried children and whispered not a word. Many wept quietly.

Ho had asked that no monuments be built in his honor and that he be cremated, with his ashes sprinkled on three unmarked hilltops around the country. He wanted trees planted where his ashes lay because they would "multiply with the passage of time and form forests." If he died before the end of the war against the United States, he said, it would please him if some of his ashes were sent to the "compatriots in the South."

But Party leaders had no intention of allowing their most important symbol of struggle and nationalism to slip from public consciousness. When Ho died in 1969, at the age of seventy-nine, with the war still raging, his body was secretly whisked to a farming town thirty miles from Hanoi. He was embalmed by Russian technicians and the town was placed off-limits. He was not seen by the public again until 1975, the year the war ended, when the Party put him on display in the recently completed mausoleum, modeled after Lenin's Mausoleum in Moscow's Red Square. No doubt Ho, an unpretentious man who lived modestly and never cared about wealth or pomp, would have been appalled by the ornate marble-and-granite edifice. But it is impossible to look at this small, fragile man who lies under glass, his brown suit without a crease, his pale face relaxed as though in sleep, without remembering how much he influenced the lives of those of us who lived through the Vietnam War era.

One of my neighbors in Ngu Xa was Mai Van On. He lived in a lakeside shanty—his home as long as he could remember—with his wife of forty-two years, two unemployed adult sons, and several grandchildren. The house was small and dark with no electricity or running water. On had retired from his factory job on a pension of $18 per month, enough to barely eke by, and except for one day in October 1967 he had led a cautious, uneventful life.

On that eventful day, On was working with the volunteer militia guarding Truc Bach. The dike road on the lake's western shore was lined with antiaircraft batteries. When they began firing and the Soviet-made surface-to-air missiles (SAMs) screamed skyward, locked on to the silvery images of approaching U.S. warplanes, On dove into a bunker. He hated such raids. They terrified him, and sometimes he would shake for an hour after calm had returned. One of the missiles struck the right wing of a plane piloted by U.S. Navy Lieutenant Commander John McCain. The Skyhawk fighter-bomber plummeted into the lake, 100 yards from where my apartment building now stood, followed moments later by the parachute that carried the semiconscious McCain, the future Arizona senator and Republican presidential candidate.

"I still don't know why I did what I did," said On, a frail, paper-thin man of more than eighty years. He stroked his wispy Ho Chi Minh beard as though that might help him offer a plausible explanation. "Sometimes you do things without thinking. It has nothing to do with being a hero or a coward. You just act, not thinking if you're doing right or wrong."

Before he knew it, On was in the water, clinging to a bamboo pole and paddling toward the injured pilot, who was tangled in, and weighted down by, his heavy gear and was in danger of drowning. On, with several others, pulled McCain to shore. An angry crowd poured out of the small brick homes once owned by Ngu Xa's bronze casters and beat McCain with rifle butts and sticks. "Please don't kill him," On pleaded with the mob. "He is nearly dead already. We must turn him in." The frenzied shouting dulled to a murmur. The crowd backed away and the police arrived to cart McCain to prison, where he would spend five years as a prisoner of war (POW).

On had gathered up the rope from McCain's parachute. He could think of a hundred uses for it in his home. As the police were leaving, one of the officers turned back to claim the rope. "It belongs to the state," On remembers him saying. At the factory On's fellow workers accorded him a hero's reception, applauding him enthusiastically as he took his place on the assembly line. But his fame was brief. A few days later, when Hanoi officials discovered McCain was the son of the admiral who commanded U.S. forces in the Pacific, and thus an important bargaining chip—"the Crown Prince," they called him—Ngu Xa's security forces began claiming credit for the capture. They even had the rope from McCain's parachute to back their claims. And after the war, as McCain's political fortunes grew and he became a leading advocate of reconciliation between the United States and Vietnam, numerous Hanoi residents began taking credit for saving the U.S. senator, apparently hoping for a reward from Washington.

Mai Van On sighed and poured another cup of tea from his Thermos. "I never wanted compensation," he said. "I just wanted recognition as a patriot. But life is life. Everything happens for a reason. Consider: I save an unknown pilot. He becomes a famous man and leads the way for America and Vietnam to become friends. If I had let him die, would we still have become friends?" He paused, offering no answer.

Taking my arm to steady himself, On walked with me through Ngu Xa's maze of sidewalk markets to what had been McCain's target three blocks away: a coal-fired power plant. Inside its high stone walls on this day there was a buzz of activity. Workers were hurrying to convert the plant to an electrical facility before winter's arrival. As we walked, On told me about the thrill of meeting McCain in Hanoi some years before. On, who had dressed in his only suit for the occasion, was so on edge with excitement that he showed up an hour early. He remembers McCain being a "very fine, wonderful man with a good face." He still keeps the fifty-cent Senate key chain McCain gave him as thanks for saving his life.

"What's done is done," On said. His life was not greatly changed by either the war or the war's end. He remains poor. He worries about paying his $2 monthly rent. He would like to buy his wife a new dress. He thinks life has treated him fairly. "I never hated Americans, only the American government. But the war's past now. It belonged to my generation, not my sons'. I never regretted saving Mr. McCain, though a lot of people wanted to kill your pilot that day."

Much to my surprise, On hugged me in farewell. I walked on alone. It was still early, but the marketwomen had already arrived from the countryside, lugging their produce in large baskets attached to wooden shoulder yokes. They were hunkered along the curbs, surrounded by neat stacks of tomatoes, lettuce, onions, and flowers. An old woman I saw every day pedaled by on her bicycle, clanging her bell and calling out, "Bread. Warm bread." Behind her pedaled a pint-sized newspaper boy named Hung, announcing the day's headlines over an amplifier attached to his bike's handlebars. I saw the familiar figure of a gaunt peasant in sandals and a conical hat carrying her bathroom scale, which she would occasionally set on the pavement in hopes a passerby wanted to know his weight. She told me if she earned 7,000 dong per day (about fifty cents U.S.), her time had been well spent.

Everywhere I turned, the streets were alive with energy. No one was idle. People were sawing, welding, jackhammering, repairing, building, lugging, selling, cooking. They arose at 5 A.M., were at work by 7 A.M., and often did not set down their tools until deep into the evening. Everyone seemed to have a purpose. Battered by war, invaded, occupied, colonized, Hanoians moved with the confidence of victors—warriors who time and again had defeated more powerful outsiders. There was a swagger in their attitude that fell between arrogance and confidence. They were prudish and proud. They had a tough edge but were not cold or distant. I asked the young bartender in the Polite Pub one evening what he thought of his city, and he replied, "Hanoi is like being in the center of the universe."

Not many non-Vietnamese would put it quite that way. Actually, Hanoi is pleasingly dull and quiet, far removed from the center of anything. But his reply reflected the reverence that all Vietnamese—even those in Ho Chi Minh City, as Saigon is now called—harbor for the City on the Bend in the River. More than a seat of government, it is the spiritual heart of a reunified country. If Ho Chi Minh City is New York, with its up-tempo beat and economic clout, then Hanoi is Boston. It is smaller, more refined and austere than its southern sister-city. In this place, who your family is counts more than what your salary is. The Southerners think and do; the Northerners think, then they think some more. The entrepreneurs live in Ho Chi Minh City, the poets in Hanoi.

The odes to Hanoi that make Vietnamese teary-eyed lose much in translation, but Phan Vu's song, even in English, conveys Vietnam's attachment to Hanoi. Set to music by Phu Quang, a widely known composer who now runs a restaurant in Hanoi, it tells of the 1946 winter when the city rose up against French rule and battles raged in the Old Quarter for two months.

> *Oh, my dear Hanoi streets.*
> *I still remember you with the perfume of orchid.*

*I still remember you with the perfume of milk flower.*
*The quiet street whispers with rain.*
*A girl waits, her long hair wet, covering her shoulders.*
*I still have you, Hanoi, and the memory of the lonely tree in winter.*
*I still have you, the lonely street corner in winter.*
*And a lonely piece of moon in winter.*
*That winter, in a collapsed house, sounds of a piano echoed.*
*The afternoon prayer is over, but why still echoes the bell?*
*I still have you, ever green, though time has gone by.*
*In an afternoon when the girl waits, her hair radiant,*
*the artist wanders on streets*
*suddenly unable to remember even a street name.*
*I still have you, the old streets covered by moss.*
*And uneven tile roofs fill my heart with memories.*
*West Lake in the afternoon echoed with waves.*
*Twilight came unexpectedly.*
*Oh, my dear Hanoi streets.*

The older generation of Hanoians found a certain pleasure in their country's ability to suffer and survive hardship. And these people had known no shortage of tough times, particularly in the decade that followed the war when Vietnam's humorless, hard-nosed government pursued doctrinaire communist policies with the fervor of a fundamentalist preacher. Hanoi became dispirited and bleak. The shelves of state stores were empty and the streets were deserted, save for a scattering of bicycles and the occasional Soviet truck that rumbled by. Residents were not allowed to speak to foreigners on the street, much less sit with them in cafés or their own homes. The glorious old Metropole Hotel—once the center of French colonial life—was renamed Thong Nhat (Reunification) and fell into such disrepair that guests could look into the room a floor above through holes in the ceiling. One former guest recalls being awakened in the middle of the night by rats gnawing on his suitcase. Squatters moved into the stately villas along Dien Bien Phu Boulevard; the turn-of-the-century Opera House was boarded up; and economist Do Duc Dinh remembers queuing for hours for a handful of rice. On the rare occasions when meat or a few pairs of new shoes went on sale at a government store, prospective customers would stampede the door. Most went home empty-handed.

Several families lived in each house, usually with just a curtain separating their living quarters. Nothing had been repaired in years. The old French colonial buildings appeared in danger of collapse. Everything was in a state of poverty and decay. "The human landscape was equally wrenching," Truong Nhu Tang, a Viet Cong (VC) official, wrote after visiting Hanoi in the 1970s.

> People walking or biking in the streets shared a look of grim preoccupation. They seemed poorer than they had three decades earlier. They walked slowly, as if resigned to their lives of poverty and constant toil. Though the streets were crowded, there was none of the bustle or vitality that Asian cities usually display. In its place was an air of melancholy given off by people who seemed to have aged prematurely. The scene was somber and colorless, like the clothes that almost everyone was wearing—both men and women in dark or khaki pants and white shirts (industrial textile dyes were an unaffordable luxury). A surge of pity came over me for what Hanoi's citizens had gone through, for the sacrifices that the war had demanded of them, not just for years but for a full generation.

Once, a young Australian diplomat traveling to Vietnam on temporary assignment called his embassy in Hanoi when he reached Bangkok to inquire if his colleagues wanted him to bring anything. "Their only request was for colored posters to put on the wall," the diplomat, Michael Mann, remembered. "I didn't know what they were talking about but I brought them posters. As soon as I got to Hanoi I understood. Everything was so gray—the mood of the people, the rundown city itself—they just wanted something to brighten their lives."

By the time Mann returned in 1998 as Australia's ambassador to Vietnam, Hanoi was a different city, tingling with activity and entrepreneurial spirit. Its renaissance was rooted in a single government decision: to follow China's lead and gradually open up Vietnam's economy to make room for private enterprise. The decision gave birth to a tourist industry and foreign investment. Western and Asian businessmen began arriving, first with only their suitcases, then later with their families. Ground was broken for a half-dozen five-star hotels. Hoa Lo—the dark, French-built prison that became known as the Hanoi Hilton, housing American POWs in squalor and terror—was razed to make way for a high-rise residential-commercial complex. One small section of the prison was retained as a museum. In it authorities posted a shamefully untrue sign: "American pilots suffered no revenge once they were captured and detained. Instead, they were well-treated, with adequate food, clothing, and shelter." Construction started on a real Hilton Hotel next to the refurbished Opera House. Ford Motors opened a plant to manufacture cars, Compaq an office to sell computers. Construction began on Western-style homes and apartments for stratospheric rents—$7,000 per month, two years' payment in advance.

On block after block, the industrious Hanoians transformed their street-front living rooms into tiny shops, from which they stitched dresses and suits, sold food, peddled electrical and plumbing wares, served tea and noodles, hung vast arrays of sneakers and shoes for sale. Art galleries and restaurants offering Australian beef and Japanese sushi soon followed. Prosperity grew. The luckier Hanoians bought Honda Dream motor scooters and TVs, and electric appliances were piled in the storefronts along Hai Ba Trung Street. The Thong Nhat—which in an earlier era had counted among its guests Graham Greene, Somerset Maugham, Bertrand Russell, and Charlie Chaplin—became the Metropole again and, after a $40 million renovation, glistened with restored elegance.

People spoke of Vietnam as an emerging "tiger" during the economic boom that blossomed throughout Southeast Asia in the 1980s and 1990s.

But Hanoi stood its ground. While other capitals fell to wrecking balls and bulldozer shovels, Hanoi's historic charm lingered. The boulevards were still wide and tree-lined. The catacombs of narrow, bustling lanes in Hanoi's Old Quarter seemed unscathed by modernity, still ringing with the voices of artisans and merchants who for 400 years had worked on thirty-six streets bearing names that reflected their businesses: Silk Street, Gold Street, Broiled Fish Street, Jewelers Street, Paper Street. Along the shores of downtown Hoan Kiem Lake—where legend has it that a golden turtle returned to heaven the magical sword that Emperor Le Loi used in driving out the Chinese in the fifteenth century—elderly Hanoians by the hundreds still gathered at dawn to exercise and play badminton. Sometimes I'd stop my bike to watch a spirited game. Ripples would glide across the lake, and I'd wonder if the golden turtle was about to emerge.

In the village of Bat Trang, just across the Red River from Hanoi, I met Le Van Cam, one of Vietnam's most admired ceramic artists. Nearly seventy years old, he wore a black beret and a hearing aid; a cane helped him rise from a big stuffed armchair in greeting. "Please don't get up," I said. But he struggled and eventually stood upright. He had lost his left leg fighting the French in 1954 and had seen his two sons go off to war— one as a teenager to fight the Americans in 1968, the other to fight the Chinese in 1979.

"So long ago," he said. "And that is just as well. There is so much lost time to make up for." He spoke in Vietnamese and sprinkled his conversation with an occasional French phrase. He said all the village's 3,000 inhabitants worked in the ceramics trade, as had their ancestors for six centuries. "For me it really doesn't matter any more. I am old. But for my sons, this is a new time of opportunity. For the first time in my life, ordinary people have the chance to prosper."

Cam had been the chairman of the local pottery cooperative in the postwar years. That system had been dismantled by the government's decision to open its economy, and now the potters of Bat Trang were on their own and business was thriving. Cam's shelves displayed rows of pottery that he and his sons had made, and outside his door, on a dirt street, a bicycle was being piled so high and wide with brightly colored ceramic vases, pots, cups, plates, and figurines that the owner would have to walk the bike into Hanoi, balancing it by clutching a long pole that rose from what had been the seat.

"You give people incentives and they are going to produce more," said Cam, whose heart belonged to communism but whose wallet carried the rewards of capitalism. "There's not much doubt about that. As a cooperative we were very poor. We cared about surviving, not prospering. We did not make good decisions because people's interests and abilities were not always the same." He compared life today: "Now I have ten people working for me. I have this new house. I just bought the television and the refrigerator. I may even get a Honda Dream, although I am not sure I could ride it well with one leg." He hobbled to the door to give instructions to his bicycle-walker, who set off down the road to Hanoi. "I'm not saying we've made up for the lost war years when we didn't have the time or the resources to develop, but I am saying this is just the beginning. Everything is changing."

ing defiance and perseverance, not victory. Perhaps the reason is that the Vietnamese, once Ho Chi Minh died, shunned the cult of personality. They celebrated the struggle of the faceless masses, not the achievement of individuals.

The United States spared most of Hanoi in its blitzkrieg from the air, despite the claims of antiwar activists who visited the capital in the 1970s and reported it had been nearly leveled. Bombs didn't fall around Hoan Kiem lake or in the Old Quarter. So Hanoi's nonmilitary areas survived the war remarkably intact, its French-influenced architecture—villas with tall, narrow windows, high-ceilinged rooms, small balconies, and wrought-iron gates—still form as pleasing a sight today as a century ago. Down an alleyway off Doi Can Street I happened upon a pond in a working-class neighborhood, and from its murky waters protruded a B-52 bomber, aged with rust and neglect. It had become part of the landscape, and no one paid it much notice. I asked a vendor in the outdoor market that wraps around the pond why the plane hadn't been removed, like other remnants of war in Hanoi. "Oh," she said, "more important things to do, I guess."

To the south a couple miles away, Bach Mai Hospital had barely survived the Christmas bombings of 1972, during which the B-52 had been shot down. The hospital, now Hanoi's largest, is fully operational again, its war scars covered under fresh mortar and brick, its orthopedic clinic supported in part by a grant from a U.S. veterans group. Flowers lie on a statue's pedestal of clustered figures, representing the thirty patients and staff killed by a bomb the Pentagon said was mistakenly dropped that holiday season. The director of the clinic is Nguyen Xuan Nghien, Vietnam's top rehabilitation specialist and a member of the Communist Party. I had gone to see him, with a government interpreter, to talk about the rehabilitation of Vietnamese with wartime disabilities. I had to wait in his office for nearly an hour while a procession of people streamed in to seek his advice—young doctors carrying envelopes of x-rays, nurses with prescriptions to sign, patients wanting reassurance of relief from pain. He hurried no one and did not seem impatient when another person would burst in unannounced just as he thought his office had been cleared and he could turn his attention to me.

Dr. Nghien was sixty years old. He wore Coke-bottle glasses and was chunkier than most Vietnamese. He spoke some English but often turned to my interpreter for the specific word or phrase he was looking for. He mentioned how grateful he was for the support Americans were providing his clinic and never mentioned that Americans had nearly leveled the place a generation earlier. In our exchange of niceties and inquiries about the well-being of each other's families—an exchange that forms the foundation of every conversation with a Vietnamese—he mentioned that his mother was ninety-three years old; he planned to visit her the next week in her village home near the old Demilitarized Zone (DMZ). His two brothers, who had fought for the Saigon regime and still lived in what had been South Vietnam during the American War, would also be at the family reunion. I was still new to peacetime Vietnam at that point and was apprehensive about how I'd be received by the war-battered peasants of the countryside. But I asked if my presence at the reunion would be an imposition.

"Not an imposition, an honor," he replied.

{{{ }}}

FIVE DAYS LATER I took a Vietnam Airlines flight to Danang, hired a driver for the two-hour drive to Dong Ha, and, after making the required courtesy call at the People's Committee headquarters, followed a dirt road to a small village. It was monsoon season, and the river had swelled above its banks. The road soon became impassable. I got out of the car and walked along a path, my notebook and a newspaper shielding my face from the rain. At the edge of the bamboo thicket a clearing had been cut. Dr. Nghien told me his mother's house would be the second on the right. The house had a tiled courtyard in front, two rooms, and a narrow, covered porch, on which Mrs. Nguyen Thi Nhien sat in a wooden armchair. She nodded and smiled when I greeted her but said nothing. I could not tell if she could see or hear me distinctly.

The old lady had done a lot of waiting for her sons over the years, and now she was waiting again. Her sons had not arrived. She fidgeted, smoothing the pleats of her purple dress, and peered out into the rain. The bamboo saplings moaned with each gust of wind. Maybe she had the wrong day, she worried. Or maybe it was the rain. How could anyone travel, even to a family reunion, in such weather?

Then she saw the first two sons—the two who had been soldiers in the South Vietnamese Army (ARVN)—sloshing up the muddy path to her home. And behind them, sheltered by an umbrella, their older brother, Dr. Nghien, who as a teenager had crossed the Ben Hai River into North Vietnam and spent the war patching the wounded and burying the dead.

"Hurry, children," she called out, "or you will be wet." And Dr. Nghien shouted back, "But Mother, we are already wet!"

Dr. Nghien bent to kiss his mother's cheek and hugged Nguyen Xuan Kien, eleven years his junior. "Ah, my little brother," he said, squeezing hard, and turned to Nguyen Xuan Tinh: "And you, Tinh. How lucky we are to be united. I wish Father was alive to see us together again."

For two decades, when Vietnam was a country divided by the Geneva Accords, the separation and silence between Dr. Nghien and his family was so vast that neither knew if the other were alive or dead. But on this morning, Mrs. Nheh's home once again glowed with the warmth of small talk, just as it did whenever the Nguyens gathered to share bonds restored by peace and to consider their good fortune in surviving a war they never voluntarily spoke of any more.

Compared to many families—one mother who lived close by had lost eight of her nine children in the war—the Nguyens had been lucky: No one in their family was killed. But like the Mason-Dixon Line of the U.S. Civil War, the Ben Hai River that split Vietnam into North and South from 1954 to 1975 pitted brother against brother. The story of how families like the Nguyens dealt with the division and the eventual reunification is the story of modern-day Vietnam itself.

I asked Mrs. Nheh if, having children on both sides, it hadn't been difficult to know whether to support the North or the South. Her jaws worked hard on a wad of betel nut gum. "Oh, really, I never distinguished between North and South," she said after pondering the question a moment. "What was the difference? I wasn't interested in politics. I just wanted my sons back. And peace. I wanted peace."

The Nguyens had lived in Quang Tri Province along the DMZ for, well, forever, Mrs. Nheh said, and the war—or wars, really, first against the French, then the Americans—had dragged on "for longer than I can remember. I lived with war most of my life."

French soldiers had burned down her house and most of her village in 1952, and she hated the former colonialists for it. "They didn't even ask the people to leave. They just burned," she said. "I could never understand why the French were in Vietnam in the first place." But at night she didn't have to deal with them. They withdrew to the safety of their base camps, and the Viet Minh—the forerunners of the Viet Cong—would sneak into the village to instruct the children in propaganda and basic skills like reading. On rare occasions, they brought medicine. In the process they began winning hearts and minds, just as the Americans would try to do more than a decade later without much success.

On May 8, 1954, a day after the defeat of the French garrison at Dien Bien Phu, representatives of eight countries met in Geneva and, after two months of negotiating, partitioned Vietnam at the Ben Hai. The division was to be temporary, until free elections could be held in 1956 to reunify Vietnam, under either the North's Ho Chi Minh or the South's leader, Ngo Dinh Diem, a devout Catholic who once contemplated the priesthood and a fervent anticommunist whose brother had been assassinated by the Viet Minh. Like Ho, Diem's nationalistic credentials were beyond reproach.

Mrs. Nheh's husband, Nguyen Xuan Nghinh, believed Vietnam had not seen the last of war with the departure of the French. Nghien, the future doctor, was his brightest son and the only one in the family who could read, and the father started making plans for him. He sent him to Dong Ha to learn to be a tailor. When the boy had learned the craft well, the father gathered his family one evening and said he wanted his son to go to the North. The schools were better there, and they were free. "You will stay only two years, until the election," the father said. "Then you will come home and we will be waiting."

The next night, just after dusk, young Nghien waded alone across the waist-deep Ben Hai, carrying only a plastic bag with a change of clothes he had sewn in the tailor shop. He was thirteen years old and knew not a soul beyond the river's northern banks.

Neither South Vietnam nor the United States had signed the Geneva Accords. Washington wanted free elections and democracy in Vietnam, but not if that meant the communists would come to power. And Diem, believing, probably correctly, that Ho would win a popular vote, refused to hold elections. The country remained divided, and the DMZ—a buffer zone thirty-nine miles long and five miles wide that roughly followed the 17th Parallel—became to Vietnam what the Berlin Wall would be to Germany. For the next twenty-one years, Nghien would not see or communicate with his family.

He moved in with a family of peasant farmers in the village of Vinh Linh. "Oh, I was homesick, so homesick, at first," he said. "My brothers, my parents, my village, I missed terribly." Nghien tended the farmer's cows in the morning, went to school in the afternoon, and studied until late at night. Each year the state gave him two shirts and two pairs of pants. Food and health care were free. No foreigners bossed him around. All in all, life was better in the North than it had been in the South, he thought. He liked the communal spirit and sense of shared dreams he found in his new home. People helped each other without being asked. Was that because of communism? He wasn't sure.

"I had heard a little about Ho Chi Minh," he said, "but I didn't know anything about him being a communist. I didn't even know anything about communism. I just knew he was promising independence. I thought of him as a patriot."

Nghien was a good student and upon graduating from high school was chosen to study medicine, an honor reserved for no more than a handful of boys. Five years later, in 1966, he became a doctor and took a step critical for anyone who expected to make career advancements in North Vietnam: He joined the Communist Party. "I thought communism, or socialism, provided a good example for working, studying, helping when you're trying to build a country," he said.

By then the American War was raging in the South, and the North was under heavy U.S. bombardment. The rice paddies and villages south of the DMZ had become a no-man's-land, but unlike most of the DMZ's inhabitants, Dr. Nghien's mother and family decided to stay put rather than seek safety farther south. "Where would we have gone?" Mrs. Nheh asked. "This was home. Besides I was old, even then. So we lived with the war."

Mrs. Nheh sat quietly, hands folded on her lap. Thunder rumbled overhead. Her three sons, laughing and chatting at the little kitchen table next to her, had to raise their voices to be heard over the drumbeat of rain pounding through the bamboo thicket. Mrs. Nheh tilted her head to better hear their stories but said little.

"I always believed one day my brother and I would meet again, because we were separated by a border, not by our hearts," said Tinh, a farmer with callused hands and skin darkened by years in the sun-baked fields. "Really, it made no difference who fought for which side. That was just circumstances."

In the North, Dr. Nghien met a beautiful young nurse named Hop at a lecture for treating war wounds. They were married two years later. By foot and bicycle they moved from town to village to commune and finally to the forests as the U.S. bombing intensified in the late 1960s. They dug shelters for patients, conducted operations by candlelight, and, Nghien said, never once considered the possibility the North might lose the war.

Years later Hop would say, "I believe I'm a stronger person today for what we went through. That's my generation's contribution to the young—strength and peace and a better standard of living. I just hope they have the wisdom to avoid the trouble my generation knew."

Hop was pregnant with their first child when Nghien went off to East Germany on a scholarship to study physical rehabilitation in 1971, a year before the United States bombed the hospital where he would eventually take up residency. Nghien felt guilty being in Europe while his homeland was in flames. "I was very afraid Hop would be lost in the Christmas bombing," he said. "So many hospitals and doctors and nurses and patients were. But, except for my worries and loneliness, I liked East Germany. The professors were good. The people were very kind to us. Living standards were high and I saw more freedom than we knew in Vietnam. I realized how little knowledge we had in Vietnam. Catching up with the rest of the world was not going to be easy once peace came."

By the time Nghien took up his studies in Berlin, young North Vietnamese volunteers were pouring down the Ho Chi Minh Trail toward southern battlefields. But the call to duty that was answered so willingly in the North met a less enthusiastic response in the South.

Nghien's youngest brother, Kien, managed to avoid South Vietnam's draft for four years by using a doctored identification card that showed him to be too young for military service. His other brother, Tinh, the farmer, was just as reluctant to fight a war that stirred no passions except the will to survive. He refused to volunteer.

"The Americans had pulled out of Quang Tri Province by the time I was old enough for service," Tinh said, "and before, when I was a boy tending water buffalo, I mostly only saw them at a distance, on patrol in the paddies. They scared me. They were so big, their skin was so pale. They had so many weapons. They appeared strange. I thought they had come to invade our country."

Eventually both boys were drafted into the South Vietnamese Army, Kien as a tank driver and Tinh as a bugler. Kien was in Ban Me Thuot on March 9, 1975, the day Hanoi's tanks rolled into town, beginning the rout of South Vietnam's forces from the Central Highlands. Seven weeks later

Tinh watched the North's soldiers march into Saigon. "I really didn't care who won or lost the war," he said.

Both brothers had the same reaction to Hanoi's victory. They discarded their South Vietnamese uniforms, stole civilian clothes and food, and by foot, bicycle, and bus made their way back to their mother's village outside Dong Ha, on the doorstep of a Demilitarized Zone that no longer existed.

"I returned to Hanoi from East Germany about that time," Dr. Nghien said. "My first son had been born while I was gone. I had never even seen him. Hop met me at the airport. We embraced. She was very thin and wearing a torn dress. She told me she had lost thirty-five pounds while I was gone. Everyone was so thin, so gaunt. They were so very, very poor. I was very moved. I couldn't imagine how much they had suffered. On the way back to our home I cried."

It had been twenty-one years since Dr. Nghien had seen—or had any word of—his family. He journeyed south in late 1975, crossing a rebuilt bridge that spanned the Ben Hai. The river had been swollen by a month of rain, and he wondered if it was now too deep for a small boy to wade across. After two days of travel, he reached his village. There was nothing left, not even a house.

But in a lean-to, covered by a mosquito net, he found an old woman who peered at him with a glimmer of recognition. Heavy-set with thick glasses, he bore little resemblance to the thirteen-year-old who had left home so long ago. Not until he showed the woman his birthmark—a brown spot on the right side of his neck—did Mrs. Nheh know for sure that she had reclaimed a son. She could offer him only a sweet potato in celebration for dinner, but all night, unable to sleep, she sat by his bed, touching his hands, his feet, his face.

The unified Vietnam that Nghien returned to was a dark-spirited place. Everything smelled of poverty. Everyone was hungry. No one smiled. Just owning a bicycle qualified a man for middle-class status. Nghien sold the motorcycle he had brought back from East Germany and with the money rebuilt his mother's house and supplemented his family's monthly rations: thirty-five pounds of rice, half a pound each of sugar and vegetables, one pound of meat. Mostly the meat was Mongolian lamb fat.

Dong, the son born to Dr. Nghien while he was in East Germany, went to school dressed in old, ripped clothes and shoes with flapping soles. The only boy Dong knew who did not wear a badge of poverty was the son of a high Communist Party official. He always had nice shoes, new jeans, and clean shirts. Dong said to himself one day, "Wow, that's amazing. How does he get them?"

Slowly, ever so slowly, the Communist Party took the first timid steps toward a free-market economy in the late 1980s. The fog of desperation lifted, and the Nguyens realized some fruits of peace. Dr. Nghien's brother Tinh received a one-acre plot from the government and earned enough from his plentiful rice harvests to buy ten oxen. His other brother, Kien, became the communist equivalent of a city councilman, a member of the Dong Ha People's Committee, and worked on plans to promote tourism in Quang Tri Province. Dr. Nghien's wife got a television, then a refrigerator, and finally a motor scooter, which, as in most Vietnamese homes, she parked in the living room. Dr. Nghien's international reputation as the talented head of orthopedics at Bach Mai Hospital spread. By the time I met him in Dong Ha, his salary had reached $50 per month.

The better things got, the more the lingering animosity toward the United States faded. It was replaced by a sense of relief that life was on the mend. Hating took energy—energy the Vietnamese wanted to expend in more productive pursuits. "I tell you this from the bottom of my heart, and I think I also speak for the Vietnamese people when I say this: We never hated the Americans," Dr. Nghien said. "It was the American leaders who set out to destroy us, not the people. We got great support from your people. They were of service to Vietnam. They protested against the war policy and the Voice of Vietnam gave us news every day of the demonstrations. It encouraged us. Your people were an important force in stopping the war. So were the reporters. They were the social conscience of a country."

It was ironic to hear this from a member of the Communist Party. What Dr. Nghien so admired in the United States—the right to dissent, to freely challenge the policy of elected leaders—was precisely what his own government denied him. Nghien and his countrymen did not elect their leaders. They did not have access to a press that debated policy. They could not demonstrate. Strangely, that lack of basic freedoms did not seem to bother him.

Sometimes Dr. Nghien talked to his sons about the benefits of joining the Party. The boys were grown now, in their twenties. Dong had become a doctor, and his younger brother, Ha, was finishing his university economics studies. Their father would tell them that the Party was about nationalism, not theory, that it was a vehicle for development. "If I could pay back my country a hundred times for educating me and giving me independence, that would not be enough. I would still owe," he told them. The boys would listen politely and silently, their eyes wandering, before focusing on the floor. Once Dong whispered to Ha: "Another generation talking."

I became good friends with Dong as the months passed and asked him one day if he wanted to join the Party. "I was in the Youth Association, but I'm not a communist," he said. "In my father's time, if you wanted a good job, wanted to get ahead, you needed to be in the Party. All good people were in the Party. So I can understand why it is important to him. But times have changed. You can get ahead now by knowledge, and you don't really need to be a communist. Right now you just need to abide by the law and try to be of service. That is enough to do well."

And times had changed for the Nguyens because the enmity between the Americans and the Vietnamese was melting. Not only had the U.S. veterans' grant been a godsend for the Bach Mai clinic; English had replaced German as Dr. Nhgien's second language. Pepsi, Marlboro, Compaq, and Procter & Gamble were brand names that were now part of the family's daily life. Dong was preparing to leave for Baltimore to study at Johns Hopkins University. And he had brought home to introduce to his parents the first real love of his life—a young American woman who worked for the Vietnam Veterans of America Foundation in Hanoi. Her father was a former Marine who had fought in Quang Tri Province.

"Life is easier if you have a Vietnamese girlfriend," Dong said. "But my parents are supportive of my relationship with Sarah. Even if we marry. They like Sarah because she is very nice, very polite and she speaks Vietnamese. And like a good Vietnamese, she is respectful of elders.

"I was a very good boy before we met at a seminar. I think maybe she was lonely at the time. We had a good conversation and talked about everything very frankly. We agreed to go out on a date. We went on a trip to the countryside. I'd had no experience with love before. American girls respond in much stronger ways than Vietnamese. We agreed to spend time together but we never talked about tomorrow. Maybe things will work out, maybe not. I do not yet know if my love is an endless love."

The improving relationship between Hanoi and Washington even enabled Dr. Nghien to visit the United States twice. "Who'd have guessed I've ever be in America?" he mused, still a bit bewildered by the improbability of it all. During one visit, he found himself standing in front of the Vietnam Veterans Memorial, wiping away a tear as memories of war and separation and an old woman living in a lean-to came flooding back.

"When I touched the names on what you call the Vietnam Wall," he said, "I thought, 'What beautiful people they would be if they were alive today.' All the bitterness left me at the moment. I understood that if some visitors there knew I had been on the other side in the war, I could have been beaten up. But I didn't care. I just wanted to think about how much both sides had lost."

At their mother's home on the Hieu River, Dr. Nghien and his brothers toasted me with cups of tea on the day of their reunion. "I wish my father was alive to see an American in his home because he would be very honored," he said. The words made me wince. I had trekked through the rice paddies around Dong Ha many times with U.S. Marine patrols thirty years earlier. How could I once have considered these same decent people the enemy? Outside the rain still fell in sheets. The brothers talked on. Finally Dr. Nghien said, "Mother, we must be going, or we will have to swim."

Dr. Nghien spread his umbrella, and his two brothers squeezed in under it. They linked arms. "We'll be back soon, Mother. I promise," the doctor said. Then the three of them headed back down the muddied path. Mrs. Nheh watched them go and did not avert her gaze until they had turned the bend and disappeared beyond the bamboo.

# 3

# THE MAKING OF
# VIETNAM

I N LATE AUGUST 1945, with Japan defeated in World War II and its
occupation of Vietnam ended, Ho Chi Minh, disease-ridden and
fifty-five years old, was carried on a stretcher from his jungle hideout
to a house at 48 Hang Ngang in Hanoi. The son of an itinerant teacher
who had worked as an official for the imperial court in Hue, Ho was unknown to most Vietnamese. He had left Vietnam in 1911 as an assistant
cook on a French passenger ship and spent thirty years abroad: first on
the high seas, then in Paris, Russia, China, and Hong Kong. He went to
America, working briefly as a pastry chef at the Parker House Hotel in
Boston and making a brief tour of the U.S. South where, he said, he witnessed the Ku Klux Klan lynching blacks. His name when he left Saigon

on the *Admiral Latouche-Treville* liner was Nguyen Tat Thanh. Later he would adopt the pseudonym Nguyen Ai Quoc (Nguyen the Patriot) and, in the 1940s, Ho Chi Minh (He Who Enlightens).

Asia and Africa had already been divvied up among the colonial powers of Europe, and there is little doubt that young Ho steamed out of Saigon filled with nationalism and a burning hatred of the system that had turned Indochina—Vietnam, Laos, and Cambodia—into a labor camp for France's economic and expansionistic aspirations. Before his departure from Vietnam, Ho had been a teacher in Phan Thiet. He wore white pajamas and wooden sandals to classes and filled his lectures with Vietnamese history and recited poetry. One of the poems he was fond of quoting included the stanza:

> *Oh, Heaven! Can't you see our suffering?*
> *The nation is in chains, languishing in grief,*
> *Foreigners have doomed it to hunger,*
> *They've robbed it of everything it had.*

Popular legend in Vietnam today has cloaked Ho in so much mythology it is difficult to know where fact ends and fable begins. In 1994, the publisher of *Tuoi Tre* (Youth) newspaper lost her job for printing that Ho might have once had a wife. (He was indeed briefly married as a young man to the daughter of a wealthy Chinese merchant; he was romantically involved with several other women.) According to the Party, Ho's only marriage was to the revolution. The official line on Ho, based on his scattered reminiscences and the Party's propaganda, contends among other things that he left Vietnam on a mission to save his country from colonialism. But Ho's personal history has been airbrushed over time to enhance his image, and one of Ho's biographers, William J. Duiker, cautions: "Given his notorious proclivity to dramatize events in his life for heuristic purposes, it is advisable to treat such remarks [as his reason for going abroad] with some skepticism."

During his brief visit to the United States Ho expressed admiration for the energy and industriousness of the American people but distaste for capitalism, which he found exploitative. In Paris in 1919, inspired by President Woodrow Wilson's doctrine of self-determination to "make the world safe for democracy," Ho sent Wilson a petition asking for support in establishing a constitutional government and democratic freedoms in Vietnam, but making no reference to independence. "All subject people," Ho wrote, "are filled with hope by the prospect that an era of right and justice is opening to them . . . in the struggle of civilization against barbarism." What Ho didn't understand was that Wilson was talking about democracy for Europe and North America, not the rest of the world. His petition went unanswered.

Ho once recalled his reaction to reading a copy of Lenin's "Thesis on the National and Colonial Questions" that a friend had given him in Paris: "There were political terms difficult to understand in this thesis. But by dint of reading it again and again, finally I could grasp the main part of it. What emotion, enthusiasm, clear-sightedness and confidence it instilled in me! I was overjoyed to tears. Though sitting alone in my room, I shouted aloud as if addressing large crowds, 'Dear martyrs, compatriots! This is what we need! This is the path to our liberation!'"

In the end Ho found support in the one place that would offer hope and refuge to Asia and Africa's anticolonial revolutionaries for the next fifty years—the Communist Party. Four years later, in 1924, he left Paris for Moscow to become a full-time communist agent. He spent the next seventeen years in the Soviet Union, China, Hong Kong, and Thailand, organizing the Indochinese Communist Party, recruiting organizers and strategists, and stitching together the fabric of his revolution. In 1941, he returned covertly to Vietnam, setting up a headquarters in mountain caves near the Chinese border.

In the Hanoi house where he had been brought on a stretcher, after four years in Chinese prisons and in the malaria-infested jungles with the Viet Minh fighting French colonialists and Japanese occupiers, Ho sat at an ironwood table, chain-smoking 555-brand cigarettes and tapping out a statement on his portable typewriter. A week later, on September 2, 1945, he put on a khaki tunic and rubber sandals and made his way to Ba Dinh Square to declare Vietnam's independence. Hundreds of thousands of Vietnamese, from mandarins to peasants, milled about. Ho stepped onto a wooden platform and, speaking into a microphone, began with words that any American would recognize but that surely must have mystified his audience: "We hold the truth that all people are created equal, that they are endowed by the Creator with certain unalienable rights, among them life, liberty and the pursuit of happiness. This immortal statement was made in the Declaration of Independence of the United States of America in 1776. In a broader sense, this means: All the peoples on the earth are equal from birth, all the peoples have a right to live to be happy and free."

Ho had chosen his words deliberately, hoping Washington would recognize what he saw as the rightness of his cause. Washington had, after all, supplied Ho's guerrillas with grenades and rifles to fight the Japanese, and the U.S. Office of Strategic Services (the forerunner of today's CIA) had supplied Viet Minh partisans during the war. But within months of Ho's declaration of independence, President Harry S. Truman had thrown his support behind France's claim to Indochina. The French returned as rulers, and over the next decade the United States would pour $2.5 billion into France's ill-fated campaign to keep Vietnam a colony. When the French left, the Americans took their place, confident they could bring Ho's communist army of peasants to heel in short order. At the time General George Decker, the U.S. Army chief of staff, stated, "Any good soldier can handle guerrillas."

The reaction I received in Vietnam as an American was perplexing. It was as though the United States had accepted Ho's overtures and that our countries had been friends through the ages. The American War was seldom mentioned in conversations unless I brought it up. My reception in the "new" Vietnam was more gracious and welcoming than the one I remember receiving in the "old" Vietnam, on whose behalf much of my generation had fought. People who had lost two or three sons in the war invited me into their homes and treated me as an honored guest. Families whose villages had been leveled, like Mrs. Nguyen and her three sons outside Dong Ha, took me briefly into their lives and thanked me for caring. Strangers smiled when they asked my nationality and I answered My—"American." Almost every male I knew in Hanoi over the age of forty-five had been a soldier—and almost all had fearful tales of battles and bombings along the Ho Chi Minh Trail—but no one gave the vaguest hint of considering me or the United States an adversary. When I told former combatants I had covered the war as a reporter thirty years earlier they would often place both hands on my shoulders as though to say, "I traveled those roads too." My admission established my credentials as someone who had shared bad times.

It would be easy to dismiss my observations as those of someone who had discovered only what he wanted to hear or see. But every American I met in Vietnam, whether tourist, businessperson, or former GI, had the same reaction: The Vietnamese *liked* Americans. They had forgiven, if not forgotten. They had lost 3 million citizens, been pummeled with 15 million tons of munitions—twice the tonnage dropped on all of Europe and Asia during World War II—and lived through a war that created 7 million refugees in South Vietnam and destroyed the industry and infrastructure of North Vietnam. Yet they had put the war behind them in a way that many Americans hadn't. Their hospitals weren't full of veterans with postcombat trauma, and they had no national mourning memorials like the Vietnam Wall in Washington. They didn't write books about the war. Veterans didn't gather over beers to talk about it. Schoolchildren studied it as only a brief page in their country's 2,500-year history.

Perhaps the Vietnamese of the North weren't haunted by the war because they had won it. Perhaps humility belongs to the victors. Yet it was difficult to understand how a country could consider itself victorious after it had paid such a terrible price. Sometimes I'd look for an opportunity to challenge Hanoi's contention that it had won a military victory. Before I went to see a former North Vietnamese colonel whose battalion had attacked Hue in the Tet Offensive of 1968, I jotted in my notebook a comment General Norman Schwarzkopf had made in his autobiography: "The United States military did not lose the war in Vietnam, period. In the two years I was in Vietnam, I was in many battles. I was never in a defeat—came pretty close a couple of times, but we were never defeated. The outcome of the Vietnam War was a political defeat, but it was not a military defeat." I read the retired colonel the quote and asked his reaction. "That's irrelevant," he replied without dropping a beat. "Whose flag do you see out there?" And indeed, outside the window the flag over the citadel of Hue bore the yellow star on a red background that once represented North Vietnam and was now the symbol of the unified country.

Usually when I asked a Vietnamese why he harbored no animosity toward Americans, the answer had something to do with Ho Chi Minh. Uncle Ho, I'd be told, said that the enemy was the U.S. government, not the American people. Or Uncle Ho said independence was worth any price and the American War was a cost the Vietnamese were willing to pay to claim what was rightfully theirs. Sometimes, more to the point, they'd explain that Vietnam had spent a good part of the past 2,000 years at war and that the decade they'd fought the Americans added up to no more than a blip in history.

Another reason the Vietnamese hold no apparent grudges against Americans is that they believe U.S. servicemen were forced to fight in Vietnam against their will and that the majority of Americans were on the streets protesting Washington's policies. Their interpretation of history ignores the fact that two-thirds of the GIs in Vietnam were volunteers, not draftees, and that in a poll taken after the war 91 percent of Vietnam vets said they were "proud" to have served. Jane Fonda and other activists who visited Hanoi to denounce the war are remembered with fondness in Vietnam, but many Vietnamese admit privately they had a difficult time respecting the activists: To the ultranationalistic Vietnamese it was unfathomable that anyone who campaigned against his or her government in time of crisis was worthy of esteem.

Plus, times have changed. Vietnam now seeks U.S. investment and assistance, technology and expertise. Americans are a welcome sight. Their
presence is confirmation that better days lie ahead—and evidence that
Vietnam's international isolation, engineered by the United States in the
postwar years, is over. What consumes the people's energies now is economic development. To achieve it, they know they have to look forward,
not backward.

Although I searched for explanations, I never doubted that the Vietnamese affability was sincere. Just as they didn't much take to the gruff
and somber Soviets who overran Vietnam after the American War, they
genuinely liked the gregarious and curious Americans who traded jokes
with them, asked them about the war, and knew the value of a smile. And
I think they were just as aware as I was that Americans and Vietnamese
share an almost inexplicable bond. It is not the bond of natural friendship
that Americans might feel for, say, Australians, or a bond of cultural linkage as some Americans feel for Africa or Great Britain. Rather, it is something deeper and more mysterious. It is a liaison woven in tragedy and
common suffering, a tie strengthened by the flight of hundreds of thousands of Vietnamese to the United States, who, having generally prospered in their new home, now return to the land of their birth in large
numbers each year, as visitors and businesspeople, to showcase the American Dream. Perhaps as much as anything, the bond is rooted in the realization that the war changed the United States as much as it did Vietnam.

{{{  }}}

MY FIRST SPRING IN PEACETIME VIETNAM arrived and, with it, my
fifty-eighth birthday. I remembered that when I'd gone off to cover the
war, shortly after my twenty-eighth birthday, my friends considered me a
wise-guy, always joking and full of mischief. I was a night owl who could
party and drink until dawn. I came home more serious and, perhaps for
the first time, sensitive to pain in the world around me. So I guess Vietnam had changed me, too. Or maybe the passing years would have done

that anyway. Sandy and I had dinner at the Press Club in Hanoi, where I ordered Australian wine and a black Angus steak imported from the United States. I had insisted on no birthday cake, but, as I knew would happen, one still arrived at the end of dinner, a single candle burning on top. Then a few days later I headed off to Vinh, a drab port city 190 miles south of Hanoi. Vinh isn't much of a place—it's known as the ugliest city in Vietnam—but the real miracle of Vinh is that it survived at all. To the Northern communists, Vinh was "the throat that fed the stomach," the main supply point for the Ho Chi Minh Trail, whose network of paths and roads carried Hanoi's soldiers and equipment to the southern battle-fields. The French started bombing Vinh in 1931 and didn't stop until 1952. Then, a decade later, the Americans took over. By the time they had finished, all that still stood in the once-proud city were a provincial guest-house and two college dormitories. Vinh had entered history as the only Vietnamese city totally destroyed by the United States. Except for a de-tachment of antiaircraft gunners, its population in 1972 was zero.

"I can tell you exactly when the first American planes came," said a seventy-one-year-old veteran, Nguyen Van Ngoc, who was showing me around and, despite all conventional wisdom, talking up Vinh's potential as a tourist destination. "It was August 5, 1964. I was bicycling back from the port. This place was alive then. We had enough supplies coming through Vinh by rail and sea to equip 100 armies. We'd been bombed on and off by the French for twenty years so we knew what bad times were but we thought they were over. Then on that day, August 5, in the morn-ing, I caught a glimpse of six or seven planes, American planes it turned out, headed for us and I said, 'Uh-oh, here we go again.'"

Ngoc and I piled into a four-wheel-drive vehicle driven by a member of the People's Committee and drove over to see the two abandoned col-lege dormitories. They seemed in danger of collapsing. Trees and vines clung to crumbling brick walls, branches slithered in and out of shattered windows. The outside walls were studded with gaping holes. I peered in a ground-floor window, at what I imagined had been a bedroom. Its ceiling had disappeared and plaster littered the floor. There was a door frame leading to a long corridor but no door. I wondered what had become of the students who had once lived there. Had they ever returned to remember what university life had been like before the war? How many had gone off to war? How many had died?

I asked Ngoc if he knew and he said, no, he had no idea. Those were questions, he said, best addressed to the provincial People's Committee. He said all he could be sure of was that Vinh was nothing but a pile of bricks after the war. "We had to rebuild the city from the ground up, from zero," he said. But he had great hopes for Vinh. The population now topped 200,000. A bank had opened; the Huu Nghi (Friendship) Hotel had been renovated and expanded to seventy-four rooms; the port was being upgraded, boosted by the trade of smuggled goods, from timber to cigarettes, that flowed out of Laos on Highway 9 and ended up in Vinh for transshipment. And then there was tourism: Once foreigners learned there was a good hotel in Vinh and that Ho Chi Minh had been born in 1890 in a three-room thatched-roof house a few miles away, the city would be hard-pressed to handle all the visitors, he boasted.

We made our way through streets congested with bicycles. The markets were bustling, and shops sold a wide array of secondhand electronics from South Korea and Taiwan. Economically Vinh seemed to be doing fine. But I didn't share Ngoc's enthusiasm for the potential of tourism. First, Vietnam Airways had cancelled its Hanoi-Vinh flights due to lack of demand, leaving Vinh's airport idle save for three flights a week to Danang by a propeller-driven plane. Second, I didn't know what tourists would do or want to see in Vinh. Hanoi was an anomaly with its charm and beauty. Vinh, like most of Vietnam's towns and cities, was architecturally uninspiring and, everything considered, decidedly forgettable. But Ngoc would have none of such pessimism.

He had spent his entire life in and around Vinh, although he dreamed of one day visiting Hanoi. "I might even take the train, but I doubt I'd want to stay more than a few days," he said. I asked him what he thought tourists might like to see in Vinh. "The market," he said. "It's got vegetables you can't even find in Dalat. And the port. You know some of those ships come from Japan? Of course, the house where Uncle Ho was born. And I imagine they'd want to stay at the Huu Nghi if they can get a room."

The Communist Party occupies the grandest, and often the newest, structure in almost every Vietnamese city, and so it is in Vinh. Some of the buildings, as in Ho Chi Minh City, had been inherited from the French. Others were built after the war, and their gaudy elegance is a reminder of the Party's role in daily life. At first I found them distasteful, a flashy advertisement for communism. But their presence isn't much different than the stately city halls that overlook downtown squares in so many American towns, and I entered the People's Committee headquarters in Vinh with hardly a second thought. Ngoc introduced me to the three members of the Party chosen to welcome me.

Foreign journalists do not make spontaneous visits to towns outside Hanoi, and my trip to Vinh had been arranged well in advance, after I submitted a written request to the government press department saying where I wanted to go and what I wanted to talk about. I didn't find the restriction particularly burdensome because over the course of four years I usually managed to get where I wanted to go. And I wasn't bothered by the government's requirement that foreign reporters could set up offices only in Hanoi, even though Ho Chi Minh City was more spirited and economically significant. The fact is that Hanoi was a much more pleasant place to live, even if being there made it easier for the government to keep tabs on me and meant that my stories were more apt to reflect the Northern perspective than that of the South.

So I had told the press department I wanted to talk about the reconstruction of Vinh, and the three Party members who awaited me carried stacks of blueprints and a thick twenty-year master plan and had filled up the chalkboard with graphs and information that offered considerably more detail than I wanted. We drank tea and bottles of springwater. They talked, each in turn, at great length until I felt in danger of nodding off. But I admired the inclination of Vinh's residents to plan and dream because it would have been easier to simply walk away and leave Vinh the pile of rubble that it was. I came to think of Vinh as a feisty place. And I could understand the gratitude the residents felt for their deposed communist comrades in Berlin.

In 1972, after the United States quit bombing and three years before the war officially ended, East Germany proved to be Vinh's only outside friend. It sent in scores of engineers, technicians, planners, and laborers to haul away the rubble and build a new city. Unfortunately, that's how Vinh came to be known as Vietnam's ugliest city. The first project that went up comprised twenty-one five-story concrete apartment buildings, including a kindergarten, schools, and a food market, for 6,000 Vietnamese workers. The Vietnamese like to live close to the ground, with doors open to the street and breezes that blow unencumbered through their homes; no one was happy living in these bunkerlike concrete blocks. Still, month after month, square look-alike buildings sprung up, block after block, until Vinh resembled a Soviet gulag.

The problem was no one factored in maintenance costs, and when communism collapsed in Eastern Europe in the late 1980s, Vietnam lost $1 billion a year in assistance. Bonn had little interest in underwriting the Vinh project. The sprawling housing complex soon looked like something born in the Bronx. "This is a problem, no doubt about it," Nguyen Van Luc, one of my hosts, said after the briefing had mercifully ended and we'd left the office to drive around the city. "We've talked about razing the project, but you can't just make 6,000 people homeless. If we can get the money it'd be better to renovate." Luc took me inside one of the buildings. Scores of children appeared out of nowhere. They were clean and neatly dressed and eager to try out the few English phrases they knew: *Where are you from? What is your name? Do you like Vietnam?* Luc and I were careful to avoid the electrical wiring that protruded from stairwells.

Big chunks of plaster had fallen from the ceilings. Lightbulbs dangled from cords. The apartments rented for $3.50 per month. Some of the better-off families had a mattress in the bedroom. As in other cities, the mattress was a new amenity in Vinh and sales were booming. You could hardly drive a block without seeing someone lugging a mattress out of a shop, wrestling it onto his motor scooter for transport home, displaying a broad smile of anticipation. I wondered if mattresses would be Vietnam's downfall. The Vietnamese were among the most industrious people I'd ever seen. They got up with the dawn and thought nothing of laboring twelve or fourteen hours. What was going to happen when an entire nation realized thread-thin mats stretched over cement floors were lousy for sleeping, that big, deep mattresses provided a powerful incitement for not getting up early to go to work?

Luc offered to drive me to the Huu Nghi Hotel; as we passed the two college dormitories I visited earlier, he asked if I were an American. I told him yes, and he said, "I have one question. Is it OK to ask it?" It was a question I would only hear once in Vietnam: "Why did America do this to us?" His tone was neither hostile nor challenging. I think he was simply bewildered and, even after so many years, had never heard a satisfactory explanation.

I wasn't going to get suckered into apologies. "You have to put it into the context of the Cold War and what the world was like in the 1960s," I said. "The Korean War had just been fought to stall the spread of communism in Asia. The United States and Soviet Union were confronting each other with proxy wars in Asia and Africa. Washington viewed Ho Chi Minh as just another Soviet-backed communist trying to take over a democratic country. No matter how great the miscalculation might have been, the United States didn't do business with communists. There is little Ho could have done to change that. We came to save the South, not destroy the North. But we got drawn in deeper and deeper. It was like poker. The pot got too big, and for a lot of reasons, no one was willing to walk away and leave all those assets on the table."

Luc listened without commenting, and I knew my explanation had fallen short. He asked what the American people thought about the war now. I said, "Everyone agrees it was a great tragedy for both sides." Luc nodded and let the subject drop.

The state-owned Huu Nghi Hotel was quite acceptable, though it could hardly be described as a tourist draw. I was the only guest. The cavernous dining room, with its metal chairs and long, uncovered tables, had the ambiance of a Soviet mess hall, but it was clear the new local chef had attempted to spruce up the menu, which included chicken testicles with ginger, sautéed frog with banana, and turtle with leg of pork. The turtle dish apparently was not in demand, and the sole star of that entrée splashed around its tank by the cashier's register, awaiting the inevitable. It was 7 P.M. A waiter approached; I ordered water buffalo steak. "I'm sorry," he said. "We close at 6:30." He found me a loaf of French bread and filled a glass with ice cubes. I repaired to my room, where my dinner companion was a bottle of whiskey.

A list of hotel regulations was posted in English on the wall. Number 7 warned: "No harboring the social evils: prostitution, gamble, criminal." It made no mention of the massage parlor just off the ground floor, where, I assumed, social evils were readily available at a reasonable price. Number 8 stated: "The hotel just taken upon oneself about guests money and wealthies when both of sides are having the transfer between the guest or receptionist or room servant."

Clearly, Vinh's tourist industry was still in its infancy.

{{{  }}}

THE DILAPIDATED APARTMENT COMPLEX Nguyen Van Luc had shown me was called the Quang Trung Quarters, named for an eighteenth-century emperor who had routed Chinese invaders. The name was no surprise: The Vietnamese name projects, streets, and temples for their ancient partisans, some of them women, who fought China for a millennium to protect Vietnam's cultural and national identity. The first major insurrection against China was led by the Trung sisters, Trac and Nhi, who liberated Vietnam in A.D. 40 and established an independent state that reached from Hue to southern China. One of their commanders, a woman named Phung Thi Chinh, was said to have given birth during the battle and continued to fight with the baby strapped to her back. Another woman, Trieu Au, wore armor and rode an elephant into battle against the Chinese in A.D. 248, leading a force of 3,000 warriors. "I want to rail against the wind and the tide, kill the whales in the sea, sweep the whole country to save the people from slavery, and I refuse to be abused," she is remembered as saying. Defeated at the age of twenty-three, she committed suicide. Like the Trung sisters, as well as other heroes and heroines who fought the invaders from the north, she remains venerated by a people whose recorded history is engraved with bloodshed and struggle.

Archaeologists have unearthed basalt tools and handaxes showing that Vietnam was occupied during the Bronze Age, between 5,000 and 3,000 B.C., by fifteen tribes of small, dark-skinned people of Melanesian or Austronesian stock. The dominant group was known as the Viet. The word *nam* means "south," meant to distinguish the region from China. Actually there never has been a country named "Vietnam," any more than there has been one named "Greatbritain." It is Viet Nam, just as it is Ha Noi, Sai Gon, Plei Ku, and Da Nang. The compression of the words is the result of a cultural insensitivity taken by headline writers at U.S. newspapers during the early stages of U.S. involvement in Vietnam.

The beginnings of Vietnam, like that of many Asian countries, are buried in myths of mystical emperors and 4,000-year-old kingdoms— folklore that pleases the Vietnamese by reinforcing their belief that the country's roots are as deep and old as those of their traditional rivals in China. Vietnam's recorded history, in Chinese annals, dates back to the second century B.C. when Trieu Da, a renegade Chinese general, conquered Au Lac in the northern mountains of Vietnam and proclaimed himself emperor of Nam Viet, a kingdom that stretched nearly to present-day Danang. A century later Nam Viet was annexed as the Chinese province of Giao Chi.

It was not long before the Vietnamese rebelled against China and its attempts to introduce new taxes and to tighten administrative control. Starting with the Trung sisters' military campaign, Vietnam would struggle to resist Chinese domination and assimilation for 1,000 years. Invariably, the Vietnamese absorbed many elements of Chinese culture. They became Buddhists and Taoists and followed the moral and social doctrine of Confucianism: Community is more important than the individual; your worth as a person is determined by your public actions; parents and elders are to be honored, ancestors worshipped; spontaneity is a sign of disrespect; education is nearly as important as family. They borrowed from Chinese institutions and from the Chinese language. But in the end a distinct Vietnamese culture, heritage, and language were put in place.

Throughout the first century A.D., Vietnam knew periods of independence and subjugation, each accompanied by terrible battles. Despite dynastic squabbles and their own expansionistic goals, the Viets (the predominant ethnic tribe) were always quick to respond to charismatic leadership. Often one man—Emperor Le Loi, in defeating the Chinese in 1426 in a battle near Hanoi, or Ho Chi Minh, in taking on the French and the Americans nearly 500 years later—was able to harness public sentiment and energy as a powerful fighting force. In each case the cause was Vietnam's independence. Le Loi celebrated his victory over the Chinese in 1426 by providing the defeated army with boats and horses to carry its soldiers home. A Vietnamese poet, Nguyen Trai, commemorated the triumph with these words:

> *Henceforth our country is safe.*
> *Our mountains and rivers begin life afresh.*
> *Peace follows war as day follows night.*
> *We have purged our shame for a thousand centuries,*
> *We have regained tranquility for ten thousand generations.*

With their northern border secured by Le Loi—every major city has a major boulevard named for him—the Viets turned their attention to the enemy in central Vietnam, where the Champa Empire had flourished for 1,000 years. In 1471, the Viets killed 60,000 Chams in a decisive battle and captured 36,000 others, including the king and fifty members of the royal family. The Champa Empire slowly disintegrated. The remaining 80,000 Vietnamese who today trace their origin to the Chams are fully integrated into society, as one of Vietnam's fifty-four minority groups, and have little left to remember their kingdom by except temples and sculptures, 300 of which are preserved in a museum in Danang.

About that time Vietnam began its golden age under Emperor Le Thanh Tong. (Most foreign journalists in Hanoi today have their offices in a government building on Le Thanh Tong Street.) According to historian Stanley Karnow, Tong was a Confucian scholar who fielded an army of 200,000 men and "devoted much of his tireless energy to the advancement of learning." He expanded the national university, organized poetry contests, banned the practice of branding slaves on the face, and developed a liberal legal code that protected citizens against abuses by the elitists and bureaucrats in the royal court known as mandarins. Women were given near equality with men. What emerged was a distinct country whose history had been forged in its resistance to China.

Nguyen Trai wrote:

> Our country, Dai Viet, has long been
> A land of ancient culture,
> With its own rivers and mountains, ways and customs,
> Different from those in the north [China].

But his hope that 10,000 generations would know peace was premature. Ruling families fought each other for nearly 200 years, starting in the mid-1500s, and Vietnam slipped into turmoil, divided north and south along roughly the same line that would mark the DMZ during the

American War. In 1772, three brothers began a seven-year peasant revolt, known as the Tay Son Insurrection, against the Nguyen Dynasty's feudal rulers. Their ragtag rebel army captured the tiny port of Saigon and killed 10,000 Chinese merchants. Fearing that the brothers might take over all of Vietnam, China sent another army south, in 1778, to crush the rebellion. With peace restored, the emperor ordered his soldiers to exhume one of the brothers' bodies and urinate on it in front of the man's widow and son. Internal conflicts continued, but the Vietnamese managed to push the southern Khmer people out of the Mekong Delta and into Cambodia. By the mid-eighteenth century Vietnam's borders had been extended to about what they are today.

Vietnam's strategic location—a 1,900-mile coastline on the South China Sea, straddling the sea-lanes that link the Indian and Pacific Oceans—soon caught the attention of sundry foreigners, from traders to pirates to potential occupiers. By the late eighteenth century, Hoi An near Danang was already bustling with ships from Portugal, Holland, and England. Jesuit missionaries were prowling the interior, converting Buddhists to Christianity. France was casting covetous glances. In 1861 France captured Saigon and began extending its influence north and west. By 1879 Saigon had a French governor, and by 1883—seven years before the birth of Ho Chi Minh—France had divided Vietnam into three entities, running Tonkin in the north and Annam in the Central Highlands as protectorates and Cochinchina in the south as a colony.

Ho Chi Minh did not live to see the reunification of Vietnam. He died having seen the South only briefly, in 1911, when he set off for Europe to become an expatriate, never having known a Vietnam free of foreign influence. He presumably understood little about his Southern countrymen, except those who shared his vision of a unified communist nation. But in a message to Americans during the war in the 1960s, he said, "We will spread a red carpet for you to leave Vietnam. And when the war is over, you are welcome to come back because you have technology and we will need your help."

# 4

# SAIGON

*From Wartime Turmoil to*
*Peacetime Prosperity*

THE UNIFICATION EXPRESS RUMBLES into the former ghost town of Vinh at 1:30 every morning, hissing and clanking to a brief stop during its 1,078-mile journey from Hanoi to Ho Chi Minh City, or Saigon, as it's still called on the schedules. Vinh is dark and deserted except for a few enterprising men who have shown up to meet the train on their cyclos—taxis that consist of a two-person carriage attached to the front of a bicycle—and a handful of women who clamber aboard and scurry down the aisles with baskets of lukewarm soft drinks and rice cakes. Business is bad at this hour. Dozing passengers look at the vendors through squinting eyes and give a quick shake of the head. In less than five minutes conductors with kerosene lanterns are yelling instructions up and down the length of the train, and the old Czechoslovakian diesel engine, followed by eight Indian- and Romanian-made coaches, make their way slowly out of the station, bells clanging.

Although the state-run Vietnam Railway has cut the travel time between Hanoi and Ho Chi Minh City from seventy-two to thirty-four hours while doubling the average speed to fifty-four miles per hour in recent years, this is not a journey for the faint-hearted. Toilets are holes in the floorboards, which grow slippery before many miles have passed. The heat takes a toll on everyone, with men stripping down to their boxer shorts and T-shirts, the women with comatose expressions waving small fans in a futile attempt to move the thick smoky air. I had not packed a supply of food or water, and every time I inquired about the possibility of a meal the conductor kept saying, "Saigon." It took me a while to understand he meant I'd have to wait a day for some sustenance, until we reached Saigon.

Still, I have always liked trains and the sense of nostalgic adventure they conjure up, and the Unification Express was no exception. We cut through the night at a noisy, steady clip toward the now-unmarked DMZ and the South beyond. Sleeping children stretched across their parents' laps. Small towns flashed by. Sometimes a silhouette of the Truong Son Mountains appeared briefly in the distance. I dabbed at my sweaty forehead with my shirtsleeve and thought about a steak (medium-rare with béarnaise sauce), but I was not unhappy.

This was only the second time I had ridden a train in Vietnam. The first was in 1969. South Vietnam had reopened the rail line on its side of the DMZ after a rash of Viet Cong ambushes, and the Saigon government, wanting to show that it controlled the countryside, invited a dozen reporters on a press trip from Hue to Danang. Our engine pushed two flat-bed cars designed to take the brunt of mines and towed another flat-bed on which we crouched. We had only gone ten or twelve miles when the train seemed to explode and stopped dead in its tracks. I dove for cover off the side and cautiously peered ahead. The lead minesweeper had hit a deuce-and-a-half truck on the tracks and flipped it upside down. Two Americans inside scrambled out the windows, apparently only their dignity bruised, while photographers snapped away. "We just stopped for a piss," one of the soldiers said. It was an amazing feat: Ours had been the only train over the track for more than a year, and the two GIs were waiting there for a dead-on hit. The South Vietnamese army officer escorting us cranked up his field radio, and a truck soon arrived to take us back to Hue.

Construction on Vietnam's rail system—known as Transindochinois during colonial times—began early in the twentieth century. By law, every bolt and rail came from France; by custom, every drop of sweat from Vietnam. Not until 1936 did the line south from Hanoi and north from Saigon link up, with Vietnam's last emperor, Bao Dai, and the French governor general, Rene Robin, pounding in the ceremonial silver spike near Tuy Hoa. Engineers called the completed project a marvel—a ribbon of rail that negotiated steep mountain passes, crossed scores of rivers, and, following the densely populated coastal corridor along the Mandarin Road, connected Southeast Asia's two great rice bowls, the Red River Delta of the north and the Mekong Delta of the south. A French company, Compagnie Francaise Immobiliere, ran special cars for weekend excursions to colonial resorts in Haiphong and Dalat and, for a while, tried to promote the line for luxury passenger travel. But the fine-dining cars and wooden-paneled sleeping coaches never paid their way. What made the system indispensable was war.

The line enabled France to move military materiel cheaply and efficiently during the colonial war. It proved a benefit as well to the Viet Minh, who controlled several spurs such as Yen Bai to Lao Cai and Ha Tinh to Quang Binh in northern "zones of freedom." In the end Ho Chi Minh's guerrillas neutralized whatever advantage the system gave France by forcing the French to fight the war's decisive battle in the isolated outpost of Dien Bien Phu, so far from the nearest rail line that troops had to be supplied by airdrops.

After the French departed in defeat in 1954, China sent thousands of laborers and several hundred engineer troops to Vietnam to upgrade the line and help Hanoi prepare for its war against South Vietnam. By the mid-1960s, Eastern-bloc military supplies were pouring through China into Lang Son and Lao Cai on North Vietnam's side of the border and into the port of Haiphong. From there the trick was to dodge relentless U.S. bombing and get the munitions and equipment by rail to the redistribution hub at Vinh. For seven years the route I now traveled, bouncing along in the Romanian-made coach, was the deadliest stretch of track in the world. Hanoi authorities say the U.S. aerial attacks on the railroad between 1965 and 1972 killed 758 people, wounded 1,721, and destroyed 430 bridges.

{{{  }}}

A QUESTION FROM ACROSS THE AISLE STARTLED ME—"How old are you?" I had been chatting casually with the young man only for a few moments, and it seemed an odd way to start a conversation. He had laid out bean curds and rice with noodles on a paper napkin. The train was shaking and making a holy mess of his meal. I told him I was almost sixty, and he asked, "How many children do you have?" I told him I didn't have any. "Then you're not married," he said. "You must be lonely." No, I told him, I'd been happily married for a long time, and Sandy and I just didn't happen to have kids. A look of sadness swept his face. "I am very sorry for you. That's terrible. What happened?"

Ho Van Trinh offered me some bean curd, which I declined. I was new enough to Vietnam to be taken aback by his directness but would learn there are three questions Vietnamese constantly throw out of the blue at every stranger. The one he had missed—Where are you from?—he had probably answered on his own because I was reading a month-old copy of the *Los Angeles Times*. His first question made perfect sense, because the

Vietnamese language has more than twenty words for "I" and doesn't have a simple word for "you"; age and status defines one's relationship and how people address each other. Trinh was merely being respectful in wanting to use the proper noun. If I were about his age, I would be older brother, *anh*; if younger, I'd be younger brother, *em*; if I were about his father's age, I'd be uncle, *chu*, and if I were older than his father or of high status, I'd be senior uncle, *bac*; if I were his Grandfather's age, *ong*.

And inquiring about the size of one's family is a form of respect as well, for the Vietnamese attach sorrow—and sometimes bad luck—to anyone bereft of children. I think it has something to do with loneliness. Vietnamese hate the idea of being alone, living alone, even eating alone. Perhaps because of this or because they lost so many sons in the wars, they shower children with more outward affection than I've seen in any society. Fathers dote on children with unabashed love. Big brothers carry around young siblings, hugging them and swapping baby talk, like they're holding something they themselves created. Grandfathers coddle babies, in sidewalk cafés and on street corners, with a tenderness that seems almost motherly. As a childless husband, I was afforded so many expressions of sympathy, followed by so many probing queries—my explanation of shooting blanks never seemed to clear up the issue—that I eventually adopted a fictional family. I had two children, a boy Sebastian and a girl Aileen (names that, conveniently, the Vietnamese found difficult to pronounce), and they were back in the United States, recently married and about to start their own families. This response would elicit beaming approval from my inquisitors. "Ah," they'd say. "A boy and a girl. Perfect. You are very lucky."

Trinh was twenty-six and didn't yet have a girlfriend. He was *em* to me; mercifully, he determined I was *chu*, not *ong*. He had a degree in English from Hanoi University but, having had no luck finding a job, was unsure whether to pursue another degree or look for a job in the hotel industry. Marriage was out of the question until he had secured his future and built up a nest egg, he said. Trinh had been to Saigon twice and not been impressed.

"The Southerners are different," he said. "Money, money, money. That's all they care about. Sometimes you can't always trust them. They talk more than we do in the North but they think less. In Ho Chi Minh you look at the people and they're fatter than we are. They've had an easier life. I mean, we're all Vietnamese, but they're just, well, just different."

The Vietnamese share a language, culture, and national identity, but the differences between North and South are as distinct as those in the United States between, say, New England and the Deep South. The Vietnamese of the North are more conservative, calculating and cocky proud; those of the South louder, more laid back, and at ease with foreigners. Busts of Ho Chi Minh are everywhere in the North; in the South you seldom see one outside a government office. The regional accents are so different that Vietnamese often have difficulty understanding one another. In the North, for instance, *Giap*, as in General Vo Nguyen Giap, is pronounced *Zap*, with a soft *a*. In the South, it has a *j* sound as in "Japan." The Northerners speak in a clipped, precise manner, the Southerners with a drawl that drags words out and lets vowels run together.

"My father would kill me if I came back to California with a Northern accent," said a Vietnamese American who works in Hanoi and whose parents—boat people from the 1975 exodus—remain disdainful of anything that smacks of Northern communism.

One reason for the regional differences is that life traditionally has been harder in the North. Its Red River Delta is more densely populated than the Mekong Delta, and Hanoi's winter is as chilly-gray and drizzly as Seattle's. Farmers can harvest only two rice crops a year in the North. If they have a good yield or a bountiful fish catch, they save some profits to get them through tough times. They build substantial homes of cement and brick designed to last a lifetime. They often live in villages surrounded by bamboo hedges that discourage social integration while encouraging xenophobia.

In the South, where the climate is sticky-hot year-round, farmers get three harvests and seldom have to worry about meeting their food needs.

If they make a profit, they'll spend it, perhaps on rice wine to share with neighbors. They build flimsy homes along the tributaries of the Mekong, and if one falls down in a howling gale they'll throw up another. The South has a better infrastructure, thanks in part to the immense network of roads, ports, and airports the Americans left behind; it also has had a longer, closer relationship with the West, ranging from France's takeover of Cochinchina as a colony in the nineteenth century to the transformation of Saigon into a quasi-American city in the 1960s and 1970s. When the communist leadership decided in the mid-1980s to put Karl Marx and Adam Smith into an economic blender and see what came out, Southerners, exposed to capitalism for decades, were far more comfortable than their northern brethren in adapting to the demands of free markets.

Over the years, starting in the eleventh century, the migration of people in Vietnam has been north to south. First, it was to escape overcrowding in the Red River Delta. In 1954, it was to escape communism, when upward of 1 million people, including many Catholics, crossed the Demilitarized Zone into South Vietnam, their panicked flight encouraged by CIA leaflets that spoke of a coming bloodbath of Christians. Finally, in 1975, it was to export communism when a huge cadre went south with missionary zeal to cleanse the land of capitalism and wrong thoughts. The migration and the north-south differences probably do not portend political instability because, unlike the Soviet Union when it imploded, deep ethnic and religious forces do not divide Vietnam. Still, authorities in Hanoi try to ensure no one region becomes too dominant by choosing a president, prime minister, and party secretary-general, each of whom has roots to one of Vietnam's three regions: the North, the Central Highlands, and the South. One usually represents the army, one the conservatives, one the reformers.

Ho Van Trinh and I ran out of conversation by Hue. I walked through the eight coaches, and as far as I could tell I was the only Westerner aboard. Families were sort of camping out now. Children had taken over the aisles as playgrounds, and parents lay sprawled across the wooden bench seats. No one paid me much attention. I tried the toilet but was driven back by powerful odors. A man asked for a Marlboro, and I gave him two. He asked me in broken English where I was from and how many children I had. The names Sebastian and Aileen did not seem to register with him. The windows in each coach, protected by grates because children like to throw stones at passing trains, were open. The breeze was heavy with humidity and heat. The countryside passed in a blur of emerald-green rice paddies and sky-blue waterways. We rolled on through the day and into the night.

By dawn on the third day, the seemingly empty landscape had given way to clusters of villages, then tightly packed rows of homes upon homes, and finally a jungle of urban sprawl with glass-fronted high-rises on the horizon. A conductor walked through the carriages, yelling first in Vietnamese, then in English: "Saigon, Saigon, five minutes now."

Once a fourteenth-century Cambodian village surrounded by mangrove forests, Saigon, as the French would name it, did not come under control of the southward-advancing Viets until 1698. They in turn were conquered a century and a half later by France under the pretext of wanting to stop the Nguyen Dynasty's persecution of Catholics. Using forced labor, the colonizers set out to create a French city in a wasteland of tropical swamps. The French filled in canals, built wide boulevards and tree-shaded roads—not a single one carried a Vietnamese name or was named for a Vietnamese person, place, or event—and designed grand villas landscaped with palm trees, glitzy casinos, and exclusive sporting clubs. Notre Dame Cathedral with its twin spires went up on the site of an ancient pagoda on Rue Catinat, and a state-run opium factory opened on Rue Paul Blanchy three blocks away. The French never loved Saigon the way they did Algiers, but it was as close as you could come to finding Paris in Asia.

"Saigon is very small and referred to proudly by the French as the Paris of the Orient," sniffed Noel Coward after a pre–World War II visit.

"This, I need hardly say, is an overstatement. It is a well arranged little town and it has several cafés and a municipal opera house, but it is not very like Paris."

District One—the downtown commercial core—is still officially called Saigon, but the greater megalopolis, with a population of 6 million, was renamed Ho Chi Minh City in 1976, a year after peace came to Vietnam. The name never really caught on. It was like renaming Boston "John F. Kennedy City." It was cumbersome and just didn't sound right. It brought to mind no images of tamarind-shaded boulevards or summer days around the pool at the Cercle Sportif or high tea on the veranda of the Continental Hotel, where Graham Greene's cynical, middle-aged British newspaperman warns the idealistic young American diplomat Alden Pyle—the Quiet American—about the perils of involvement in Vietnam. "I hope to God you know what you are doing there," he says. "Oh, I know your motives are good, they always are. . . . I wish sometimes you had a few bad motives, you might understand a little more about human beings. And that applies to your country too, Pyle."

The name didn't even carry a reminiscent whiff of the French and American Wars that so shaped the city's character. So to most people, in informal conversation at least, Ho Chi Minh City was still Saigon. During the war 17,000 Americans lived in Saigon, and the city had all the trappings of a tiny Fort Bragg. Tu Do (Freedom) Street was full of GIs, many in fatigues with M-16s slung over their shoulders, and they swaggered from bar to bar, where comely young women lurked in the doorways, calling, "Hey, Cheap Charlie, you buy me Saigon tea?" Now Tu Do had been renamed Dong Khoi (Uprising), and the Americans on the street were businessmen in white shirts and ties and tourists checking out upscale boutiques that sold Rolex watches and Calvin Klein jeans and Gucci leather. But I wasn't ready to write an obituary for the seductive Saigon I had once known. Strip away the thin veneer of communism, and there, among the ghosts of a wartime past, was a city that still had the soul of a hustler.

Before boarding the train in Vinh, I had made several appointments in Saigon. The first was at 10 A.M. with Trinh Thi Ngo, who had moved from Hanoi to Saigon in 1975 with her husband, a retired engineer, and now lived in a modest three-bedroom apartment near the former Presidential Palace, which she had often referred to as the "den of puppets." I had never met Mrs. Ngo but often heard her voice—smooth as silk, her English impeccable—flowing from the radio into the nighttime darkness of some outpost where I was holed up. In those days she was known as Hanoi Hannah.

"This is Thu Huong calling American servicemen in South Vietnam," she would begin her daily thirty-minute broadcasts that ran from 1965 to 1973, using an alias that translated as Autumn Fragrance. Then she would play a melancholy song ("Where Have All the Flowers Gone?" was a favorite), read news of antiwar protests in America, and, on Fridays, recite the names of Americans killed in action that were printed in the U.S. military newspaper *Stars and Stripes*.

Mrs. Ngo greeted me in a white *ao dai*, the figure-hugging trousers worn under a knee-length tunic, split up the side. She was sixty-seven, dark-haired with perfect posture, and quite lovely. Her English had grown a bit rusty with lack of use over recent years, but it was certainly serviceable, and her voice was still soft enough to sound mysterious, even sexy. Listening to her broadcasts, we used to speculate what Hanoi Hannah looked like. "Aw, she's probably a dump," one GI offered. "No way, man," his friend said. "She's gotta be a babe. Check out that sweet voice."

I told Mrs. Ngo—skipping, of course, any mention of the occasional vulgarities that would pop out when they heard her alluring voice—that soldiers used to wonder if she was beautiful and that many considered her North Vietnam's most prominent figure after Ho Chi Minh. In fact, Hanoi Hannah and Ho were the only two North Vietnamese most GIs had ever heard of.

She giggled, feigning surprise. "Oh my," she said, "I wasn't a celebrity. I did love that time in Hanoi, but I was just an ordinary citizen trying to contribute to my country. I'd been doing the broadcasts for about four years before I even found out the Americans were calling me Hanoi Hannah. How in the world did they come up with that name?" I told her some GI just made it up and it caught on, like the names of propagandists in other wars: Tokyo Rose in World War II, Seoul City Sue in Korea, Baghdad Betty in the Persian Gulf.

In many ways, Trinh Thi Ngo seemed an unlikely candidate to become the voice of communism. She grew up in Hanoi, under French colonialism, the daughter of a prosperous owner of a glass factory. She took private English lessons and perfected her command of the language watching French-subtitled Hollywood movies, among them *Gone with the Wind*, which she saw five times. After working as a volunteer at the Voice of Vietnam, she was chosen, largely because of her unaccented English, to begin broadcasting to U.S. troops as Autumn Fragrance.

"Yes, I wanted to make them a little bit homesick," she recalled. "But my real goal was to tell GIs they shouldn't participate in a war that wasn't theirs. I tried to be friendly and convincing. I didn't want to be shrill or aggressive. For instance, I referred to Americans as the adversary. I never called them the enemy."

Her scripts were written by propagandists in the North Vietnamese Army (NVA) who lifted their material from articles in *Time, Newsweek*, and the *New York Times* that Hanoi's diplomats in Eastern-bloc countries sent home. Sometimes activists from the United States brought the articles when they visited Hanoi.

She paused, perplexed. "You know," she said, "Jane Fonda never came back at all after the war. I wonder why. She made a tape I played that was very good. I heard that some years ago she made a public apology in the United States for coming to Hanoi during the war. Do you know if that's true?"

I said yes, she had made a televised apology to Vietnam veterans and their families for her 1972 visit when she was photographed at a North Vietnamese gun emplacement. Mrs. Ngo seemed puzzled. "I never read that in the newspapers here," she said, and I didn't think it appropriate to add that this was not surprising because Hanoi told its people only what it wanted them to know.

Neither did I mention that the problem for Hanoi Hannah was that her broadcasts weren't very credible. In fact, GIs liked her music but didn't believe a word she said. Even North Vietnamese officials didn't believe what they heard on Voice of Vietnam. If they spoke English, they tuned in to the Voice of America (VOA), the BBC, or U.S. Armed Forces Radio for news. But Mrs. Ngo was politely insistent: Her reports were not exaggerated, and her scriptwriters only used accurate accounts from the southern battlefields.

One of those accounts, which I heard one night on a fire support base with a unit of the 101st Airborne Division, told of the annihilation of a U.S. battalion and the loss of fifty U.S. planes in a battle near Ashau Valley. It struck the soldiers gathered around the radio with me that it was *us* she was talking about. "Hear that, dude? Fuck, man, we been blown away," one said. As far as I could tell, not a shot had been fired on the perimeter all day.

After the war, Mrs. Ngo was awarded the First Class Resistance Medal for her work, then she slipped quietly into anonymity, surrounded by young Vietnamese at the Voice of Vietnam who had never heard of Khe Sanh or Hamburger Hill, much less Hanoi Hannah. Occasionally the station asked her to do some voice-overs or translation, but mostly she was free to keep her own hours and come and go as she pleased. Demands were few.

With her career winding down, Mrs. Ngo said she hoped she would have the time and money to visit the country she had spent eight years talking about. "San Francisco has always been a dream," she said. "And the Golden Gate Bridge and Hollywood, I'd love to see them, too."

I asked if she could make one final broadcast to GIs who had been in Vietnam, what would she say? "That's easy. I'd tell them: 'Let's let bygones be bygones.'"

{{{   }}}

IT DIDN'T TAKE LONG TO FIGURE OUT that Saigon was still a free-spirited place marching to its own drummer. If Hanoi was Salt Lake City, strait-laced and restrained, Saigon was New Orleans, flashy and a bit wicked. The sex trade was booming, and hookers virtually hunted down their clients, cruising the sidewalks on motorbikes. The city's most famous bar, Apocalypse Now, was packed until 2:00 or 3:00 A.M. every night with twenty-something expats and locals. ("I don't think the Vietnamese here understand the significance of the bar's name," the bartender said. "They're too young. They just like the place.")

The country's first air-conditioned mall, the Superbowl, was drawing throngs of shoppers. Industrial parks were springing up. The monument that South Vietnam had erected to "our gallant allies"—a huge statue of a GI with several allied soldiers at the gate of Tan Son Nhut Airport—had disappeared, replaced by an open-air market. The six-story, fortresslike U.S. Embassy on Le Duan Street—its roof the point of departure for the last Americans in 1975—had been torn down and in its place, a stone's throw from the Club 2000 disco and a Mercedes-Benz dealership, stood an attractive new rambling building that housed the U.S. Consulate General. The staff was so swamped with visa applications from Vietnamese who lined up at 7 A.M. each weekday that within weeks of opening it had become the fifth busiest U.S. consulate in the world.

Across from the Majestic Hotel, on the far banks of the Saigon River—where Viet Cong guerrillas used to move freely through shanty-towns and no American dared venture—towering neon signs blinked out a red-letter message for the future: HITACHI . . . FUJI . . . COMPAQ. Their reflection shimmered across the nighttime waters, bathing anchored freighters and gliding sampans in an eerie glow. The placards of progress, or at least change, were everywhere.

I had spent my first night in Vietnam at the Majestic nearly thirty years earlier, camping out in a small corner room with a single light that hung from the ceiling. I had eaten dinner in the rooftop restaurant. My waiter wore a frayed tuxedo. I watched illumination flares dropped from U.S. planes cast slivers of light across the dark river. I had no idea what awaited me in the months ahead. Never had I felt so alone or so far from home. Now, the Majestic had been remodeled and the rooftop restaurant was gone. I sat in the lobby, amid tropical plants and wood paneling. I called Sandy in Hanoi on my portable phone. She was going to dinner with a group of Vietnamese friends. "When are you coming home?" she asked. I said I'd be back in Hanoi in a couple of days. Around me foreign and Vietnamese businessmen sat at marble-topped tables, drinking cappuccino and talking money. Commerce was in the air.

The marriage of communism and capitalism was an odd one, and anyone who thinks communism is the stronger partner is naive. Ho Chi Minh City is driving Vietnam's economy. Its per capita income is more than three times the national average (about $1 per day). The city contributes one-third of both the national budget and the national output. It accounts for two-thirds of the nation's wealth and 80 percent of the tax revenues. The North had won the war, but the South was winning the peace. Vietnam was being "Southernized." The Old Guard communist leadership of the North can bury its head in the sands of Marxist economic theory all it wants, but its constituency wants the model that Saigon symbolized—an economy that rewards initiative, encourages private enterprise, values liberal ideas, and frees itself from rigid government control.

"Ho Chi Minh is different because the city's long exposure to France and the United States affected the people's mentality," says Nguyen Son, who operated a clandestine Viet Cong radio station in the Mekong Delta during the American War and now was the spokesman for the Ho Chi Minh City government. "The people have been accustomed to a market economy for decades.

"If you asked me, from someone's appearance, who is a capitalist and who is a socialist, it would be difficult to tell. But I don't see any conflict.

To build socialism, you have to use capitalism and take from it what is good. To some extent, a market economy doesn't belong exclusively to capitalism but instead is an achievement of all mankind."

In Saigon, the party didn't even bother to string red banners with revolutionary slogans or flood neighborhoods with amplifiers to broadcast its messages. No one would have paid the slightest attention. The young generation had swapped its ancestors' conical hats for portable phones, and Saigon was now alive, pulsating to jackhammers and the vibrations of entrepreneurial spirit.

"What this generation has, and mine didn't, is opportunity," says Ho Si Khoach, a professor of history at Ho Chi Minh University. "We looked ahead to war. They look ahead to peace. They're much more independent, dynamic, creative than their fathers were. They don't want to study the subjects we did—history, philosophy, poetry. The majors they're choosing now are business, economics, English language, computer sciences."

{{{  }}}

I WALKED DOWN DONG KHOI STREET, toward the river, passing dirt-poor cyclo drivers who had once been soldiers in the South Vietnamese Army, as well as a travel agency run by a former Viet Cong cadre who catered to groups of returning former U.S. servicemen. I turned left on Ngo Duc Ke Street and entered a fast-food fish restaurant at Number 19, the location of the UPI office during the war. Back then it was filled with the chatter of telexes and old Royal typewriters, field reporters and photographers coming and going, and it seemed strange to find the place without chest-high sandbags protecting the entrance and floor-to-ceiling U.S. military maps on the walls. I would have given the world to see Bert Oakley, UPI's legendary rewrite man, still hunched over his typewriter, two packs of Salems and a bottle of Jack Daniel's on his desk, and hear him rasp, without looking up, "Hey, Davis. I need a lead. You got anything?" He had once seen an envelope that referred to me as Davis, and I am not sure he ever learned that my first name was David.

The owner said she had opened the restaurant here at the former UPI site four years ago. I told her that the storage closet used to be UPI's telex room and that the kitchen was the photo shop where Kent Potter and the other shooters processed their negatives, shouting with elation when an image they were proud of emerged. I'd briefly lived upstairs, in a third-floor cubicle with no window and an air-conditioner that iced over and rarely worked. But she wasn't much interested in wartime history, and perhaps that was just as well. Kent had been killed when his chopper was shot down over Laos near war's end, and Bert had died some years back after collapsing at the bar of the Foreign Correspondents Club in Hong Kong. That chapter in my history had nothing to do with her; I politely left, looking for a drink.

On Dong Khoi Street, a sweet-faced woman wearing a conical hat and carrying a baby brushed by me—and *pfffft*, as if by magic—the Mont Blanc pen in my shirt pocket was gone. I should have known better. The hotels were full of warnings not to carry valuables where they were accessible to pickpockets. This was, after all, Saigon, and the Saigonese were survivors. They had a tough edge that contrasted with the sense of innocence one found in Hanoi. Hanoi had the dreamers, Saigon the doers. The Saigonese had made the transition from wartime turmoil to peacetime prosperity not without peril—pollution, corruption, chaotic traffic, and a widening gap between rich and poor threatened the foundations of urban civility—but in capitalizing on opportunity they had raised the bar. Thus, it is toward Ho Chi Minh City and its free-wheeling economy that the rest of the nation now casts covetous glances.

# 5

# REFLECTIONS ON THE
# FALL OF SAIGON

Y THE TIME NORTH VIETNAM made its final push to liber-
ate—or conquer, depending on one's point of view—Saigon in
April 1975, I had left UPI and was working for the *Los Angeles
Times* in Washington, D.C. My time in the army had taught me never to
volunteer for anything, but suddenly I was obsessed again with Vietnam
and its unfolding drama. I volunteered to return. I updated my will, asked
the newspaper's Washington bureau chief to notify my brother if anything happened to me, and caught a Northwest flight to Seattle with
connections to Hong Kong and Saigon. Thirty hours later I stepped off
the plane at Tan Son Nhut. Everything felt familiar: the heat, the odors,

the blinding sunshine, the swirl of military activity. It was as though I had never left.

On Le Loi Street, Lieutenant Anh, who had been South Vietnam's assistant spokesman at the daily briefing the media labeled the "Five O'clock Follies" and who, for a monthly stipend, used to call UPI—and, I suspect, AP and our other competitors as well—with daily news tips, stepped out of the shadows. His face was ashen. He clutched me with both hands but offered no greeting to span the five years since we had seen one another. "Can you get me out?" he asked. "Everyone says the Americans are putting together an evacuation list. I've got to get on it. I'm a dead man if the communists take Saigon." I said I had just arrived and had no contacts, but I'd see what I could do.

Rumors raced through Saigon, all of a pending bloodbath. "AT LEAST A MILLION VIETNAMESE WILL BE SLAUGHTERED" read the headline of one of the last editions of *Stars and Stripes* to reach the capital. The CIA was more conservative, estimating that thousands would be killed. A company that provided insurance for U.S. correspondents increased premiums 1,000 percent. Restaurants closed and merchants fortified their shops with sandbags. The black market for the Vietnamese piaster spiraled so wildly out of sight that with Yankee money a shot of whiskey cost a dime, a hotel room a dollar.

In the Palace Hotel's fourteenth-floor nightclub, I bought a bar girl a drink. She showed me a telegram she had just received from a departed U.S. serviceman she had dated. "Dear Mai," it said, "plane ticket forwarded to Pan Am office on Tu Do Street. Paperwork waiting for you at U.S. Embassy. See you in St. Louis. Love." I asked her what she was going to do, and she replied quietly, "Sorry 'bout that, GI. I Vietnamese. I stay Vietnam."

North Vietnam had started its offensive four months earlier. The draft had been expanded to include forty-year-olds. Deferments for critical jobs were cancelled. Political officers, all Party members who often had more power than military commanders, were assigned to each unit. They made sure the troops got their rations and maintained discipline. They led self-criticism sessions and assigned soldiers into categories, either progressive or backward. They were unpopular, and the troops frequently called them "Mr. Argument." The North Vietnamese Army swept south out of Quang Tri Province in the first days of 1975, a violation of the treaty signed two years earlier in Paris. The Paris Peace Agreement ended the U.S. combat role in Vietnam and was hailed by President Richard Nixon as "peace with honor." South Vietnam's cities fell like dominoes in a Cold War nightmare: Ban Me Thuot, Hue, Danang, Chu Lai, Quang Ngai, Qui Nhon, Nha Trang. South Vietnam's troops threw down their weapons and fled, followed by panicked mobs of refugees that numbered in the hundreds of thousands. Hanoi kept only one division, the 308th, in the North as a home guard. As I sat drinking with Mai, eighteen divisions were closing in on Saigon, with tanks, artillery, and *bo doi*—peasant soldiers in threadbare uniforms and sandals cut from rubber tires, men who had passed from adolescence to adulthood in the jungles and likely as not hadn't seen families in the North for four or five years.

On the outskirts of South Vietnam's capital, NVA Colonel Vo Dong Giang received a coded message from North Vietnam's army headquarters, saying an all-out attack was imminent. It ended: "Good luck. See you in Saigon."

Twenty-one years earlier, in 1954, when Vietnam defeated France at Dien Bien Phu to end colonial rule, French soldiers were marched over the Doumer Bridge spanning the Red River in Hanoi. As one disarmed Frenchman passed by, a Viet Minh guerrilla kicked him in the ass. The Frenchman stopped, turned, and saluted; the Vietnamese returned the salute.

No such symbols of respect awaited Americans this time around. Americans were to gather on April 29 at prearranged pickup points in Saigon upon hearing a secret warning broadcast by Armed Forces Radio—Bing Crosby singing "I'm Dreaming of a White Christmas." Over a span of nineteen hours, 100 helicopters evacuated 5,595 South Vietnamese and 1,373 Americans. U.S. security guards used their rifle butts to beat back many more Vietnamese trying to scale the walls of the embassy compound and scramble aboard a chopper. Now the last chopper in OP-ERATION FREQUENT WIND—the largest helicopter evacuation in history—was skirting over Saigon, carrying the remnants of a U.S. force that once numbered 543,000 troops. The eleven U.S. Marines aboard had their weapons trained squarely on their former allies below.

Within minutes, the chopper was over the South China Sea. The U.S. Seventh Fleet came into view as Saigon faded from sight. For the first time since the French attacked Danang in 1858, Vietnam was free of foreign influence. For the first time in a generation—since a Cold War compromise divided the country at the 17th Parallel—there was no North Vietnam and no South Vietnam—only Vietnam.

For some this date—April 30, 1975—would represent a hopeful prologue to a lifetime of aspiration, for others, a dreadful epilogue to a decade of dashed dreams, broken promises, and unachieved goals. But no one—Vietnamese or American—would be untouched, and to this day Vietnamese in the South speak of the fall of Saigon as a milestone that divides everything in life into two eras: "before '75" and "after '75."

{{{   }}}

"OF COURSE I REMEMBER IT. My life changed that day. All our lives did." This was from Duong Cu, a former South Vietnam Supreme Court justice. He was sixty-five years old now, a scholarly man with a trim white beard and a professorial manner. His home, not far from the city center, had a garden patio off the second-floor sewing room and a bedroom lined with bookshelves. Neatly displayed on them were countless volumes on law, philosophy, and literature. Except for a few minor consulting jobs, Cu had not been able to find work for years.

I had come to Ho Chi Minh City just prior to the twenty-fifth anniversary of Saigon's fall, taking a two-hour jet flight from Hanoi, to ask people what they remembered of the day the communists won the war and what had become of their lives as a result. Cu said he had stayed home that day, caring for his sick wife and listening to the radio for news. After the shooting subsided, the streets fell so still he found the silence scary. His younger brother arrived on a motorcycle and suggested he take Cu to a Catholic monastery for his safety. Cu refused. "I'm in no danger," he said.

Despite widespread fears of a massacre, some Saigonese like Cu thought the North would be gracious in victory, and in fact the invading peasant army acquitted itself with discipline and professionalism. There was no killing. Cu also thought Hanoi would reach out to all Vietnamese, whether they had supported North or South, to nurture forgiveness and healing and fulfill the last promise Ho Chi Minh made to his people in 1969: "Once the American invaders have been defeated, we will rebuild our land ten times more beautiful."

He chuckled at his naiveté. On May 2, he was ordered to report to the university with a curriculum vitae and his official papers. "I thought it was just a formality, like a census," he said. "I didn't think I was in any danger because I wasn't a military man and I hadn't done anything wrong." Six weeks later he was packed off, carrying only a change of clothes and a day's rations, to one of the forty reeducation camps the communists set up to hold South Vietnam's 400,000 "false soldiers" and "false authorities," some for seventeen years. For the first eight months he attended political lectures. It was a disturbing experience. His teachers had little intellectual capacity and knew almost nothing of the outside world or of the subjects he held dear, like philosophy. He was not beaten or mistreated, but the days passed with a deadly tedium. He studied in the morning, discussed ideology with his mentors in the afternoon, and wrote self-criticism in the evening. There was no debate, and no opinions were to be expressed. To curry favor and be judged "reeducated," one needed to repeat the "truth." Cu's diet consisted of bad rice and rock salt. After six months he was allowed to receive a gift. His family sent instant noodles, tobacco, and dried meat.

Released after six years because of failing health, Cu returned home to find that his four brothers and sister had joined an exodus of boat people, a transformative flotilla that would carry 1 million South Vietnamese—about 5 percent of the South's population—to North America, Australia, and Europe. He considered himself lucky to find a job as legal adviser to an agency the communists established to attract foreign funds. His salary was $5 per month and food stamps. "I was so delighted," he said. "I thought I'd be able to get back in touch with my overseas friends." But he was forbidden to use the telephone or have any contact with foreigners. It was the penalty for being a southern "puppet." He quit after one year and, like most educated Saigonese of his generation, knew that his career was over.

"A lot of people think the war was a fight between communism and democracy/capitalism," Cu said. "But it wasn't that. The North's point of view was there was one Vietnam. The South thought there were two. The reality is we were just protecting ourselves in the South. Our system wasn't perfect. Human rights were abused. The legal system had flaws. There was a lot of corruption. But people will fight to protect what is theirs."

Cu spent his time now at home reading and researching law as a hobby. Sometimes he wondered how far his career would have taken him had events taken a different direction. But over many years pondering works of Western philosophers in his bedroom library, he had made his peace.

"I'm not bitter at all," he said. "I could have left as a political or economic refugee, but self-respect never would have let me think of myself as a refugee, though I have no quarrel with friends who decided to go. We all have to make our own decisions. But I stayed because I wanted to. Generally, things are getting better in Vietnam. And for my son's generation, life is improved, very much improved. You just have to learn to accept things as they are."

That's what the Southerners like Cu who didn't support the Viet Cong have done. This isn't the Vietnam they wanted or expected, and communism isn't an ideology they have embraced. But the spirit to question and criticize has left them. They decided not to walk away, so what was the choice but to play the hand they were dealt? Life *had* gotten better. They no longer have to fear their government as long as they aren't interested in making a political statement—which describes the overwhelming majority of Vietnamese—and reconciliation between North and South has been achieved on a personal level. No one cares which side his neighbor fought for. After the war all the plum jobs and positions of power went to Northerners and Southern revolutionaries. Cu could even accept that fact, as long as his now-grown children were given the equality of opportunity that his own generation was denied.

{{{   }}}

NGUYEN DUC BAO WAS ON Saigon's northern perimeter at midmorning on April 30, 1975, locked in mortal combat against the last organized resistance the South Vietnamese would offer. Nine years earlier he had said goodbye to his wife and two children in Hanoi and started the long, dangerous trek down the Ho Chi Minh Trail with 5,000 men of the NVA's 141st regiment. "The jungle was nothing new to me," he said. "I'd been fighting in it better than half my life." His right forearm bore the jagged outline of the Vietnamese flag he had tattooed into his skin with a sewing needle and ink after joining the Viet Minh and fighting the French as a teenager.

"I really had no idea that we were fighting the last battle of the war," the seventy-year-old retired colonel said. "We had been fighting so long it was hard to believe the war would not go on forever. That morning the enemy fought well. The fighting was very heavy. There were dead on both sides. Then just like that"—he snapped his fingers—"the firing stopped and the war was over. That night, for the first time in months, we got to sit quietly and talk about our comrades who died, to write letters to our families in the North. It was strange having the time to do that and not having to worry if patrols would see the lights of our campfires. I was so happy I couldn't sleep. I had not seen my wife and children in almost ten years. Ten years. That was several lifetimes in those days."

Bao had made notes about his military career in preparation for my visit, and sometimes when he dwelt on some minor happening with painfully exact detail I'd try to push him along a bit. He always seemed disappointed but would turn the page. We sipped Cokes. His daughter, a teacher, stood behind him, occasionally supplying missing words when his memory slipped. At my request he brought out his NVA uniform. He put it on as he does each April 30 and on other national holidays. His daughter helped him line up the buttons with the proper buttonholes. "Now that looks better," she said, straightening the collar.

I asked him what he had done after the war. "I was in charge of a re-education camp," he said. "We had 40,000 South Vietnamese soldiers, including twenty-three generals."

"How did you treat them?"

"In a very humanitarian way. We didn't kill them or knock them down. I always thought of them as victims of the war. But they were not broth-ers. They had been brainwashed by the puppet regime in Saigon. Our job was to teach them how to make progress and become good persons. If they were good at studying and good at laboring, they got to go back to their families early. Each time I came to visit them on work details, they were happy. They treated me with respect. In the fields they worked with-out shirts. They'd put their shirts on when I came and they'd call me 'Mr. Colonel.'"

He made it sound as though the inmates were at summer camp and had a pretty good time being remodeled into citizens of the new Viet-nam. I doubted his interpretation yet accepted that history sometimes plays tricks; we all tend to remember events long past in a way that is fa-vorable to our actions. I liked Colonel Bao. However vile the reeducation camps were, they were no more vile than the tiger cages South Vietnam had used for some of its political prisoners. I could not judge what Colonel Bao had been, but I believed the man I met was a good man. He was spending his retirement working on health and veterans committees for the Communist Party, and on several occasions he hosted groups of returning U.S. vets asking to meet their former enemy.

"We've had good talks with your veterans," he said. "I think they were impressed with us. I know we were impressed with them."

His daughter brought out a bowl of tangerines, and Bao and I sat in the small garden of his home talking long into the afternoon, he wearing the blouse of his NVA uniform. In an army career that spanned thirty-four years, he spent nine years fighting the French, ten the Americans, and six Pol Pot's Khmer Rouge in Cambodia. What he most appreciated now, he said, was the peacefulness of his life. His pension—$72 per month, a comfortable sum in Vietnam—provided for all his material needs, and he had no more real concerns, he said, other than to ensure that the next generation had opportunities his didn't and that his children prospered.

Funny. That is how Duong Cu, the former South Vietnamese judge, put it too.

{{{   }}}

AT 10 A.M. APRIL 30, 1975, Pham Xuan An was in *Time* magazine's office with several South Vietnam intelligence officers, listening to Radio Saigon. "Citizens, stand by," the broadcast said. "The president will shortly make an important announcement." *Time*'s American staffers had left Saigon two days earlier on an evacuation flight; now, reporting the city's final hours was left to An, the most trusted and respected of the Vietnamese reporters who worked for Western news agencies. I hadn't known An well during the war, but whenever I'd asked a colleague a question about the history of the Viet Cong or needed an analysis of a political event, the reply invariably came back, "Go see An over at *Time*."

An had worked for Caltex in 1952, spent two years studying in the United States, and joined the U.S. Military Advisory Group as an adviser in Saigon in 1954. He was one of the few Vietnamese reporters who had

U.S. press credentials, and his reporting was considered rock-solid: accurate, insightful, forward-looking. He shared his knowledge generously even with those of us who didn't work for *Time* and was good company when you could grab him for a beer on the veranda of the Continental.

The radio announcement—that President Duong Van Minh was surrendering to North Vietnam—didn't surprise An. In fact, very little surprised An because his intelligence was as sound as his reporting. An, it turned out, was a Viet Cong colonel and had worked for the resistance movement since 1945.

"I don't think anyone suspected," An said when, twenty-five years after the war's end, I walked through the green iron gate surrounding his house that the government provided him for $6 rent per month. "Even my wife. She knew I was involved with the liberation front, but she didn't know any details."

An had greeted me at the doorstep barefoot, smoking a Marlboro. He was seventy-two years old, with jet-black hair and a thin, tired face. The two German shepherds that had accompanied him everywhere had died, and his companion now was a Rottweiler named Bella. He took me into his library. The shelves were packed with books in Vietnamese, English, and French: Bernard Fall's *Last Reflections on a War*, David Halberstam's *The Best and the Brightest*, Neil Sheehan's *A Bright Shining Lie*, Nayan Chanda's *Brother Enemy*, Stanley Karnow's *Vietnam: A History*. Two other titles caught my eye: *Is South Vietnam Viable?* and *How to Stay Alive in Vietnam*. His desk was piled with papers and letters, and it was difficult to know whether he was very busy or just hadn't gotten around to doing all that needed to be done.

"An, I don't know quite how to put this," I said, "but being a double agent, didn't it make you feel pretty uncomfortable with yourself? I mean, weren't you betraying the friends at *Time* who trusted you?"

"No, it was simple, really, not complicated at all. I had my national obligation and I had my job. I was an analyst, not an operative. For instance, before the Tet Offensive, the front wanted a detailed report about the military situation around Saigon. How strong was the ARVN? What was their discipline, morale? What was the U.S.'s likely reaction? I did that. The research I did was strategic, not tactical. It was like working at RAND. I didn't do espionage. I wasn't supposed to plant stories. That was for the propaganda section. I never did anything that endangered the life of any American. I was loyal to the revolution but I had friends and sources to protect on both sides.

"To work for *Time*, you had to be objective. Learning that helped me with my national obligation. The American press was different than any I'd known. You are a reporter. A good reporter reports exactly what he sees and you get it right. You should not rationalize. So when I wrote for the front, I'd ask myself, 'Am I being objective in this?' I learned a lot being a correspondent. And I learned a lot from America. It helped me open up my way of thinking."

An had gone into the forests with the Viet Minh in 1945 as a seventeen-year-old platoon commander. Seven years later he started work in a strategic intelligence unit set up by Hanoi in the South. An said that with Vietnam under colonial rule, the decision to join the resistance was a no-brainer.

"The front was about nationalism then. Communism came later. The front stood for two things: It was against the French, and it was for social justice between landowners and tenants. That's why it was so compelling to people my age. It promised justice. We had to study French history in those days. We studied the French Revolution, and we'd say, 'If the French can do it, why can't we?' That's the irony. The French inspired us how to make a revolution against France.

"For a young person like me, it was easy to be against injustice. But as you grow older, you realize it's not so black and white. Now it's like I've seen the beginning of the revolution and I've seen the end. I understand that you can't crush social injustice overnight. I'm not an optimist or a pessimist any more. I'm just a realist. I try to look at things objectively like *Time* taught me to do as a reporter."

An's six-year-old grandson came over and sat on the arm of my chair. He didn't smile or frown. He just looked at me quietly with big brown eyes. An lit another Marlboro.

For ten years during the American War, An's Viet Cong liaison contact was an older woman whose name he never knew and with whom he never exchanged more than a casual hello. Their paths would cross momentarily in the Central Market or on Nguyen Hue or Le Loi Street—but never twice in the same place—and the messages they passed were written in invisible ink and hidden in biscuit tins or packs of cigarettes or bouquets of flowers.

Three days after Saigon fell, a North Vietnamese captain and a sergeant came into *Time*'s office. They were polite, even friendly, and told the man Hanoi referred to by the code name Hai Trung to register, along with others who had worked for U.S. companies, at the former South Korean embassy. An never told them he had spent the war on their side because that would have been only partly true. What he had worked for was the justice of independence. He did not want to see the North dominate the South, or the South the North. He was not anti-American. He believed Vietnam could learn many important lessons from the West. He wondered if communism were best for Vietnam.

The men from the North promoted An to general and offered him a job in censorship. "When you work for a free press, you don't want a job in censorship. I turned it down," An explained. He kept listening to the BBC and Voice of America. He spoke often of his departed American friends. There were even reports that in Saigon's final hours he had helped several disoriented South Vietnamese soldiers flee to safety by boat, taking from his bookcase the *Indochina Geographic Handbook*, written in 1943 by British naval intelligence. He showed them how the currents flowed in April, where weather depressions were likely, when monsoons struck—and he suggested an escape route. An wasn't against anyone. He was simply for the Vietnamese.

So the revolutionaries who now ran Saigon set An up in a nice house and put him out to pasture. His career ended. His double life was uncovered by French intelligence in 1978; the Party told An not to give interviews about it. When an occasional American journalist returned to Vietnam and asked the government for permission to visit An, he was told An was sick and unavailable. An seldom left his home, and the mail on his desk grew higher.

"I owe so many letters to friends all over the world," An told me. "I guess I haven't written anyone in twelve or thirteen years. That's too bad because I'm a little sentimental and I miss those journalists a lot. Jack Foise, Dan Sutherland, Stan Karnow. Those were good people. I have good intentions to answer but my English is getting rusty. And my French is worse. I don't even know where my typewriter is. Karnow tried to get me to write my memoirs. Random House was interested. I said nothing doing. I'm poor but I don't need money. Besides, I don't want to embarrass people on either side. Even if they were dead, what would their children think if I wrote unflattering things about their fathers?"

An, the good soldier of the revolution, had paid a price for believing the revolution was over once the French and the Americans left. He regretted that freedom of expression was still controlled but thought Vietnam was making economic progress and slowly becoming more free. I asked him what was the biggest mistake the Americans had made in Vietnam.

"Look," An said, "some of the influential Americans I dealt with, like Colby, Lansdale, they were beautiful people. They were very smart. They weren't ignorant about Vietnam. But being smart and making the right decision are different things. The big mistake the Americans made was not understanding the Vietnamese's history, culture, mentality. They were so sure military strength would win the war, they never bothered to learn who they were fighting."

{{{   }}}

ON APRIL 30 AT 11:10 A.M., the first communist T-34 tank, driven by Bui Duc Mai and carrying a crew whose helmets bore the words "*Ve*

*Saigon*" (Onward Saigon), crashed through the gates of the Presidential Palace. President Minh, having trouble summoning his cabinet because the switchboard operators had fled, sat with his thirty top advisers in two rows of chairs, awaiting the victors. "The revolution is here. We have been waiting for you all morning," he said.

In the fourth-floor Associated Press office on Nguyen Hue Street, George Esper heard Minh's surrender broadcast over Radio Saigon and typed a one-paragraph bulletin with hands trembling. He handed the bulletin to the telex operator, who read it quickly. The operator's jaw dropped, his eyes became saucers. He bolted for the door. Esper and his colleague Peter Arnett wrestled him back into his chair and did not release him until he had punched the bulletin for AP's New York editors that North Vietnam had taken Saigon.

"Then I ran into the street to get reaction," Esper said, recalling events during an interview. The first person he saw was a South Vietnamese police officer, wild-eyed, arms waving, shouting, "*Fini, fini!*" Esper approached to ask a question and the man unholstered his revolver. "I thought, 'Oh, my God, he's going to shoot me. I survived ten years in Vietnam and now I'm going to die the day the war ends.' Personally, I never liked weapons. They always made me nervous." The officer put the gun to his own head, saluted a nearby statue of a South Vietnamese soldier, and killed himself. His body fell at Esper's feet.

By the time Esper got back to the AP office, three NVA soldiers were waiting. They put their Chinese-made AK-47s on the counter. "They were twenty-one or twenty-two, shy but very friendly. We had a translator so we interviewed them. They took out a map and showed us the invasion routes. They said they'd been in the field two years. They opened their wallets and showed us pictures of their wives and girlfriends. One had kids. I'd been writing all these years about the nameless, faceless communists, and here I was with three of them and they seemed very, well, human. I thought, 'Geez, so many Americans, so many North Vietnamese and South Vietnamese have killed each other, and it turns out they all have the same feelings, the same loneliness.' That's how the war ended for me."

Esper had arrived in Vietnam in 1965, an unworldly reporter from Uniontown, Pennsylvania, who worked AP's overnight desk in New York. He hadn't really volunteered for Vietnam. It was just that AP needed bodies to build up its Saigon staff; an editor asked if he'd go to Vietnam. "I said sure," he recalled. "It sounded exciting. I hadn't been following the story that closely, and I'd never even thought about joining the foreign staff. But I agreed to go for a year."

He did the year and returned to New York, back to his old job. Everything around him seemed ordinary. The domestic stories he read and wrote seemed meaningless. It dawned on him he never should have left Vietnam. Esper returned in 1967. He married a Vietnamese woman, Ha Kim Cuc. He would write a book on Vietnam and, when Saigon fell, would be one of a handful of American journalists to refuse evacuation and stay behind to cover the first weeks of Hanoi's triumph.

We stayed in touch from time to time over the years with an occasional lunch in Boston, where Esper worked as an AP feature writer, and also during a stint covering the Gulf War. He was sixty-seven years old when I last saw him, long since divorced from Ha, and had been with AP for forty-two years. He said he was thinking of retiring to accept a teaching job at his alma mater, the University of West Virginia, but was fearful. "AP's been my family. That's where all my friends are." In all his assignments around the world, nothing had ever matched the intoxicating allure of Southeast Asia or the blood-pumping high of covering the Vietnam War.

"I've searched for an answer why I stayed all those years," he said, "and what I keep coming back to was a young nurse from Upstate New York I saw on a fire base. It was monsoon season. We were under rocket attack. She was tending the badly wounded. Some died in her arms. And I said, 'Wow, a woman. Why are you here?' and she said, 'Because I've never felt so worthwhile in my life.'

"That's how I felt too. What we were doing was really important. On top of that, we were living this free-wheeling, unstructured life with so much freedom and a go-to-hell attitude. It was a very good lifestyle despite the war. It was exotic, sensual. I think that's one of the reasons some people wanted to get lost in Vietnam and why some stayed in Vietnam, mentally, forever."

Esper had been one of the lucky ones—he survived. I asked Esper if he'd been present when Senator Barry Goldwater tongue-lashed the press during a visit to Saigon in 1965. He said he hadn't. Goldwater's assessment of the press was this: "I'd like to see you pansy reporters out there in the boondocks getting your asses shot at. No guts, no guts. I wish they'd let me have my way out here. There wouldn't be a gook or a fucking reporter left in six months. . . . Our kids are dying out there right now while you guys are up here getting pissed. . . . You're nothing but a bunch of yellow bastards."

More than 320 reporters and photographers from both sides died in combat covering the war.

{{{  }}}

BY NIGHTFALL ON APRIL 30, 1975, the old Saigon no longer existed. It was now the soon-to-be-impoverished economic capital of a peasant nation. The Viet Cong flag, red and blue with a yellow star, flew over the Presidential Palace. Young, hungry NVA soldiers in pith helmets and VC guerrillas in floppy bush hats gathered around separate campfires in city parks. Saigon was dark, apprehensive. A thousand miles to the north, Hanoi lay eerily still. Unlike the liberation of Paris, where Ernest Hemingway had observed, "Anyone who doesn't get drunk tonight is an exhibitionist," Vietnam's wartime anguish ended quietly and, in the appropriately austere and disciplined manner of the men who had come south to govern, somberly. The South was exhausted by war. Its people were willing to give the Northerners a chance.

Bao Ninh, an NVA soldier from Hanoi who was in Saigon that day, would write of his protagonist, Tien, in *The Sorrow of War*: "In later years, when he heard stories of V-Day or watched the scenes of the fall of Saigon on film, with cheering, flags, flowers, triumphant soldiers and joyful people, his heart would ache with sadness and envy. He and his mates had not felt that soaring, brilliant happiness he saw on the film. True, in the days following 30 April, he had experienced unforgettable joys after the victory. But on the night itself, they had that suffocating feeling. . . . And why not? They'd just stepped out of the trenches."

That night, in their small home on Saigon's Nhieu Loc Canal, two tailors, Le Van Vang and his wife, Vang Hui Huong, arranged four bags filled with clothes and rice, preparing to flee if Hanoi's troops went on a vengeful witch hunt, as Pol Pot's murderous communist guerrillas had done in Cambodia two weeks earlier. But there was no witch hunt, no bloodshed. The young *bo doi* soldiers had not come for retribution. And soon the Vangs unpacked their bags and went back to stitching.

I found the Vangs in the same house by the canal where they had lived since 1963, the year they exchanged vows in an arranged marriage. "Our parents knew each other and Huong and I both did the same job, tailors. So they said we should marry," Mr. Vang said. His wife added: "That was the tradition then. But our children wouldn't stand for such a thing today." Their home was at the end of a three-foot-wide lane where little houses stood shoulder to shoulder and a maze of alleyways meandered in all directions. It was the type of poor, working-class neighborhood that was often a Viet Cong stronghold during the war.

Huong did most of the talking while Le Van sat at her side, nodding occasionally in agreement. "My father joined the Viet Minh," she said. "He was killed fighting the French. But really 1965 to 1975 was pretty normal here. I had no idea about anything political. I didn't think about Americans being in Vietnam. We hardly ever saw them. They must have been at other bases, outside Saigon. Mostly people here just cared about working and making business."

She said Le Van had escaped the South Vietnamese draft by hiding between two walls and never venturing out of the house during the day. He did that for almost a decade. If the police came to inquire about his whereabouts, she would tell them he had already left for the front.

For the Vangs, the bad times came after the war. The communists banned the wearing of the traditional *ao dai* dress as bourgeois, and sewing *ao dais* had provided most of the Vangs' income. Making a profit was deemed antirevolutionary. The markets ran low on food. To survive, the Vangs sold everything: the radio, then the refrigerator, their clothing, even the material for *ao dais*. "Finally we had nothing left," Huong said.

Their lives did not recover until the government started implementing free-market reforms in the late 1980s. The ban on *ao dais* was lifted, as was the taboo on turning a profit. They got the refrigerator back and bought a TV and two Honda motorbikes. Four of their seven children graduated from college. One of them had become an engineer. The People's Committee was beautifying the neighborhood, cleaning up the waste-filled canal and installing streetlights on a new pathway along the waterway. "Really, life is so much better than it was that we have no complaints," Huong said.

{{{  }}}

FOR AMERICA THE FALL OF SAIGON was an ending, for Vietnam a beginning. But when the curtain came down on the Second Indochina War, the Vietnamese did not find the peace they sought. Old rivalries and suspicions reemerged, and retribution was still to be meted out. Neither did the Americans find they were able to reclaim the innocence and faith of a past era. In a 1964 Lou Harris poll, 76 percent of respondents said they trusted their government "to do the right thing in almost all cases"; by 1976 it was 34 percent.

For years Americans would debate the question, Who "lost" Vietnam? "We really meant to help and to stabilize," Admiral Noel Gayler, commander of the U.S. forces in the Pacific, said after Saigon's fall. "But things went awry in a lot of ways." Was it the press that lost Vietnam? The politicians? The soldiers? The antiwar activists? Perhaps, in the end, Vietnam simply wasn't there to be "won" in any conventional sense. The United States had come to extinguish a revolution and ended up nourishing one. It had come to build and ended up destroying. It came to the jungles of Vietnam to win hearts and minds, and in fighting its longest war—the first war the United States had ever lost—discovered the tools of war were no substitute for the vitality of nationalism. History, not ideology, shaped the future.

# 6

# IN SEARCH OF
# A PEACE DIVIDEND

IRTUALLY EVERY TOWN AND VILLAGE in the North has a
military cemetery for its fallen soldiers. Tended by schoolchildren and groups of volunteer veterans, they are meticulously
manicured, the grass carefully clipped, the gravel pathways spotlessly tidy.
In a country where the unofficial religion is ancestor worship, a country
where relatives visit and talk with their departed loved ones on special
days of the year, these resting places are more than memorials. They are
shrines—to the bonds of family, to the sacrifice of nation, to the cycles of
life. At the foot of many small headstones, incense sticks burn and freshly
cut flowers and bowls of fruit are neatly arranged. Some of the stones are
marked with a name, others with just the words *liet sy*—"martyr" or "un-

known soldier." In these cemeteries, by the tens of thousands, lie the "nameless, faceless communists" the AP's George Esper spoke of; I suspected if I had known them thirty years earlier, in circumstances other than a war, I would have found many friends, just as I had in Hanoi among their sons and daughters.

The largest of the graveyards is Truong Son, near Dong Ha in Quang Tri, a war-ravaged province that was part of South Vietnam until "liberated" by the North in its Easter Offensive of 1972. (President Nixon responded to the offensive with the comment: "The bastards have never been bombed like they're going to be bombed this time.") The headstones stretch row after row in perfect symmetry as far as the eye can see, more than 10,000 of them spread over 300 acres. The grave markers start at a stone monument whose three towering columns—visible from a long way down the road—resemble the stems of a flower and reach up the slopes of a grass-covered knoll and slip off toward a clump of trees to the east. The cemetery, opened in 1975 soon after the fall of Saigon, became the final home of soldiers who died on battlefields throughout the South, their bodies brought to Dong Ha in groups of five and six as corpses turned up here and there over the course of many years. Occasionally there is still a burial. At the end of the path near the entrance is a small visitors' center where many foreigners and Vietnamese stop to sign the guest register.

I toured the cemetery the first time with Bobby Muller, who had come to Vietnam in 1969 as a gung-ho Marine lieutenant and gone home as a paraplegic. "We were meant to guard the Cam Lo bridge that night and I just got whacked," he said of the bullet that severed his spine. Muller, who now was fifty-four years old and president of the Vietnam Veterans of America Foundation, maneuvered his wheelchair past rows of headstones. He paused occasionally by one of the headstones, then would have to apply extra muscle on the handgrips to get his wheels moving again on the gravel. I'd offer to push and he'd say impatiently, "Naw, I got it." Muller had been lifted by chopper from the battlefield and spent a year at the

Veterans Administration Hospital in the Bronx. "The place stunk, it was overcrowded," he said. He left the hospital as an antiwar activist. I asked him if he remembered what he was doing the day Saigon fell in 1975.

"Yeah," he said. "I was where I was every afternoon. At the track. I'd reached the stage in my life where I'd pretty much said fuck it. And when you're trying to figure out a daily double and a couple of perfecta bets at Belmont, the collapse of Vietnam was pretty much a background piece.

"To be truthful, I didn't like the Vietnamese. Sorry. But that's how I felt. In First Corps, up north where the Marines' AO [area of operation] was, the Vietnamese didn't see us as liberators. We were the people bringing down the reign of terror. Frankly they'd fuck with us all the time. And I'd think, 'Excuse me. I've just come 10,000 miles to save you from communism. So what's with this attitude you've got?' The ARVN, I worked with three of their battalions. Every single time there was a firefight, the ARVN would split. But the NVA were absolutely the toughest, most dedicated sons of bitches you'd ever want to fight. Everything I had to do with the Vietnamese was a negative experience."

Muller's arms were getting tired now as the wheels of his chair crunched through the gravel. We turned down a path to the left and headed back toward the visitors' center. I don't know why, but I jotted down some names on the markers we passed: Nguyen Van Luc, Phan Tien Lam, Liet Sy, Ho Khac Nghi.

"When I got involved with the vets' antiwar movement," Muller said, "my attitude was that I couldn't flip-flop and go from having my guys die fighting communists to, 'Ho, Ho, Ho, the NLF [National Liberation Front, i.e., the Viet Cong] is going to win.' I just said, 'This is wrong. We shouldn't have gotten involved.' Back in '70, '71, it was absolutely stunning to me that I, who had killed more communists than anyone I'd ever met, would be called a communist for opposing the war by people who were still waving the flag, my country right or wrong. I'd ask them why they weren't against the war and they'd say, 'We support our boys.' My rejoinder was: 'Excuse me, *we . . . are . . .* the boys.'"

The boys came home, but the wounds of war didn't really heal. Muller believed the antidote was reconciliation between the United States and Vietnam and that it was the veterans, not the government, who were the appropriate ones to begin a dialogue with Hanoi. In 1981, he led the first group of U.S. vets to return to Vietnam since the war. He could find only one business willing to underwrite the trip—*Penthouse* magazine.

"Vietnam was really off-limits then," Muller recalled. "*Good Morning, America* gave me a camcorder and said, 'Shoot anything.' But we were received with total grace and friendship and courtesy. I was blown away. And I went home and told vets, 'Come on, you can do this. You gotta do this.'" Before leaving Hanoi, Muller and his delegation laid a wreath at the memorial for North Vietnam's war dead, with the agreement no photographs be taken. The card they attached to it said simply, "With respect, Vietnam Veterans of America." Two hundred death threats poured into Muller's Washington, D.C., office.

Muller has come back to Vietnam often since then, to oversee the health-related projects his nonprofit group operates, including one that provides prosthetic limbs to landmine victims. Vietnam's countryside is still strewn with 3.5 million unexploded landmines, which, since the war ended, have claimed the lives of 38,000 civilians—just a third less than the total number of Americans killed during ten years of war.

It was getting toward late afternoon, and shadows swept over the cemetery. The only sound was a barking dog somewhere down the road. The gardeners had gone home, leaving the caretaker to await our return. Around us the world felt peaceful and lonely. Muller wheeled his way up to the visitors' center. *Crunch, crunch, crunch.* He opened the guest register and wrote:

> The magnitude of the Vietnamese people's suffering is hard to imagine even though we are so connected in our history and hearts. Let these sacrifices inform and inspire all of us to continue working for peace, healing and to prevent anything like what happened here from happening again.

{{{ }}}

A NYONE WHO ISN'T MOVED by military cemeteries has a stone heart. I can lose myself for hours in U.S. Civil War burial grounds. I have wandered through the U.S. World War II cemetery in Manila and Egypt's desert graveyard at El-Alamein and Thailand's cemetery in Kanchanaburi for the Allies who built the bridge over the River Kwai. I think the manner in which a nation honors its war dead—and, indeed, treats its living who have answered the call—says something about the traditions and civility of the country. In Hanoi, I arranged a half-dozen interviews with veterans groups and government officials to talk about benefits for military families and the role of former soldiers in society. Vietnam had 4 million veterans after thirty years of war, and the Veterans' Association of Vietnam was one of the country's most powerful mass organizations. Vietnam, I was told, had not forgotten the sacrifices. Mothers of soldiers killed in battle received a one-time payment of $272 and a lifelong monthly pension of $21 dollars, in addition to free medical care. They were honored as "Heroic Mothers"—similar to Gold Star Mothers in the United States—and, along with war widows, afforded priority in getting jobs. The government ensured that their boys were buried in pristine cemeteries, like the one near Dong Ha, and that families received support in the search for sons and husbands whose remains had never been found.

"There is a saying in Vietnam that when you drink the water, you remember the source," Huynh Van Trinh, an official with the veterans association, told me. "And the men and women who served their country are the source of our strength. For those who fell, taking care of their mothers is the duty not just of the government but of all society."

I was impressed. But I made a naive assumption. I assumed that since Vietnam was unified and Ho Chi Minh had long advocated reconciliation between the two Vietnams, all mothers received the same respect and all former soldiers were entitled to the same dignity. So I never said,

"We're talking about all Vietnamese, right, whether from the North or the South?" Had I asked that, I would have been told, no, just the ones from the North. The Southerners who hadn't been revolutionaries grieved silently. They received nothing, not even a burial place for their sons and husbands. The North had *liet sy* (martyrs), the South had *nguy* (puppets).

When the U.S. Civil War ended with the surrender at Appomattox Court House in 1865, Ulysses Grant told his Union soldiers, "The rebels are our countrymen again." He sent General Lee's troops home with their horses and sidearms and said he hoped they would make it in time to plant new crops. The South would have good cause for resenting their postwar treatment under Reconstruction, but Grant's gesture sent a powerful message of reconciliation and forgiveness. North Vietnam couldn't bring itself to do the same. To its leaders, the words "honorable" and "patriotic" were misnomers if used to describe the supporters and combatants of the South.

> *There are no more sharks in the sea,*
> *There are no more beasts on earth,*
> *The sky is serene,*
> *Time is now to build peace for ten thousand years.*
> —fifteenth-century poem written after the Vietnamese
> drove the Ming invaders of China out of Vietnam

During the war, we reporters spent 90 percent of our time—maybe more—covering the American aspects of the conflict, generally treating South Vietnam as something of a nonentity. When weekly casualty figures were released at the Five O'clock Follies on Thursday, we'd write 600 or so words wrapping up U.S. fatalities: *The U.S. Command announced today that 16 Americans died and 57 were wounded during the week in fighting that raged through.* . . . The ARVN's losses were mentioned almost in passing, often in a single paragraph tagged onto the end of the story: *Meanwhile South Vietnamese officials put ARVN losses during the week at 95 dead and 160 wounded.* Journalistically, I understood our bias. Our readers were Americans, and the only reason they cared about Vietnam was because of U.S. involvement. It was the only reason we were interested, too. If it had been a civil war between, say, the Wa and Shan in Burma, no one would have shown up to cover it. But morally our tilt was difficult to justify. We shortchanged a people who endured terrible hardship, often courageously, as did the Vietnamese of the North, and in doing so we failed to convey the true cost of the war and its impact on towns and cities whose names most Americans couldn't pronounce.

One morning in the late 1960s I took the forty-five-minute drive from Saigon to Bien Hoa, the site of a huge U.S. airbase, to cover the burial of an ARVN soldier. The four-lane road, built by the Americans, was in tip-top shape and packed with a steady stream of military traffic: jeeps, deuce-and-a-halves, flat-beds hauling tanks and munitions, trailer trucks whose cargo was covered with canvas. This cemetery, the South Vietnam equivalent of Arlington National Cemetery, was just off the highway in Bien Hoa and marked clearly with a sign. I don't remember the soldier's name, but I know he wasn't anyone prominent. He was just part of a number, in our weekly *meanwhile-South-Vietnamese-officials-put-ARVN-losses* paragraph. In giving him a name and a face and a family, I hoped in some small way my story would personalize the suffering of the Vietnamese. I pulled into the cemetery in the minimote—a sort of miniature, open-air jeep—I was driving, passed a huge stone memorial that was under construction, and headed toward a half-dozen civilians gathered around an open grave.

More than thirty years later, a month after visiting the cemetery near Dong Ha, I made the same trip with an interpreter, hailing a taxi in Ho Chi Minh City and retracing my route to Bien Hoa on the same highway, now clogged with bicycles, motor scooters, three-wheeled tuk-tuks, and all manner of civilian trucks lugging food, steel, machinery, and electronics. There was no sign pointing to the cemetery any more, and we had to stop in several villages to ask directions. Most people didn't know what we were talking about, but by following a series of rutted side roads we finally reached a large, gated expanse and, inside, a memorial that had never been completed.

The cemetery was deserted. The pagoda for family prayers was empty, its roof in a state of advanced decay. Weeds ran wild among the graves, and everywhere I looked headstones were chipped and cracked, sometimes toppled as though struck by a blunt instrument or rifle butt. A generation earlier, when these boy-soldiers died, bereaved mothers encased their photographs and attached them to the stone markers. Surprisingly, many of the pictures had not faded, and the faces I saw—clear-eyed, clean-shaven, proud soldiers—looked exactly like those of the young men I now passed on the streets of Hanoi. Their names were the same as those I might have seen in the Dong Ha cemetery: Nguyen Van Hung, Do Van Son, Pham Van Tien, all buried as teenagers. There was, of course, one big difference: These were the faces and the names of the vanquished. What they had felt about the war I do not know, but they fought for the Republic of South Vietnam, and for answering their government's call to duty—as nobly as Northern soldiers had answered Hanoi's—they had been dishonored by victors who desecrated their headstones and let the crabgrass run wild over their graves. In a country whose pride and dignity and sense of nationalism I had come to greatly admire, the cemetery stood as a symbol of national shame.

My translator and I wandered through the eerie stillness, populated only by the ghosts of the wartime past. Then my eye caught sight of a bicyclist approaching from the nearby village. He pedaled along the dirt road that had once been lined with handsome trees but was now barren, the trees having been cut for firewood. He passed a sprawling water-bottling plant, recently built on the western section of the hallowed grounds, and came up toward us on the gravel path. *Crunch, crunch, crunch.* I thought he was a government security man who had come to shoo us away. But Nguyen Tan Trung, who was twenty-five, said he was unemployed and was one of a handful of volunteers in the village who came once a year, usually on the lunar new year, to cut knee-high grass entangling the tombstones. Once in a while, he said, the villagers got letters from Vietnamese families in North America or Australia, asking them to search for the grave of a loved one. Usually they couldn't find it, but if they did, they would place incense and a flower on the grave.

I asked Trung why the cemetery had been forsaken, and he replied: "Who cares about this place? It belongs to the time before 1975."

The families of those buried in the cemetery, Trung said, never came to visit because they didn't want to admit to their former association with the South. Their attitude was a hangover from long ago, but there was no longer cause for fear. Over the years Vietnam has loosened up, gotten more relaxed and forgiving. People talk freely on most matters except those involving criticism of communism or the government. The officially articulated policy was always that all Vietnamese were equal; it's just that it didn't turn out that way. Ironically the communist leadership found it easier to reach out to its former enemy in Washington than to its own brethren in the South, and in the contrast between the cemeteries in Dong Ha and Bien Hoa one saw the seeds of an unspoken conflict: reconciling North and South on a political level.

Normally things don't rattle me much. Years ago I witnessed an execution in San Quentin and went home and slept soundly. I was thrown into one of Idi Amin's Uganda jails at a time when he was killing a lot of people, and I fell asleep on the stone floor while awaiting my interrogators. I came within an inch of getting my head blown off in Beirut—the bullet, fired from two feet away, lodged in my car-door jamb—and was fine by the time I ordered a drink at the Commodore Hotel's bar. I attribute this not to insensitivity or the absence of fear but to some gene that drops a curtain between my personal and professional lives, helping me separate past from present, the personal from the political. Yet I was steamed about the desecration of the Bien Hoa cemetery. I would have been just as angered had Saigon's soldiers shown the same disrespect for the burial grounds in Dong Ha. I went to see the Communist Party's vice director for ideology in Ho Chi Minh City. He opened a notebook and began reading a long list of accomplishments—1,135 new schools, the Party's youth league swollen with 200,000 members, a robust city economy. . . . It took a while before he ran out of breath and I could ask: "Why hasn't someone made the respectful gesture of cleaning up the cemetery?"

"Even before 1975," Trung Minh Nhai replied, "we considered the young soldiers who fought for the puppet Saigon regime victims of war. We understand they were forced to take up arms. We think it is the same for the American soldiers—they were forced to come here against their will. Our policy has always been to treat all Vietnamese who suffered equally. But it is natural to pay more attention to those who died for their country."

Hold on. If Vietnam were one country, as Ho Chi Minh said, whose country did the Southerners fight for? Was it possible South Vietnam's entire million-man military fought against its will? And what were South Vietnam and its 20 million people being liberated from? The Americans? The Saigon regime? Oppression? Poverty? Democracy? The right to honor their dead? I started to raise those questions but didn't make any headway. All the Southerners were puppets, Nhai said. With ideologues, I'd found, you didn't get common sense, just ideology. After a while I put away my notebook. Our interpretations of history were too different to be reconciled.

{{{  }}}

Nguyen Thi Le hadn't talked about her husband's role in the war for twenty-three years, until I showed up at her house with my interpreter. Sheets of monsoon rain swept over Ho Chi Minh City that day, and the narrow alley where she lived, several hundred yards from the main street, was so badly flooded I took off my shoes and socks, rolled up my pants, and waded through the knee-deep water.

Le was fifty-one and had lived in her two-room, government-owned house for half her life. Twelve children and grandchildren were crammed with her into the clean, simple quarters. She was two years in arrears paying her $5-per-month rent and often had trouble scraping together enough money for the next bowl of rice. She sat drinking tea on one of the ten-inch-high plastic stools the Vietnamese favor, near the door through which her husband had last passed in 1972 to join an ARVN artillery unit.

"I don't know how he felt about the war," she said. "We never talked about it. We just hugged and said goodbye when he went. That was it."

For a while he wrote faithfully every month. (June 10, 1973: "Time has gone by so fast, hasn't it, honey? It is already three months on the front. I am so sad that our lives are so far apart." July 20, 1973: "Life is difficult here but I have good friends. Do not worry. I miss you always.") Then the letters stopped, and one day in November an ARVN officer came to her door bearing a telex sent by her husband's unit. Truong Van Hai, age twenty-five, was missing in action.

"My life was over," Le said. "I kept waiting, thinking perhaps he would return, but the days came and the days went, and now my children are grown, and I am still here, waiting."

Most of her neighbors burned letters from their husbands and scrapbooks that held pictures of smiling, cocky young men headed off for war, fearing they somehow could be used by Hanoi's cadre as incriminating evidence. Le kept hers, hidden at the back of a kitchen cabinet and secured in a plastic bag. She did not know where Hai fell, or how he died, or if he received a proper Buddhist burial. She would like to have searched for his remains, she said, but that would require money for travel and food, so she had put the thought out of her mind.

Le did not begrudge the communist government for not giving her a military widow's pension. The Saigon government hadn't given her one either. I asked if she weren't uneasy talking to me about Hai and the ARVN. She said no, it didn't matter any more. Ten years ago, she said, she wouldn't have breathed a word, but Vietnam had changed, and she had no fear of the authorities.

"I've heard that Northern widows get pensions and mothers of the dead and missing are called 'Heroic Mothers' of martyrs," she said. "Here we get nothing. Our husbands and sons were considered traitors. Hai, I can tell you, was no traitor. He loved Vietnam."

*Open your eyes and look around here.*
*Who's left who is Vietnamese?*
*A million people have died.*
*Open your eyes and turn over the enemy corpses,*
*Those are Vietnamese faces upon them.*
*Going over the human corpses,*
*Who have we been defeating all these years?*
*The homeland has withered.*
*Brothers and sisters of North, Center, South:*
*Go forth to preserve the mountains and rivers,*
*Have hope in your hearts for a tomorrow*
*Looking at this land,*
*Joyfully cheering the flag of unification,*
*With footsteps passing over all three regions.*
*Open your eyes and look around here.*
*Who's left who is Vietnamese?*
*Artificial hatreds,*
*Open your eyes.*
*Look at this day of Vietnam.*
*So many years of tattered lives,*
*Our people bathed in fresh blood.*

—ballad written and sung by Trinh Cong Son,
a Southern poet and peace activist, in the final years of the war
(translation by Neil L. Jamieson)

To this day, Hanoi's Party leadership insists the conflict that led to Vietnam's reunification was not a civil war. It was, according to the official line, an uprising of Southern indigenous people—the Viet Cong and its supporters—against a corrupt regime that answered to imperialistic invaders, the United States. Hanoi's negotiators even managed to sit straight-faced through the Paris Peace talks, contending there were no North Vietnamese soldiers in the South, only Viet Cong. Its support of the Viet Cong, Hanoi said, was in direct response to U.S. aggression. But Hanoi was preparing for civil war in the South—planting agents in the countryside, starting work on the Ho Chi Minh Trail, repairing the rail line, building one of the world's largest armies—years before the first U.S. Marines landed at Danang in 1965. America's involvement raised the stakes and complicated Hanoi's game plan to control the South but otherwise probably didn't affect the eventual course of history.

With the Americans gone in the early spring of 1975, Hanoi had a golden opportunity to achieve reconciliation between the war-weary peoples of North and South. "It wasn't that I wanted communism, but when Saigon fell, I thought, 'Thank God, no more fighting. Now everyone will join to rebuild the country.' That was our dream," said Hoang Van Cuong, a Saigon photographer who had thrown his arms around a group of NVA soldiers at the Presidential Palace on April 30. But the dream was an illusion. So was true reconciliation. A lifetime of struggle had made the Hanoi leadership paranoid. What it wanted was conformity, a country of true born-again communist believers, and to achieve it Hanoi instituted unforgiving policies that would set Vietnam back thirty years or more.

"At every station the loudspeakers blared, blasting the ears of the wounded, the sick, the blind, the mutilated, the white-eyed, gray-lipped malarial troops," Bao Dinh wrote of the time he and other NVA soldiers left Saigon on a train that would carry them home to Hanoi. "Into their ears poured an endless stream of the most ironic of teachings, urging them to ignore the spirit of reconciliation, to beware of the 'bullets coated with sugar,' to ignore the warmth and passions among the remnants of this fallen, luxurious society of the South. And especially to guard against the idea of the South having fought valiantly or been meritorious in any way. But we 'meritorious' and victorious soldiers knew how to defend ourselves against this barrage of nonsense. We made fun of the loud-speakers' admonishments, turning their speeches into jokes, ridiculing them."

Based on the scores of conversations I had, as well as everything that my instinct says, I am sure in the heart of virtually every ordinary Vietnamese, Northerner or Southerner, civilian or soldier, was the spirit of reconciliation. But for officialdom, that was not a high priority. Part of the problem was that Ho Chi Minh was dead by the time Saigon fell. He was a dedicated communist and no soft touch, but he was a pragmatic man and, above all else, a nationalist. I think he would have turned over in his mausoleum if he had known of the disastrous path his hand-picked successor, Le Duan, decided to follow.

Four hundred thousand South Vietnamese—soldiers, teachers, writers, student activists, businessmen, intellectuals, along with some common criminals—were sent off to reeducation camps. Conditions varied widely. Executions were rare, and systematic brutality was not a pattern. But thousands of prisoners died before seeing freedom, and mistreatment was common. Recalcitrants were kept in wooden boxes that served as isolation cells, measuring six feet long, three feet wide, and six feet high. A single lightbulb shone overhead throughout the night. A pith helmet in each cell served as a toilet. Prisoners were manacled, the right hand cuffed to the left ankle, the left hand to the right ankle.

"I am not sure how many days I stay; ten or twelve, I think," Doan Van Toai wrote of his time in solitary confinement. Toai was a Saigon student activist who supported the Viet Cong but was arrested after refusing to cooperate in the expropriation of all property in South Vietnam after the fall of Saigon. "I remember noticing the symptoms of beriberi: my legs seem to be asleep or partially paralyzed, and I am afraid I will never be able to move again. At first hallucinations come sporadically, Ho Chi Minh appears, then my mother, then gray-skinned, long-haired ghosts. At some point I begin to feel a fever coming on. I know I am going unconscious for periods of time. I vaguely remember being unlocked and propped up in a standing position, my legs buckling under me. Though I can't seem to see, I know I am being carried across someone's shoulders. Then a familiar, nauseating smell overwhelms me, and just before I lapse into darkness I remember where I smelled it before. It's the smell that wafts out of the Zone C cells when you open the door to hand in their pail of rice."

A number of antiwar activists in the United States had an unusual take on all this. In an open letter published in the *New York Times* in June 1979 and signed by, among others, Harry Bridges, Corliss Lamont, and Karen Ackerman, they praised "the remarkable spirit of moderation, restraint and clemency with which the reeducation program was conducted" by the communist authorities. The letter went on to say: "Vietnam now enjoys human rights as it has never known in history as described in the International Covenant on Human Rights: the right to a job and safe, healthy working conditions, the right to join trade unions, the right to be free from hunger, from colonialism and racism. Moreover, they receive—without cost—education, medicine and health care, human rights we in the United States have yet to achieve."

That may have been true for those in the communist ranks of True Believers. Everyone else was shortchanged—even the Viet Cong, who had played a crucial role in reunifying Vietnam even though their ranks had been decimated in the 1968 Tet Offensive and by the CIA-sponsored Phoenix assassination project. (The phoenix, or *phuong*, symbolized all things virtuous and graceful in Vietnam; it is the emblem of queens and a sign of peace.) The VC fighters were thanked and sent home to their villages, denied any significant say in Vietnam's future. Hanoi's men arrived by the planeload to take over every aspect of society. On Hanoi's orders 2 million people were involuntarily moved into ecologically unfriendly "economic zones" for cooperative farming. Food production soon plummeted. Another order was to take over the administration of the education system and revise the school curricula and textbooks. Vietnam's new world view was through the lens of Marxism, and in this new society jobs went to Northerners, university slots to the children of Northerners.

Without firing a shot, the communist leadership managed to achieve what a generation of war had not: the flight of discontents; more than a million Vietnamese left their homeland in three waves between 1975 and 1989. Never before in any country had so many people fled peace. Among those leaving were Vietnam's best and brightest—the writers and scholars and statesmen and economists and merchants, the very people Hanoi desperately needed to build a new society incorporating all Vietnamese. The exodus included a half-million people of Chinese origin—coal miners from Quang Ninh, fishermen from the Gulf of Tonkin, pottery workers from Mong Cay, merchants from Cholon. Many of their families had lived in Vietnam for generations.

"These Chinese hegemonists and expansionists have always been our enemies," Le Duan said. "I have known that ever since Nixon went to Peking in 1971. . . . We have to be on our guard and watch out. The Chinese have been our enemies and will remain so for hundreds of years to come."

In Cholon, Saigon's prosperous Chinese quarter, truckloads of soldiers and volunteers wearing red armbands descended on the maze of teeming, narrow streets to inventory private property—everything from gold watches to factory machinery—that was to be turned over to the state in the name of destroying free enterprise. Within days the property was confiscated and South Vietnam's currency was abolished. Overnight millionaires became paupers.

"They took everything but who knows what happened to it," a garment maker in Cholon told me. With turning a profit suddenly illegal, he survived the 1970s by hiding the spools of thread he produced by candlelight under his shirt and asking friends in the market to trade them for food.

The newspapers, brothels, and restaurants in Saigon closed. The Continental Hotel, on whose veranda Graham Greene, Colonel Pham Xuan

An, and countless writers, diplomats, and spies had gathered to exchange information, was renamed the Hotel of the General Uprising. Writers, poets, and intellectuals who had not fled in the first exodus were scooped up and dispatched to camps to learn the language of Marxism. One of them was Cuong, the photographer who had wanted to join in rebuilding Vietnam. His crime: He had worked for an American wire service. Trinh Cong Son, whose antiwar songs had been as popular in the North as in the South, was sent off to a camp near his hometown of Hue to grow sweet potatoes and cassava. His crime was speaking of the conflict as a civil war. Library shelves were emptied, and more than 100 authors and nearly 1,000 specific titles, including Mario Puzo's *The Godfather*, were banned. To fill the cultural void, Hanoi sent 170,000 books to the South—mostly about Marx, Lenin, Engels, and the accomplishments of communism—and 450,000 pictures, almost all of them of Ho Chi Minh. The newspapers disappeared, then the bookstores closed. At the banks, safety deposit boxes were sealed, accounts frozen. The price of rice soared from thirty cents a pound to nearly $2. Westerns and martial-arts action pictures were replaced by films about revolutionary heroes. Audiences were forbidden from leaving the theater before the end of the shows.

"The Communist Party of Vietnam . . . armed with Marxism-Leninism, is the only force leading the state and society, and the main factor determining the success of the Vietnamese revolution," read the constitution drafted for the newly united country, which today is known as the Socialist Republic of Vietnam.

As if there weren't enough problems at home, Vietnam twice went to war within four years of Saigon's fall. Provoked by cross-border attacks, Vietnam invaded Cambodia in 1978 and overthrew Pol Pot's murderous Khmer Rouge regime. Vietnam stayed on in Cambodia for eleven years as an occupying power. China decided to teach Vietnam a lesson for invading its Cambodian ally and sent 600,000 troops south. China managed to penetrate only twenty miles into Vietnam and was forced to

periment: communism. To what could they point and say, "See, I told you this works"? Certainly not Cuba, Laos, North Korea. China? Maybe. But the Vietnamese had hated the Chinese for centuries. Party bosses presided over one of the world's poorest countries: Ninety percent of the roads were unpaved; farmers in the most impoverished provinces got by on the equivalent of perhaps $5 per month; nationally, bicycles outnumbered cars forty-to-one. But—and I am quite certain—the leadership still believed Vietnam was at the center of the universe, as it had been briefly during the war. These contradictions surfaced on a personal level, too. People were stunningly direct in asking how much money you earned or how old you were yet so concerned with being polite and avoiding confrontation that "yes" often meant "maybe" and "no" didn't always mean "no." Contradictions were many. The Vietnamese poetry and music spoke of loss and melancholy, but the contemporary, brightly colored pastoral scenes that artists painted reflected none of the anger and darkness that surely must have dwelled in Vietnam's war-torn soul. All the men and none of the women smoked. Everyone I met seemed to carry the family name of the Nguyen, Le, or Tran Dynasties. On my desk was a *Who's Who in Vietnam* directory that covered 147 pages; fifty-nine pages were filled with people named Nguyen, Le, or Tran.

Even the language—basically monosyllabic with romanized script—looked invitingly accessible yet was devilishly difficult. For instance, in the unlikely event you wanted to say in Vietnamese that three busy friends were selling four dirty tables, it would be, with diacritical markings to indicate tonal differences: *ba bạn bận bịu bán bốn bàn bẩn*. If your voice didn't tweeter like a bird's, if it soared when it should have dipped, forget it. The word would take on an entirely different meaning than what you intended or would have no meaning at all. The Vietnamese would smile politely but have no idea what you were talking about. And the language basically was written and spoken in the present tense, making little distinction between "walk," "walking," and "walked." It was pretty much left to the reader-listener to figure out if past or future was intended.

My Vietnamese language skills did not proceed far, particularly given limitations imposed by my Boston accent, but I took solace in the fact I had improved on my wartime efforts. Like most journalists, then, my vocabulary was restricted to *didi mau*, an abrupt way of telling kids to scram; *bao chi*, or "newspaper," which we thought meant "journalist" and might save us if stopped by the Viet Cong; and *mamasan*, or "older woman," a Japanese term we must have taken from World War II movies but wasn't used in Vietnam. I don't think I knew the words for "thank you," *cam on*.

Although some words were of Chinese origin, the language that Vietnam developed was unique, with a script originally based on Chinese ideograms. In the seventeenth century, European missionaries, led by Father Alexandre de Rhodes, created the system of romanized writing, doing me a huge favor in that I could read the street signs but, I'm afraid, not advancing my progress as a linguist. Depending, for instance, on where you placed the markings and what you did with your voice, *le* could mean a tear, a kind of bird, margin, a pearlike fruit, or fast. If you use a falling tone, *binh* means peace; with no tone, it means soldier. Robert McNamara made the mistake of trying to say a few words of Vietnamese when he spoke at the National Cathedral in Saigon during the war. He wanted to say "Long live South Vietnam." But he missed all the tones. It came out as "The Southern duck wants to lie down."

So I came to accept that I was always to be the interloper. I could chip away at Vietnam, but I would never reach the inner sanctum. Time passed quickly, pleasurably. Winter returned to Hanoi. The temperature dipped into the sixties, and Hanoians started shivering. They donned motorcycle helmets, which they wore on the commute to work not because of the appalling death toll on the nation's roads but to keep warm. They zipped up parkas thicker than any I'd seen since Alaska. The darker the December skies got, the brighter seemed the fresh flowers that women from the countryside pedaled into Hanoi each morning. A dozen chrysanthemums cost seventy-five cents. I would sit on my balcony with a cup of Vietnamese coffee and watch the clouds and rain sweep in across

West Lake. Sometimes I'd jot down notes about people I'd met or things I'd seen that day.

One of them was about a young bartender whose name was, of course, Nguyen (pronounced "n'whin"). He had asked me, "How would you describe the Vietnamese people?" It was a question I'd heard before. I said I could think of many adjectives. One of the first that came to mind was industrious.

"Everyone says that about us. That we're industrious," said Nguyen Van Hoa, who worked two service jobs and had an engineering degree. "But if we're so industrious, why are we so poor?"

{{{  }}}

VIETNAM HAD HAD A LOT OF EXPERIENCE with being poor and with seeing its leaders use harsh means to accomplish revolutionary goals. One of the harshest—land reform—began in 1955, at the end of the French War, and continued for a decade, until the beginning of the American War. In the process of breaking the power of the landed gentry and distributing land to 2 million families, Ho Chi Minh's cadre executed as many as 50,000 North Vietnamese, usually by firing squad, immediately after conviction by village tribunals. There are indications Ho disapproved of the methods his zealots used, and the Party did acknowledge "a number of serious errors," but the campaign still tarnished the revolution's image, confirming, to some, the heartlessness and hypocrisy of communism once it was put into practice. In her book *The Sacred Willow: Four Generations in the Life of a Vietnamese Family*, Duong Van Mai Elliott writes of that era:

> After they [the cadre] arrived in a village, they linked up with the poorest of the poor peasants. The moved into their hovels, lived and worked alongside them to win their trust. Once they had become accepted, they would draw out the peasants' unhappiness over their wretched lives and their

grievances against the landlords. Then, they told the poor that if they joined in the land reform, their problems would come to an end. By bringing the resentment of the poor to a fever pitch, they created a groundswell for land reform. Finally, together with the most militant of the peasants, they took over the village. They arrested landlords accused of having ruthlessly exploited and oppressed the poor, and sealed their assets.

They tried the landlords in a kangaroo court, carefully staged to make it look like it was the will of the people. About a dozen poor peasants who had suffered the most and who harbored the deepest hatred of the landlords were chosen and coached in advance to denounce them at this trial. While these peasants took turns denouncing the landlords in front of this tribunal, other poor peasants would shout: "Down with the landlord!" to reinforce the atmosphere of hostility. If the sentence was death, the landlords would be executed on the spot. If the sentence was imprisonment, they would be led away. The property of landlords found guilty of crimes—including land, houses, draft animals, and tools—would be seized and distributed among the most needy peasants.

The Hanoi leadership didn't do much better than its predecessors in managing affairs after the American War, and by 1986, the year Ho Chi Minh protégé Le Duan died after twenty-six years as the chief of the Communist Party, Vietnam was poorer than it had ever been. Almost all its 6,000 state-run companies—they ranged from heavy industry to hotels, shoe factories, cigarette plants, even beer halls—were losing money. Starvation threatened and rice imports grew. Personal freedoms had vanished for all but the communist elite. Food was rationed. A pair of shoes was beyond the means of most families, unless they were prominent Party members. Isolated by international sanctions and the leadership's xenophobia, Vietnam had become a lost frontier, like Albania or North Korea, surviving on its wits and the Soviet Union's treasury. Ho Chi Minh's most quoted credo was, "There is nothing more precious than independence and liberty," but surely this wasn't the independence and liberty he was talking about.

"Even when I came south from Hanoi with the army, I carried a sketch pad," said Ngo Dong, who today makes a good living painting reproductions of Monet, Van Gogh, and other masters in his studio in Ho Chi Minh City. "During lulls in the battle, I'd draw pictures of flowers and rice paddies and dream of being a great artist.

"After '75, no one could survive as an artist. I got a job painting store signs. At night I painted for pleasure. My parents, my children lived in the apartment where I painted. Three generations. If I had an idea for a painting, I had to submit a rough sketch to the government. If I got approval, they'd give me a canvas—maybe it would be torn, maybe not—and a packet of paints made in Eastern Europe. The paint was old. It was often rock hard and unusable."

Dong told me he no longer needed to submit proposals to the culture ministry for approval. He had ample canvas and paint. He saved Sundays to work on his originals, but the other days, from eight in the morning until six in the evening, he was on Pasteur Avenue—one of two streets, along with Alexandre de Rhodes, whose French name survived the communist takeover of Saigon—churning out his reproductions. An Italian businessman had just commissioned thirty reproductions of paintings by Fernando Botero, the Colombian artist. Each would take Dong about a week and earn him a handsome return: $75. "You could say this isn't real art, but I think I'm helping the Vietnamese appreciate the great painters," he said.

Up and down the streets around Pasteur stood dozens of studios, with doors that opened onto the street, filled with young artists duplicating the masters. Much of their work drew praise from art critics. A generation earlier graduates of the Indochina Fine Arts Institute, which France had set up in Hanoi in 1925, had been pressed into wartime duty as propagandists to paint posters and design leaflets in the name of nationalism and communism. Now they were part of a flourishing free-enterprise mini-industry, and because their work did not end up as "originals" in the international marketplace and they didn't sign the originator's name, no one paid much attention to copyright infringement.

What turned around Dong's life—and that of millions of other Vietnamese—was the government's decision at the Sixth Party Congress in 1986 to institute a program called *doi moi*, or "economic renovation." Given the depths of Vietnam's desperation, it was a decision made out of necessity, yet it reflected the pragmatism of a government that understood slogans don't fill empty stomachs. *Doi moi* was designed not as an ideological retreat from socialism but as an instrument to introduce elements of a free-market economy, to encourage private enterprise, and to free the entrepreneurial spirit of the Vietnamese.

Land reform—this time executed without bloodshed—allocated plots to farmers who proved themselves the most productive. A merit system that awarded points to people who merely showed up for work (even if they didn't do any work) was abolished. The government kept title to all land, but land could now be leased, traded, inherited, and mortgaged. People were given the right to "enrich themselves." The *equitization*—Hanoi couldn't bring itself to use the word "privatize"—of the state-run economy took its first timid steps. A bevy of new laws were drawn up, including one to deal with something that didn't happen when the state owned every business: bankruptcy.

I moved to Hanoi about ten years after the adoption of *doi moi* and four or five after its implementation began, more or less, in earnest. For the conservatives in the communist hierarchy, the exercise was no fun. The communist countries of Eastern Europe had made the transition to a free-market economy by focusing on all they had to gain. Vietnam's leaders could only think of all they had to lose. At the top of the list was not ideology; it was privilege. Although there were countless bright bureaucrats who worked tirelessly for Vietnam's well-being, everyone knew that the directors of the state-run industries and many of the people who ran the ministries didn't get their jobs on merit. The director of tourism, for instance, had impressive wartime credentials as a revolutionary but knew next to nothing about tourism. She refused all requests for interviews with foreign journalists, a peculiar response in a country trying to promote tourism as a major source of hard currency. But I suppose the Old

Guard had a right to be nervous. If the playing field were leveled and promotions were based on competency rather than contacts and Party commitment, a lot of senior people would have been out on the street. The thought of suddenly waking up and finding oneself with the salary of a civil servant or a teacher—about $30 a month—was as appealing as a bowl of soggy rice.

The results of *doi moi* over the first eight or nine years were dazzling. The annual inflation rate fell to single digits from 700 percent. Farmers, freed from collectivization, transformed Vietnam from a rice importer into the world's second largest rice exporter, after Thailand. The gross domestic product grew by nearly 9 percent a year. Thirty-five thousand small businesses started up in the private sector. Families that couldn't afford a new pair of shoes a decade earlier were now riding to work on Honda Dream motor scooters. Shops that didn't have a bolt of cloth or a can of paint to sell in the Dark Years were awash in goods: lamb chops from New Zealand, microwave ovens from Japan, silk from Vietnam for tailoring, kitchen utensils from China. Many homes in my neighborhood didn't have running water, but almost every one had a TV set.

All of a sudden Vietnam had buzz. It was the darling of the new emerging markets. Foreign donors tripped over each other to be among the first to shower money on Vietnam. Investors and entrepreneurs from the capitals of Europe, North America, and Asia poured into the country and snapped up apartments at $5,000 per month, two years' rent due in advance. Hanoi knew a cash cow when it saw one. It set up a dual-pricing structure, charging foreigners three times what a Vietnamese paid for rail and air tickets. Phone rates were among the highest in the world. Hanoi soon became one of the world's ten most expensive cities to live in for expatriates. But no one seemed to mind. Vietnam was the place to be.

"There was electricity in the air," remembered Jay Ellis, an American whose R&R Tavern became Hanoi's favorite watering hole for expats. Ellis put up pictures of George Washington and Ho Chi Minh over the door. "People—Vietnamese and foreigners—were excited. You had the feeling things were really happening."

The World Bank rented a villa. Tourism soared. With the end of the U.S. trade embargo in 1994—an event greeted by fireworks in Ho Chi Minh City—Coca-Cola unveiled its $24 million plant outside Hanoi with parading drummers in costumes. One U.S. company said it would develop a $243 million resort in Danang, next to the U.S. Marines' former R&R center on China Beach. Eleven recently arrived automotive manufacturers predicted they would be selling 120,000 vehicles by the year 2007. Chrysler's investment alone was $191 million. A dozen American money managers who controlled billions of dollars in pension funds for General Electric, Arco, General Motors, and other corporations prowled Vietnam looking for places to invest. "We were very excited," one of them, Kent Damon, said.

{{{  }}}

I HAD NO IDEA WHEN I ARRIVED I WAS SEEING THE END, not the beginning, of the boom. Vietnam had made stunning economic advances, and that progress would continue, albeit at a slower pace, during the rest of my four years in the country. But about the time I got to Hanoi, in the summer of 1997, the *baht* collapsed in Thailand and all of Southeast Asia slid into recession.

It became clear everyone had held unrealistically high expectations for Vietnam and that Vietnam had become a victim of its own hype. The buzz faded. The conservatives in the politburo had outlasted the liberals, and they favored caution over risk, a controlling hand over an empowering one. They took a step forward on reforms, then two backward. They appeared perplexed, uncertain. While the world rushed toward a new knowledge-based economy, they paused to catch their breath. Life, in a strange way, had been easier, even safer, during the war. "Those were the days," Bao Ninh wrote, "when all of us were young, very pure, and very sincere."

North Vietnam was of single focus then. To suffer and persevere was to eventually succeed. The future didn't belong to people demanding economic opportunity, more material possessions, all sorts of things that had nothing to do with independence. It didn't revolve around complicated fiscal issues that needed quick decisions and firm commitments. The leadership had tried to develop an economic system unique to the world—a "socialistic free-market economy that leapfrogged capitalism"— and when investors tired of a business environment fraught with a lack of transparency, bureaucratic red tape, corruption, and indecisiveness, the Party bosses promised accelerated reforms that they may never have intended to deliver. They didn't understand that investor confidence was shaped by attitude as much as by policy.

"This is Vietnam," Anil Malhotra, a World Bank official, used to say to government officials, holding up a small carving of a turtle, a creature sacred to the country's old dynasties. "It represents perseverance. It never gives up. It has thick skin that deflects all criticism. In those ways, the turtle is just like Vietnam. But the only time it moves forward is when it sticks out its neck." And that's what the leadership couldn't bring itself to do—take risk. If Hanoi had been as timid and indecisive on the battlefield as it was in the peacetime boardrooms charting economic strategy, it might never have earned its liberation.

Still, I was willing to cut the government more slack than many frustrated business friends did, for the obstacles that Vietnam faced and overcame were mammoth. It had been ravaged in 1980 by typhoons that destroyed 40 percent of the North's rice harvest, debilitated by wars against Cambodia and China, devastated by the collapse of its benefactors in the Soviet Union, crippled by its leadership's ineptitude, and punished by vindictive governments in Washington that froze Vietnam's assets in the United States and declared a trade embargo within twenty-four hours of Saigon's fall, then set out to collect from Hanoi $143 million the defunct Saigon government owed the United States. But for all its shortcomings, when its back had been to the wall, the government had instituted reforms, and the reforms were significant. They resulted in changes that reduced the share of the population living in poverty from 35 to 15 percent and improved the standard of living more dramatically than even the most upbeat citizen would have dared hope. Vietnam had fought a lifetime of wars for the right to be Vietnam—to decide what road it wanted to travel and at what pace. The leadership was in no rush.

Perhaps it was easy for me to be tolerant because I had no financial stake in Vietnam's success or failure. The international business community was less forgiving. Venture capitalists were the first to pack up with investor burnout. Then went some of the medium-sized companies that couldn't afford to wait years to turn a profit. "Hanoi is a great place to live. It's just not a good place to do business," said an American insurance-company rep the day he got on a plane to Bangkok with his Vietnamese wife and son. Chrysler gave up and went home, too. The megadollar resort project on China Beach was cancelled. "The government said all the right things," Kent Damon recalled, "but we didn't see a commitment in action to match the words." Construction on Hyatt, Marriott, and Westin hotels stopped in midair, about ten stories up. Owners of the $70 million, fourteen-story Sheraton that I could see from my apartment balcony turned off the electricity two weeks before its scheduled opening and boarded up the hotel. Four international carriers cut their air links to Vietnam. Seven of my colleagues, including those representing *Time, Far Eastern Economic Review,* and *Financial Times,* packed up to relocate their bureaus in other Southeast Asian capitals. Rents fell by half. Foreign investment tumbled by 80 percent between 1996 and 1999. Five-star hotels limped along with occupancy rates of 10 or 15 percent. At Jay Ellis's R&R Tavern, where expats had once stood three-deep, it was easy to find an empty stool at the bar any night of the week.

During the war I was reluctant to make close friends because next week they might be dead. Now I was hesitant to make them—at least in the expat community—because next month they might be living in Singapore, Seoul, or New York.

Vietnam's economic downturn was a troubling portent of the future, but it had more effect on foreign investors and the moneyed citizenry than it did on the ordinary Vietnamese, most of whom operated outside the structured economy. Vietnam was a cash economy, and in an ironic twist to the legacy of the war, Yankee dollars were the favored currency. They were interchangeable, more or less legally, with the Vietnamese dong and could be used for everything from paying a cab fare to buying a house. Many restaurants and shops listed their bills in dollars, not dong.

Few Vietnamese used banks, and almost none had credit cards. The well-heeled didn't like banks because a lot of wealth in Vietnam had been created through graft, and no one wanted his illegally earned money going through the official system. Also, middle- and working-class Vietnamese didn't trust banks. They kept their money in cash or gold, under beds and in kitchen cabinets—an accumulative fortune that lay idle in a capital-starved nation. If they bought a house, they went to the seller carrying suitcases of dong—suitcases in the plural because it took 15,000 dong to buy one U.S. dollar. When my bills were due each month, I didn't write a bunch of checks. I stockpiled a drawer full of dong notes (Vietnam didn't have coins) and made some phone calls. An hour later the bill collectors—from the telephone company, the Internet service, the landlord, the butcher, the wine shop—would be knocking at my door to take payment in cash.

{{{   }}}

DESPITE THE ECONOMIC DOWNTURN, there were noteworthy achievements along the way. One was agriculture. Food production doubled between 1990 and 2000, and people no longer felt threatened by famine. In addition to its rice surplus, Vietnam became the world's second largest exporter of cashew nuts, after India, and third largest coffee exporter, after Brazil and Colombia. Nearly one-quarter of its robusta coffee went to the United States. The coffee was grown in the Central Highlands, where I had spent much time traipsing around with the 4th Infantry Division and the 101st Airborne. Even the largest of the Highlands towns, like Pleiku and Ban Me Thuot, were sleepy backwaters in those days, populated mostly by ethnic minorities. I caught one of the thrice-weekly flights from Danang to Pleiku to see what effect the coffee boom had had on one of Vietnam's most beautiful regions.

In many ways, Pleiku was where the American War began. On February 7, 1965, when the 23,000 U.S. military personnel in Vietnam were classified as advisers, the Viet Cong attacked a U.S. Army compound on the outskirts of the town with mortars, killing eight Americans. In retaliation, President Lyndon B. Johnson began the sustained bombing of North Vietnam on February 24. Hanoi announced a general mobilization. "Nothing is more precious than independence and freedom," Ho Chi Minh said—words that one day would hang in eighteen-karat gold outside his mausoleum. On March 8, two battalions of U.S. Marines landed at Danang. Johnson offered Hanoi aid in exchange for peace on April 7. Hanoi rejected the overture the next day. In the tit-for-tat escalations, you could hear the whisper of history and Charles de Gaulle's warning to John F. Kennedy in 1962: "I predict that you will, step by step, be sucked into a bottomless military and political quagmire." By the early spring of 1969, U.S. combat troops in Vietnam numbered 543,000.

Nothing looked familiar to me. Pleiku had been burned to the ground by South Vietnamese troops fleeing the Highlands in March 1975 and rebuilt with Soviet assistance five or six years later. Bulldozers had claimed all but the memories. I couldn't find the press hooch where I had awakened one night to look at a starlit sky and wonder if it could be true what VOA was reporting—that a man was walking on the moon at that very moment. The sprawling base that had housed the 4th Division was easy to find, but it had been turned into a coffee plantation. The runway of the U.S. airfield in Kontum to the north was used for drying rice and giving driving lessons to young Vietnamese, something they desperately needed. Pleiku's dirt roads had been paved, and the first traffic lights had been installed. The population had swelled from a few thousand when I had last seen the town to 70,000. A new movie theater was packing in crowds to see *Cyberbyte Monster*. New buildings were going up all over town, and instead of looking like Stalinist housing projects, as they did in Vinh, they reflected the sweeping, open style of Montagnard architecture. Everyone seemed to have a Chinese-made motor scooter. Fueled by high yields of coffee, black pepper, and rubber, Pleiku was booming.

The Highlands reminded me of Vermont, where I had spent the summers of my youth. The mountains and wooded valleys and rushing streams calmed me. The People's Committee in Pleiku knew it was guardian of a tourist treasure—the Highlands were Vietnam's last redoubt of elephants and tigers and the Javan rhinoceros—and it devised a twofold plan to attract foreign visitors and cash in on a potential bonanza: keep prices high and make it difficult for tourists to explore the region. Then the town's fathers sat back and waited . . . and waited. And when tourists flocked to beach resorts in Danang and Nha Trang and to Halong Bay and Sapa and skipped the Highlands entirely, they scratched their heads in puzzlement.

Like individual states in the United States, the provinces of Vietnam had considerable autonomy in determining local policy. And in Pleiku, the Communist Party had opted to give government control top priority, even as the rest of the country was becoming more liberal, more open, more accessible to foreigners. It forced tourists to spend the night inside city limits and required them to get a $20 permit if they wanted to visit an old battlefield or a village inhabited by ethnic minorities. Sometimes it took a week to get the permit. And it set the room rate at the dreary Pleiku Hotel at $38, about what a luxury four-star hotel cost in Ho Chi Minh City. A sign in each room warned: "Do not play games and bring prostitutes into room."

The fact that the Highlands were the last place where the xenophobia of the late 1970s still openly lingered was not surprising. For more than a decade after the fall of Saigon, the government fought a low-level war in the plateaus around Pleiku against guerrillas belonging to the United Front for the Struggle of Oppressed Races (FULRO), which had about

10,000 combatants in 1975. They were Montagnards—a generic term for Vietnam's scores of upcountry minority groups—and many had fought as mercenaries for the French and the Americans. Most were Protestants, with little affection for the ethnic Vietnamese majority. As recently as 1992, a surviving band of several hundred guerrillas remained in a remote corner of Cambodia, continuing cross-border raids. They later surrendered and were integrated into society or flown under UN auspices to the United States, bringing a delayed peace to the Highlands.

Plans to revive the coffee industry that the French had started in the 1920s began a few years before FULRO's disintegration. Like almost everything else in agriculture the government touched in the 1970s and 1980s, the early results were disastrous. "Yes, we had a small failure," admitted Thai Doan Lai, who ran a state-owned coffee company in Ban Me Thuot. "The government tried to tell farmers everything, even where to plant their trees, and it really had no idea what it was doing."

But *doi moi* allowed farmers to keep their profits and lessened the state's role in production. It offered tax incentives and subsidies when the world price fell below certain levels. And by the time I got to the Highlands, everywhere I went farmers were abandoning their beans and corn and planting coffee. Thousands of new settlers were rushing in, much to the dismay of the indigenous Montagnards, and claiming land for coffee plantations. A lot of it had been handed out by the Party to senior military men. Times were good, and an entire region was being lifted out of poverty. Some farmers were earning $3,000 per year—about ten times the national average.

"I never dreamed coffee could do this," said a thirty-five-year-old farmer, Y Mum Eban, with whom I chatted. He had built a spiffy home, bought a TV set and two motor scooters—"one of them a real luxury model"—and worked his three-acre farm with a tractor. "More coffee," he said. "That's the answer."

Success came at a price. Farmers and settlers were clearing land for coffee production at such an alarming rate that Hanoi issued a new decree to protect the forests and stop erosion. Most people ignored it. In Dak Lak Province, which accounted for 60 percent of Vietnam's coffee yield, the forest cover had been reduced from 70 to 15 percent since the end of the American War. At the same time, the acreage devoted to coffee increased eighteenfold.

International agriculturists worried that Vietnam's obsession with increasing coffee production to garner foreign currency had led to unsustainable farming practices. One example they cited: The widely used fertilizers that accelerated growth were so strong they had made Vietnam's per-acre yield the world's highest. The downside was that they "burned" the soil and destroyed nutrients the next generation of farmers would need. But having been poor so long, the benefactors of the coffee boom were willing to let tomorrow's farmers worry about tomorrow's problems tomorrow.

{{{  }}}

THERE WERE A LOT OF REASONS TO BE UPBEAT about Vietnam's long-term economic prospects. The country's 80 million inhabitants, with increasing access to discretionary income, represented a huge consumer market. The labor force worked cheap (minimum daily wage: $1.28) and had brains (the literacy rate was 91 percent). Vietnam had resources—offshore oil as well as natural gas, coal, phosphates, manganese, forests—and a 1,900-mile coastline whose waters teemed with fish. Perhaps most important, it had hard-working, reliable people who thirsted for knowledge and were obsessed with education. I had no doubt that if the government just got out of the way and let its people exercise their inherent strengths, Vietnam could have advanced light-years instead of miles in terms of social, political, and economic development. Vietnam was like a racehorse whose jockey kept yanking on the reins rather than giving the animal its head to find full stride.

The Party bosses seldom acted until their collective backs were to the wall. When they weren't sure which way to turn, they would fall back on Ho Chi Minh and ask, What would Uncle Ho have thought and done? But Ho didn't leave behind extensive writings and treatises, and the thoughts of Ho remained something of a mystery. The Party's intellectuals gathered with instructions to come up with a generalized definition of the "Thought of Ho." After months of deliberation, there was no consensus. Sixty separate definitions were offered. The search went on.

The summer of 2000 was one of those times when backs were to the wall. Just when everyone thought the turtle pace of reforms meant the politburo had fallen asleep at the switch, there was a shot of good news: Bulls started running on Chuong Duong Street. After seven years of talking, backtracking, and planning, the Ho Chi Minh City Stock Exchange—the world's newest and smallest exchange—was finally open for business, and it didn't take long to figure out that the veins of many good communists flowed with a generous supply of capitalistic blood.

"This isn't like gambling, you know," said Nguyen Thanh Tuong, a civil servant and nascent capitalist who, like most Vietnamese males, rated gambling up there with beer-drinking on the list of life's great pleasures. He stood outside the converted French villa that housed the exchange, checking information on the listed companies that had been tacked to a bulletin board. "Gambling involves risk. With stocks you can study the company and make an intelligent choice, and right now I'm sure these stocks are undervalued."

In a matter of weeks the Saigonese had become such enthusiastic big-board watchers that they'd often show up at brokerage houses at 7:30 A.M., their children in tow, and put in buy orders before heading off to work. The Party's doctrine still considered profit an unsavory accomplishment, and anyone with wealth was a target of public suspicion. But no matter. All of Ho Chi Minh City was abuzz with investor talk. The newspapers started printing stock prices and reporting the daily closing of the Vietnam Index. Within six months the index had more than doubled, even though the nervous government had decreed that stocks could not rise or fall by more than 2 percent a day.

"I stood on the floor of the New York Stock Exchange on one visit to the United States and said to myself, 'Vietnam's won't ever be this big, this active,'" the exchange's deputy director, Tran Dac Sinh, said as we looked out over the small, orderly trading floor where a half-dozen dealers, most just out of college, took telephone and computer orders at their desks. "Still, things have gone better than we dared hope, and I think more and more people will invest because of the possibility prices will go up."

Certainly Vietnam's exchange, which opened more than a decade after China's, had some catching up to do. Only four companies—an electrical manufacturer, a utility, a paper company, and a warehouse-transforwarding firm—were listed, and three of the four were state-owned enterprises. Share prices hovered at little more than $1 each. With prospective sellers reluctant to part with their holdings, total volume on some days—the exchange was open for two hours, three days a week—fell short of 50,000 shares.

But the important aspect of the Ho Chi Minh City Exchange was simply that it had opened. It was a necessary step in attracting foreign capital. And it underscored a fundamental fact in Vietnam's transition from a traditional Marxist economy: However frightened the government was about the impact of free markets, there was no turning back. Its very survival depended on delivering the improved living standards, the opportunity for meaningful employment, and general economic growth the Party had promised. A state-run economy had no hope of achieving those goals. Only free enterprise could.

## { 8

# WHO RUNS VIETNAM?

I AWOKE ONE AUTUMN MORNING to find my sleepy Hanoi neighborhood had slipped into festival mode. Convoys of pickup trucks
and motor scooters cruised the streets, Vietnamese flags waving,
loudspeakers blaring patriotic songs and messages. Large bouquets of
flowers were everywhere, on the doorsteps of shops, on the plastic tables
of sidewalk noodle cafés, on the altars of pagodas, on the sewing table of
the tailor down the street. From the schoolyard, I heard children singing
the Vietnamese national anthem, written by a Northern soldier in the
colonial 1940s:

> *Soldiers of Vietnam, we go forward*
> *With the one will to save our Fatherland*
> *Our hurried steps are sounding on the long and arduous road*

*Our flag, red with the blood of victory, bears the spirit of our country.*
*The distant rumbling of the guns mingles with our marching song.*
*The path to glory passes over the bodies of our foes.*
*Overcoming all hardships, together we build our resistance bases.*
*Ceaselessly for the people's cause let us struggle.*
*Let us hasten to the battlefield*
*Forward! All together advancing!*
*Our Vietnam is strong, eternal.*

*Soldiers of Vietnam, we go forward!*
*The gold star of our flag in the wind*
*Leading our people, our native land, out of misery and suffering.*
*Let us join our efforts in the fight for the building of a new life*
*Let us stand up and break our chains*
*For too long have we swallowed our hatred*
*Let us keep ready for all sacrifices and our life will be radiant*
*Ceaselessly for the people's cause let us struggle*
*Let us hasten to the battlefield*
*Forward! All together advancing!*
*Our Vietnam is strong, eternal.*

"What's going on?" I asked the bicycle repairman on the corner.

"The election," he said. "It's the startup to the election."

Election? Vietnam had elections? *Real* elections?

Most historians agree Hanoi had no intention of letting its citizens vote freely had elections on the future of the country been held in 1956. The communists did hold a "free" national election in 1976, but the 99 percent of the vote they won made the whole affair a bit suspect. Still, the celebratory atmosphere I had awakened to in my Ngu Xa neighborhood had engulfed the entire country. One hundred thousand candidates were running for 25,000 seats on the local People's Committees—Vietnam's version of a town council—and in the balance hung a new road for some villages and not for others, perhaps a beautification project, access to electricity or purified water, another public toilet facility or rebuilt marketplace. The campaign lasted about a week and was pretty uneventful. The candidates had all been approved by the Vietnamese Communist Party, and there was no debate on issues, or even any apparent differences of opinion. Seldom did candidates even show up to pitch their credentials to voters, although for the first time some neighborhoods were circulating petitions saying they wanted to hear from the candidates before making a choice.

The election was set for Tuesday. I walked down to the polling station in the school on Duc Chinh Street. Voting is mandatory in Vietnam, so a good turnout was never in question. Ngu Xa had 1,542 registered voters, and by 9 A.M. 1,537 ballots had been cast. I asked a friend if he had voted, and he said, "I couldn't. I was late for work. My uncle voted for me." Ah, so that's why the schoolyard was quieter than I had expected. Voters fulfilled the obligations of indisposed relatives and friends. Some cast seventeen or eighteen ballots.

Ngu Xa had the ambiance of a village, a quiet, pint-sized peninsula linked to the bustle of Hanoi by a single road, and I wanted to learn more about its political structure. I asked around, inquiring when the People's Committee met, whether meetings were open to the public, how decisions were reached. No one had any idea. Then I started asking the same questions about the central government. Who was on the politburo? How did they get there? How long did they serve? Why didn't newspapers write about the debate on any issue? Again, hardly anyone knew anything. Which raised a question: Who runs Vietnam?

The simplest answer is the Communist Party. It is an elite organization, open to newcomers by invitation only, with 2.5 million members, the majority of whom live in the North. Only 12 percent are under the age of thirty. The Party dominates all sectors of society, with trusted senior cadres controlling the ministries, the military, the media, the state-run enterprises, the instruments of policymaking. It is, says the 1980 constitution, "the only force leading the state and society and the main factor determining all successes of the Vietnamese revolution." That doesn't leave much room for interpretation, so the Vietnamese don't sit around discussing the merits and shortfalls of communism. For the most part, they have bought into the leadership's masterful sales pitch. Myths and realities of the past are presented in a manner that suggests they led naturally to the present: The innate wisdom and rectitude of Ho Chi Minh led to the formation of the Communist Party; the Communist Party freed the country from foreign domination; ending foreign domination resulted in the dramatic improvement of living standards in the 1990s. Were it not for communism, well, God only knows what misfortune would have befallen Vietnam.

Ho Chi Minh presided over the founding congress of the Vietnamese Communist Party in Hong Kong in February 1930. In his book *Understanding Vietnam*, Neil L. Jamieson quotes a French military report on how pervasive Ho Chi Minh's organizational apparatus soon became. It included:

> youth groups, groups for mothers, farmers, workers, "resistant" Catholics, war veterans, etc. It could just as well have included associations of flute players or bicycle racers; the important point was that no one escaped regimentation and that the territorial hierarchy was thus complemented by another, which watched the former and was in turn watched by it—both of them being watched in turn from the outside and the inside by the security services and the party. The individual caught in the fine mesh of such a net has no chance whatever of preserving his independence.

In recruiting rural peasants for the resistance in South Vietnam, Ho's cadres were not entirely honest in sharing their goals. They were instructed not to talk about ideological purity and never to mention communism. "Nationalism" was the only word in their political vocabulary. Neither did they ever speak of Party plans to collectivize the farms—an idea that could well have turned many peasants against the revolution. The truth is most Southern farmers didn't care whether their leader was Ho Chi Minh or Ngo Dinh Diem, whether they lived under communism or under a regime that purported to stand for democracy. They just wanted to survive and know that no one would shoot their water buffalo.

Vietnam was run by a troika during my time in Hanoi—a president, a prime minister, and the chief of the Communist Party. But President Tran Duc Luong's job was ceremonial, and Prime Minister Phan Van Khai, a decent, reform-minded man respected in international circles, didn't have much power. He could decree that Vietnam Airlines paint its planes blue but not that Vietnam accelerate economic reform or increase steel production. Many of his tasks were mundane. When, for instance, an infestation of rats nibbling through precious rice fields struck the North, it fell to Khai to issue the battle cry, "Kill rat; grow cat" and to urge the citizenry to collect the tails of dead rats it had hunted down and killed.

The rat decree was issued shortly after I arrived in Hanoi, and I was surprised such affairs of state fell on the prime minister's desk. But his office had determined that there was a good reason for the explosion in the rat population: Vietnam had eaten—or exported to China to be eaten—most of its cats. So Khai ordered the closure of Haiphong's "little tiger" restaurants, which specialized in cat (boiled or grilled), and urged the nation to start raising cats as predators. One zoo got so caught up in the antirat campaign that it released its snakes into the rice fields. Some were poisonous, raising many complaints among farmers.

A man from the agriculture ministry, Nguyen Van Tien, told me: "I know growing cats may seem a long-term solution to the rat problem. They take a long time to grow up, they don't have many children and they can run away or die from disease. But they don't like rats so it's an important option." Still, I was not convinced that cats had become eat-proof, and ours, Boomer and Paka (the Swahili word for "cat"), remained restricted to quarters in our ninth-floor apartment.

I went with Tien to Thanh Xuan, a village an hour's drive from Hanoi, where the mobilization of the citizenry had been impressive. Rats had been smoked and flooded out of their holes, chased and clubbed to death and poisoned. The confirmation of each kill was a severed tail. Just as Americans used to save green stamps, farmers were collecting rat tails in plastic bags until they had enough to warrant a trip to the local rat redemption center. Their reward for each tail was 200 dong, or about two U.S. cents. One man biked into the Thanh Xuan with 2,000 tails and went home with more money than he normally earned in a month. "This is easy work," he said. "There are rats everywhere." The national rat body count reached 20 million before I stopped paying attention.

The fact that Khai had taken the long-term cat approach to the rat problem was very much in keeping with the national character. Patience was Vietnam's long suit. It's how the Vietnamese outlasted the French and the Americans, how they played China and the Soviet Union one against the other. Patience, the older Vietnamese believed, was their key weapon. "How long do you Americans want to fight?" Pham Van Dong, a founder of the Viet Minh and one of Ho Chi Minh's closest allies, asked an American reporter in 1966. "One year? Five years? Twenty years? We will accommodate you."

Dong, who had headed the communist delegation at the Geneva peace talks that followed France's defeat at Dien Bien Phu, was prime minister of North Vietnam, then of the reunited Vietnam, from 1955 to 1987. The political apparatus he and Ho oversaw served Hanoi well in time of war. Patience, endurance, and single-minded focus were virtues. The politburo made decisions by consensus in collegial meetings with few disagreements. As in the United States during the 1950s and early 1960s, the people trusted their political leaders to do the right thing and make the right decisions. North Vietnam and its population were manageable. Discipline and orderliness were valued. The wisdom of elders was respected, unquestioned in the tradition of Confucianism, and Ho, Dong, and General Vo Nguyen Giap were already old by the time the American War started. Decisions were reached quietly, privately. The politburo, a small group of fifteen or twenty men—occasionally a woman found her way into the fraternity—didn't have to explain, cajole, or ask for anyone's approval. They were like a corporate board of directors with no shareholders to answer to.

But the system that worked so well for wartime North Vietnam proved itself ill-suited for peacetime Vietnam. In a high-tech, information-driven, globalized economy, patience, caution, and narrow focus are not virtues. What count are decisiveness, flexibility, and transparency—the very attributes that are anathema to a secretive Communist Party. The Party leadership today is composed of men who over the course of many years shared the same experiences, the same views of the world, the same joys and traumas. I'm sure they would happily go back to the past, if they could do so with pockets full of dong. They entered the future reluctantly and with few fresh ideas.

"Marxist-socialism together with nationalism helped in the primary task of liberating the country," wrote Pham Ngoc Uyen, one of the Party's respected elderly intellectuals, in an unusually candid assessment. "But after 1975, Marxist-socialism failed to help solve the crucial task of combating poverty and backwardness. Therefore, our people are silently abandoning it. The new revolution is one of brains, not guns, but Vietnam can only succeed if communism bows out in favor of the free market."

The most powerful man in Vietnam was the secretary-general of the Communist Party, Le Kha Phieu, a man of seventy who had climbed the hierarchy as a commissar within the army. He was of the old school, conservative and suspicious of the intents of outsiders, but it was difficult to discover intimate details of his personal life or how he considered the changes taking place around him. The public viewed him as an institution, not a person. Every time I'd run across one of Phieu's comments in the media, I'd make a note of it in my computer. Sometimes his remarks reflected a realization that change was both necessary and inevitable, but more often his Cold War language seemed, in a contemporary world, as outdated as Latin. Some of his comments I noted were:

- 1966: Capitalism is backward. It does not meet the people's needs for happiness. It will definitely be replaced.
- 1994: Peaceful evolution is our gravest danger. Resist all efforts by outsiders to introduce it. It will bring only anarchy, chaos from which none will profit.
- 1997: The economic reform effort must be intensified.
- 2001: We are determined to safeguard [political stability]. This is the best opportunity to build socialism and build our armed forces. Our fatherland is a focal point which hostile forces constantly seek a way to contain, sabotage, assimilate, and subvert.

The politburo was comprised of Phieu and seventeen other members. More than half were sixty-five or older. They were the Party's top power-brokers and, as a group, held unlimited authority and were basically accountable to no one but each other. They didn't give interviews and, except for Phieu and the prime minister, weren't quoted in the press. They lived in villas near Ho Chi Minh's mausoleum and met at the nearby former French colonial high school on Hoang Van Thu Street. How often they met, what they talked about, how they reached decisions—all were a mystery to virtually everyone.

Sometimes, sitting in a coffee shop or a pub, I'd ask the waiter or bartender how many members of the politburo he could name. Two or three was average; six, exceptional. When A. C. Nielsen pollsters asked the postwar generation of Vietnamese in 1999, "Do you know who your leader is?" 56 percent said "no." That didn't mean they couldn't name the prime minister or the Party secretary-general; it meant that they, like the population as a whole, didn't know who was really calling the shots.

In theory, the Party's highest organ was the National Party Congress, an unwieldy group of about 1,200 members who met every five years. It selected the 150 members of the Central Committee, which in turn decided who would be in the politburo. There was also a National Assembly that acted as the legislative arm of the politburo. But in reality it was meaningless to make a distinction between the politburo and the government. The politburo decided; the other bodies confirmed.

From time to time there were whispers of disagreements within the politburo—a wrangling between pro-Soviet and pro-China cliques in the 1980s, squabbling between the conservatives and the reformists in the 1990s—but the truth is that even the most informed diplomatic analysts didn't know what went on behind the closed doors of the old French school that served as Party headquarters. The Party's inner sanctum was a self-perpetuating fraternity, as closed to scrutiny as the Masons.

It always surprised me when a bright young Vietnamese told me he was a Party member, because communism was viewed as irrelevant by most educated Vietnamese who weren't on the state payroll. Few paid any attention to the slogans and banners. But ask ordinary Vietnamese if they were communist and they would probably say yes. What they meant was they were nationalists, not that they were advocates of Marxist economic and political theory.

If the genius of leadership is to understand the pulse of a nation and move people toward a desired destination, the politburo was distinctly lacking in whiz-kid qualities. Its members were neither well-educated nor well-traveled. Many understood little about the world. This was a severe intellectual limitation, and it is no wonder the leadership clung to the reins of privilege as tenaciously as any fading American politician no longer in step with his constituency.

Vietnam's first generation of communist leaders—Ho Chi Minh, Pham Van Dong, Vo Nguyen Giap, and Le Duc Tho among others—came from scholarly backgrounds. Some of their fathers had served the emperors. Ho and his colleagues were seen as morally diligent, administratively efficient, incorruptible. Even if they had been thieves, there wouldn't have been much around to steal. But the second generation that now ran Vietnam encountered many temptations, with big money from donor groups and foreign investors floating around as a result of the government's *doi moi* open-door economic policy. Suddenly Vietnam was awash in corruption. It reached from the policeman on the beat to the high levels of government. There had always been perks involved with Party membership—better housing, better jobs, better educational opportunity for the elite's children, funded travel abroad—but now ordinary citizens knew they had to pay the traffic cop to avoid a ticket and bribe a low-paid civil servant to get something done at a ministry. Shopkeepers knew they had to pay to stay in business. Investors knew they had to pay to get a contract approved. In this new atmosphere, the leadership came to be viewed as cynical careerists; the Communist Party itself lost its mythical aura of wisdom and rectitude, which had enabled it to govern.

{{{   }}}

VIETNAM'S FIRST CONSTITUTION, written in 1946 during the colonial era, provided for freedom of speech, the press, and assembly. Many historians question whether Ho Chi Minh intended to honor those provisions and believe he included them to give his fledgling republic a democratic flavor that would appeal to the international community. The second constitution, in 1959, after the French had left, had a more typically communist lilt, referring to Vietnam as a "people's democratic state led by the working class." The third, drafted in 1980 when Vietnam faced a serious threat from China, resembled the 1977 Soviet constitution. Article 67, however, guaranteed citizens' rights to freedom of speech, the press, assembly, and association and the right to demonstrate, with one caveat: "No one may misuse democratic freedoms to violate the interests of the state and the people." Who decided the interests of the state and the people? The Party.

Vietnam took a lot of heat from Western civil libertarians and human-rights activists. The condemnation was well deserved during the Dark Years, but the "new" Vietnam I saw emerging was as free as Indonesia had been under Washington's staunch ally, Suharto. It was less abusive of human rights than China. Its press was not much more timid tiptoeing

available at newsstands. The National Assembly, although hardly a bastion of free debate, became more than a rubber stamp for the politburo and sometimes challenged ministerial appointments and policy. Farmers with grievances sat outside the headquarters of the Hanoi People's Committee and, if they were patient, usually got to deliver their complaints to a minor bureaucrat. The Catholic churches and Buddhist pagodas were full on days of worship, and as long as the gatherings had no political overtones, people were generally free to practice their religion. Bao Ninh was allowed to publish his book, *The Sorrow of War*, that celebrated not the revolutionary glory of the war against the Americans but the distress and loss of ordinary North Vietnamese soldiers and the unfulfilled promises of an uncertain peace. (He wrote of envying his protagonist's "optimism in focusing back on the painful but glorious days [of war]. They were caring days, when we knew what we were living and fighting for and why we needed to suffer and sacrifice.") From time to time newspapers carried articles, albeit approved by Party censors, declaring that corruption, smuggling, mismanagement, and the slow pace of economic reform were hurting Vietnam. The government started receiving human-rights delegations, and senior officials would at least listen and nod politely when the issue of sixty or so political and religious imprisoned dissidents came up. The activists considered them political prisoners; the government said they were common criminals who had misused "democratic freedoms to violate the interests of the state and the people."

The last effective tool of control the Party wielded—and the one it held to most tenaciously—was propaganda. That word made me cringe, but in Vietnam, as in many developing countries, it didn't have a negative connotation. It meant news or information deemed to be in the best interests of the nation. And if there was one thing the government had always made clear, it was that a free flow of information, debate, and discussion were not on Vietnam's agenda. It was a very elitist thesis, the premise being that all wisdom belonged to the leadership. Ordinary people were too ignorant to decide for themselves the merits of an issue.

After the French left Vietnam in 1954, many Northern writers and poets looked for individual expression and creative freedom in the burst of pride and euphoria that accompanied the end of colonialism. A form of protest literature even flourished briefly. But its practitioners were soon branded malcontents and reactionaries and, like other intellectuals who dismissed the notion that the role of art was to serve the Party, were silenced. Fifty-eight writers and poets from the Arts and Letters Association, Neil L. Jamieson wrote in *Understanding Vietnam*, were sent in teams to work for six months in agricultural cooperatives, mines, lumber camps, road gangs, textile factories, and frontier outposts so their future work would reflect the new "reality" of Vietnam, as interpreted by born-again communists.

Commenting on the transition from colonialism to communism, Hoang Cam wrote:

> *Stop, write no more letters,*
> *Lest each line be one more crime.*
> *My parents have passed away.*
> *Now I have new parents.*
> *. . . . .*
> *When can I be an orphan?*

*Doi moi*—and the loosening of some state controls that came with it—led to a dramatic increase in the number of magazines and newspapers published in Vietnam. In the late 1970s, only a handful of drab, crude communist propaganda news sheets were available; twenty years later, the Vietnamese had a choice of 368 state-owned daily and weekly publications. Unlike the United States, where newspapers were losing public credibility, in Vietnam people trusted without question what they read in the papers, and almost everyone—the national literacy rate was 91 percent—read a newspaper.

Newspaper layouts got brighter as the industry became more competitive; government subsidies were cut, forcing business managers to accept advertising and look for ways to increase revenue; editors (most, but not all, of whom are Party members) became responsible for the content in their publications; a few daring reporters tried to occasionally push, if only an inch or two, the bounds of Party limitations on what was acceptable to write.

"There is no question we have more freedom today," said Nguyen Duc Tuan, an editor at *Lao Dong* (Labor), which had 80,000 daily readers and sold for twelve cents a copy. "In the old days we had no news. You never would have read stuff like this." He handed me a stack of papers. There were stories on slumping exports, rising inflation, urban power blackouts, rampant corruption, widespread drug use among teenagers, and another foreign airline—Qantas of Australia—ending service to Vietnam because of dwindling passenger loads.

A good presage. Still, no one would confuse *Ha Noi Moi* (New Hanoi) with the *Times* of London. The Party's Commission of Culture and Ideology met every Tuesday to decide what Vietnam's people should be told that week. When the commission decided enough had been written about Princess Diana's death, coverage ended overnight in every newspaper, even though she had not yet been buried. When the commission decided it wasn't in the state's interest to report that 1,000 Vietnamese troops had been sent to Laos to help the beleaguered communist government there put down an upcountry insurrection, not a word was carried in the media. (Vietnamese could have read about it in the *Los Angeles Times* or any one of a dozen foreign papers.) Ranking the top events of 1997—a year in which the Asian financial crisis began, Hong Kong was returned to China, El Niño assaulted the environment, and Russia signed a security pact with NATO—the Vietnam News Agency chose as the top story the thirtieth-anniversary celebration of the Association of Southeast Asian Nations. Number nine on the list was Cuba successfully staging the 14th Festival of World Youth and Students. It was as though the media lived in a dream bubble far removed from the realities of planet Earth.

In other developing countries where I'd worked, local journalists often turned out to be my best sources of information and most useful contacts. Vietnam was different. Reporters, who were licensed by the government, generally had chosen journalism because they wanted the security of a state job, not because they were curious about the world around them or had a calling to pluck a kernel of truth from a sack of lies. They knew little about the workings of their country and almost nothing about the countries next door. That didn't seem to bother them. In their jobs, they didn't ask why, they didn't challenge, nothing seemed to stir them to public outrage. They couldn't live on their $40-per-month salaries, so they scurried from press conference to press conference to collect their *phong bi*, envelopes stuffed with 100,000 dong ($6.60) that hosts gave local journalists for showing up and writing a (favorable) story. When 5:00 P.M. arrived, they were out the door. That saddened me, not only because they had missed all that is rewarding and worthy in an honorable profession but also because many of the young reporters I met were plenty bright yet didn't seem to realize they'd put their brains on cruise control. I asked one reporter what her idea of a good story was, and she replied, "A story that is in harmony with the people." Like her colleagues, she had bought the official line that to question or criticize was to undermine the spirit of nationalism. My professional training had taught me precisely the opposite.

"Being a true journalist," Le Kha Phieu explained to senior editors in Hanoi, "it is necessary . . . to reflect the thoughts and wishes of the public [and be] on the right political track oriented by the party."

{{{ }}}

FOR THE LIFE OF ME, I couldn't figure out why the leadership was afraid of so many things: of people having access to unfiltered information, of the intents of foreign governments, of farmers tired of being ripped off by local People's Committees, of what foreign correspondents wrote, of the Internet, democracy, religion. Vietnam was stable politically and nationalistic to the core. It had fewer dissidents in a population of 80 million than most backwoods Michigan towns had in a single block. Even the few malcontents who surfaced from time to time had no radical goals; they just wanted to help build a better country. True, the collapse of the Soviet Union had given the politburo nightmares, but Vietnam wasn't divided by religious or ethnic gulfs as was Moscow's former empire. And true, Suharto's fall from power after thirty-two years in Indonesia sent a signal that no one was immune, but the former general had stolen a Rockefelleresque fortune, let his soldiers kill thousands of citizens, and presided over a patched-together country of 17,000 islands where various groups often had little in common, historically, culturally, or linguistically.

Vietnam's government was of two minds about having people like me around. One group of old-line conservatives would have been happy to see Hanoi's small foreign press corps—there were about twenty of us: Americans, French, British, Russian, and Cuban—pack up and leave, sparing Vietnam its nosy questions, its pursuit of issues that officials didn't want to talk about, and its notion that communism was more a detriment than an asset to the country's development. But however big a pain we were, most officials, I think, realized there were benefits to our presence. Foreign investors wanted access to information that wasn't siphoned through official channels. Potential tourists wanted assurances Vietnam was stable, welcoming, and worth visiting. Overseas Vietnamese who had fled their homeland needed to know—but didn't always accept—that the Dark Years were over and that Vietnam had made progress in human rights and economic development. And Vietnam itself liked being reminded that a few newspapers still considered the country important enough to base a correspondent there and distribute his or her articles to an international audience.

I knew the government kept track of me, though I doubted that my office was bugged or that I was followed, as some colleagues insisted. I knew that my assistant—an office manager-interpreter-translator-facilitator-minder hired from the government—had a dual role: first to make my job easier, which he did, and second, to report every Saturday to the press department on whom I had seen during the week and what stories I was working on. It was a childish game because everything I knew and did was printed in one article or another in the *Los Angeles Times*, and anyone who wanted to know what I was up to could have simply read my clip file of stories in the bureau or on the Internet. But letting Western correspondents snoop around their country was a new experience for the Vietnamese, and their uneasiness was understandable, particularly given the cantankerous nature of the press as a whole. The key to professional survival, I found, was attitude. If government officials who dealt with the media thought you tried to be fair and balanced, were respectful of Vietnamese culture and history, didn't swagger with Western arrogance, and wanted the best, not the worst, for Vietnam, they would cut you a lot of slack and accept their share of critical stories. Their approach with us was more sophisticated than the overbearing one they used on their own reporters, and I never had any trouble when it came time to renew my visa every six months.

The government, of course, is destined to lose the campaign to keep its people like-minded and uninformed. Thousands of Vietnamese students have been exposed to a free exchange of information abroad. Party officials have given up their attempt to stamp out Internet cafés, and scores of shops in the cities are jammed with young Vietnamese hunched over computers, the websites of the world at their fingertips. Short-wave radio brings news from the BBC and VOA. CNN plays in hotels and the homes of Party officials. Technology is making censors irrelevant. The beneficiary is the Vietnamese people; the loser, the Old Guard that sees another pillar of the past being dismantled.

{{{ }}}

WHEN PHAM VAN DONG, the political architect of Vietnam's victories over France and the United States, died during the third year of my assignment in Hanoi, blind and frail at the age of ninety-four, only one of

Ho Chi Minh's first generation of revolutionaries still remained—General Vo Nguyen Giap. Though widely regarded as one of the twentieth century's leading military strategists and revered by the Vietnamese as the nation's last hero, Giap had long since been removed from the corridors of power, shunted aside by other ambitious men, among them the late Le Duan and Le Duc Tho. One by one he was forced to give up his positions, as commander in chief, defense minister, central committee member, politburo powerbroker. His last position, from 1984 to 1991, was chief of the demographics and family planning commission.

Giap lived quietly near Ho's mausoleum in a tree-shaded villa at 30 Hoang Dieu Street, set back from the road, his parlor filled with busts and portraits of Ho, Marx, and Lenin. He was a sort of official greeter whom the government showcased periodically for the legions of foreign visitors and dignitaries requesting an audience. Sometimes I'd catch a glimpse of him around town, a celebrity surrounded by well-wishers. I would see him at opening performances in the Opera House or coming out of a VIP reception, his brown army uniform immaculately tailored and bearing four gold stars on each shoulder. Although he was nearly ninety and needed an aide's arm to negotiate stairs, everyone who had spoken to him, in Vietnamese or French, said he still had a quick mind and a sharp memory. He could recall various military campaigns—Napoleon's and his own—in brilliant detail.

He declined most requests for interviews and only consented to press conferences on special occasions; certainly the twenty-fifth anniversary of North Vietnam hoisting the Viet Cong flag in Saigon qualified. Resident foreign reporters were told to submit their questions in advance to the government press office. At 11 A.M. three days later we were summoned to an ornate meeting hall in the foreign ministry's guesthouse. The legendary general waited there, in a large armchair, its red-upholstered back towering above his head. I was surprised how short Giap was, no more than five-foot-three, I guessed. He was white-haired with a round face and the shrunken cheeks of a chipmunk. His hands were soft-skinned, his voice animated.

Giap's name had become synonymous with battles that shaped a generation of world history. His victory over the French at Dien Bien Phu in 1954 had emboldened liberation movements from Africa to Latin America. His construction of the Ho Chi Minh Trail in the 1960s was an engineering and logistical feat bordering on the miraculous. His diversionary siege at Khe Sanh in 1968 set the stage for the Tet Offensive, which so intensified antiwar sentiments in the United States that President Lyndon B. Johnson was forced to begin the phased withdrawal of U.S. troops the next year. I was loaded with questions and excited that I finally would have an opportunity to get some long-sought answers.

"I've read your questions," Giap said to us. "I see there is a lot you want to ask. Most of your questions are about my role in the war, so let me start there." He shuffled the stack of typewritten pages he was holding and started reading. Alas, as often happens with Vietnamese officials, there were to be no questions, no exchange of dialogue—only Giap, center-stage, lecturing on history and war, repeating tired stories from a generation or two ago and carefully avoiding any of the intimate details or personal reminiscences that bring history to life. It was as though Giap's life had gone into slow motion after his troops took Saigon.

Of the three "golden milestones" in his life—Vietnam's declaration of independence in 1945, its victory over France at Dien Bien Phu in 1954, and its triumph over the U.S.-backed Saigon regime in 1975—the last was the most joyous, he said.

Speaking of the Vietnamese as "the most peace-loving people in the world," Giap said: "Finally, we were rid of the enemy. It fulfilled the dreams the Vietnamese people had held for hundreds of years. The paradox is we had to fight for our freedom, our independence. But the U.S. soldiers did not understand Vietnam. I have read their books. One wrote, 'I didn't understand why I was in Vietnam or what I was fighting for.' That was the common point between the United States and French soldiers. Their morale and fighting spirit were low."

U.S. commanders were in awe of Giap's military skills, but they were also shocked by his ruthlessness and his willingness to sacrifice legions of men without apparent guilt. The Tet Offensive, which earned Hanoi a psychological victory in the United States but represented a devastating military defeat for the Viet Cong, claiming the lives of thousands, was a case in point. "Giap was callous," General William Westmoreland, the U.S. troop commander, said after Tet. "Had any American general taken such losses he wouldn't have lasted three weeks."

Giap was a hard, uncompromising man. Victory was everything. The cost of achieving it was immaterial. "Every minute, hundreds of thousands of people die on this Earth," Giap said in 1969. "The life or death of a hundred, a thousand, tens of thousands of human beings, even our compatriots, means little."

A master logistician and skilled artillery tactician, Giap built, with Moscow's help, one of the world's most sophisticated air defense systems in North Vietnam. He saw the war against the United States as an extension of the war against France and never wavered in his belief that Washington's resolve would eventually whither, as had Paris's. "You can kill ten of my men for every one I kill of yours," he once warned the Americans, repeating what he had told the French more than a decade earlier. "But even at those odds you will lose and I will win."

Giap held court with us for two-and-a-half hours, talking nonstop except for a fifteen-minute snack break of bananas, cheese, and tea. He gestured with his hands to emphasize his points on the depths of Vietnamese history, culture, and pride. He smiled and seemed to be having a good time, pausing at times so that his translator would not be rushed. However disappointed I was that he was willing to only rehash well-known stories, I had no doubt that I was in the presence of a remarkable historical figure.

The son of scholarly parents who owned a rice farm, Giap began reading Marx at the age of thirteen. He attended Vietnam's best schools, including the prestigious Quoc Hoc Academy in Hue, whose alumni included Ho Chi Minh and Ngo Dinh Diem. He was expelled for organizing student protests against France's ban on nationalistic activities. He later earned a law degree from Hanoi University, was a teacher in Hanoi for a while, and married a communist militant, Minh Khai. Their only child, a daughter, would become a nuclear physicist and win, in 1987, the Soviet Union's Kowolenskia Prize for Science.

At the age of twenty-eight, after spending time in a French prison in the north of Vietnam, Giap moved across Vietnam's border to a communist stronghold in southern China. There, in Kwangsi Province, he met Ho Chi Minh. Although Giap had no military background and knew nothing about the strategy or tactics of guerrilla warfare, Ho entrusted him with putting together a communist army to lead the resistance against France. Back in Vietnam with his raggedy band of guerrillas, Giap lived for four years in caves, hunted by French patrols. He and his men were so short of food they often ate bark. Giap gave his camp an egalitarian structure and assigned himself the job of dishwasher.

While Giap lived in the jungles, a fugitive from civilization, his sister-in-law was arrested as a revolutionary and executed by the French. His wife was imprisoned on similar charges and died—Giap says because of ill treatment, other historical sources say because of illness—in the French prison that eventually would house American POWs and be known as the Hanoi Hilton. He later remarried and fathered three more children, but he once confided to an interviewer that the loss of Minh Khai had "ruined" his life.

Giap was not a man who knew restraint in the pursuit of his goals, and his various purges of noncommunists had covered his hands with much blood. The most murderous purge came in 1946. While Ho Chi Minh was negotiating with France outside Paris, trying to avert the First Indochina War, Giap was overseeing the extermination of thousands of noncommunist nationalists. Many were radical leftists. But that wasn't good enough. If they weren't communists, they died. The former Vietnamese ambassador to Washington, Bui Diem, once a student of Giap's at the elite Thang Long school in Hanoi, wrote in his book, *In the Jaws of History*:

Panic struck the [Vietnamese] parties as Giap's reign of terror swept their ranks with a force that dwarfed previous assassination campaigns the factions had launched against one another. While Ho and the French colonial ministers danced a slow minuet at the Fontainebleau, site of the future independence negotiations, thousands of nationalists in Vietnam died quietly.

Those dark days of terror aren't in Vietnam's history textbooks. Only victory is. Giap was never held accountable for all the blood shed on his watch. Young Vietnamese aren't even aware of it. Giap remains Vietnam's last hero, among the young and the old, the final link to Ho Chi Minh's partisans who brought the country its independence and reunification. For that, the Vietnamese are willing to overlook his transgressions.

The morning with Senior General Vo Nguyen Giap, though hardly memorable in terms of historical insights, was not time misspent. Giap was the model of the Old Guard communists whose descendants still held sway over Vietnam. Like many Vietnamese he never shared everything, always holding something in reserve. He was proud, given to lectures rather than discussions, and annoyingly self-righteous in his inability to admit that neither he nor the Party was capable of error or misjudgment. He had been weaned on the Marxism of the 1930s and 1940s, but from reading his writings and talking to those who knew him, I gathered he had found nothing new in the world of the 1990s and 2000s. The past was his present. Perhaps, given his years in the jungles, his decades on the battlefield, his loss of family, the death of so many countrymen, that was not surprising. The revolution had sustained him. It was what all life was about. But as a man of unquestioned intellect, Giap could have contributed so much leadership and inspiration to peacetime Vietnam. If only he had felt the winds of change sweeping through his beloved country and moved with them, looking for fresh ideas to accommodate all that was new, exciting, unsettling. His military achievements still stirred spirits of national honor. But to the young generation, Giap's calls for dedication to the revolution and the ideology of his past no longer resonated.

Bicyclists cross the Red River into Hanoi, transporting pottery from the nearby village of Bat Trang. The village has made ceramics for six centuries. Ever since the government started moving cautiously toward a free-market economy, business has boomed.

Can Tho's floating market in the Mekong Delta, one of Asia's great rice bowls. Hanoi's post-war decision to collectivize farming pushed Vietnam toward famine and turned the country into a rice importer. Today, Vietnam is the world's second largest rice exporter.

*Right:* The French bombed Vinh from 1931 to 1952; the Americans from 1964 to 1972. By war's end all that stood in the port city was a provincial guesthouse and two college dormitories. The dorm pictured here will be razed to make room for low-cost housing.

*Below, right:* Le Van Vang and his wife, both tailors, hold their wedding picture from 1963. Vang spent the war in Saigon, hiding to avoid the draft. They lost everything in the Dark Years after 1975 but have rebuilt their lives and their business and are once again prospering.

*Above:* When Senator John McCain returned to peacetime Hanoi, one of the men to greet him was Mai Van On, who had helped save McCain when he was shot down in 1967 and crashed into a lake. "I still don't know why I did what I did," On says.

*Right:* Nguyen Duc Bao, a retired North Vietnamese Army colonel, spent nine years fighting the French, ten the Americans, and six Pol Pot's Khmer Rouge guerrillas in Cambodia. As a teenager, he tattooed a Vietnamese flag on his arm with a sewing needle and ink.

East Germany helped Vinh rebuild after the war. The first project comprised a cluster of concrete block apartment buildings that resembled a Soviet gulag. When assistance from Eastern Europe ended, the complex fell into disrepair. Apartments rent for $3.50 a month.

For eight years during the war, Trinh Thi Ngo was the voice of the communist North Vietnam. Nicknamed Hanoi Hannah by GIs, Ngo played popular American songs and provided news that wasn't very creditable. She lives quietly in Ho Chi Minh City now.

The most respected South Vietnamese journalist to work for the Americans during the war, *Time* magazine's Pham Xuan An was a double agent who had served the resistance since 1945. But he never planted a fake story or put an American's life at risk.

Like four hundred thousand southerners, Duong Cu, a former South Vietnamese Supreme Court justice, was sent to reeducation camp when Saigon fell in 1975 and was later denied meaningful employment. He says he has made his peace and is no longer bitter.

Nguyen Thi Le holds a picture of her husband, a South Vietnamese Army artilleryman. He was killed in 1973. "My life was over," she says. "I kept waiting, thinking perhaps he would return, but the days came and the days went . . . and I am still here, waiting."

Nguyen Van Tran on the airstrip at Khe San, where U.S. Marines withstood a bloody seventy-six-day siege in 1968. Tran sells fake medals and souvenirs from both sides, but business is slow and few visitors stop at the abandoned outpost on Highway 9.

A group of U.S. veterans mingles with former Viet Cong guerrillas. They had fought each other in central Vietnam a generation earlier and conversation did not come easily at first. Before long the ice broke and it became clear this was not a gathering of enemies.

Three college professors—all former North Vietnamese soldiers—with the author in Hanoi. Nguyen Ngoc Hung, second from left, traveled to the United States in 1992 on a mission of reconciliation. He met with groups of GIs throughout the country.

Returning GI Chuck Owens meets an elderly village woman in Pho Vinh, once a Viet Cong stronghold. After years of heavy drinking, Owens got his life back on track and found that coming back to Vietnam helped lay to rest the ghosts of his wartime past.

With nowhere to go, a handful of Amerasians remain stranded at a ramshackle refugee camp in the Philippines. Fathered by unknown U.S. servicemen, many look so American one expects to hear them speaking English. "We're the leftovers of the war," says one.

Hoi Trinh with Amerasian children in the Philippines. An Australian-Vietnamese whose father escaped Vietnam after ten failed attempts, Trinh spent five years helping settle Vietnam's boat people who were scattered in refugee camps throughout Southeast Asia.

For the first time in decades, soldiers are back on the Ho Chi Minh trail—this time as unarmed engineers who are turning the legendary route into a national highway. Most of their fathers walked down the trail when it was the world's deadliest road.

Life has improved dramatically for the post-war generation and young Vietnamese like photographer Pham Ba Hung have oportunities their parents dared not imagine. Hung's family still sets a place at the dinner table every night for his uncle, missing in the war.

A boom in coffee production has made Vietnam the world's third largest coffee exporter and brought prosperity to parts of the Central Highlands. "More coffee. That's the answer," says farmer Y Mum Eban, who has built a spiffy house and bought a tractor.

Vietnam's government worries that the move toward a free-market economy could lead to moral decay and the importation of "social evils" from the West. This sign in Hanoi warns against "poisonous cultural articles," drug abuse, prostitution, and gambling.

{9

# AWAITING THE
# PASSING OF THE TORCH

S O WHERE WERE THE BRIGHT YOUNG PEOPLE who would save
Vietnam?

They were everywhere. And there were plenty of them, division
upon division of twenty- and thirty-somethings whose destiny a generation ago would have been to schlep down the Ho Chi Minh Trail and
who today had been turned loose on a peacetime banquet of opportunity
unimaginable in their parents' time. They worked feverishly, considered
education a sacred obligation, often starting on a second university degree
before they had even finished the first, and thirsted for marketable skills
and knowledge. Every morning in Hanoi when I stopped for coffee at Au
Lac Café, my waiter approached with a list of four or five English phrases

that mystified him. He was reading Jane Austen, who had been beyond my own comprehension as a student. "I don't understand this at all," Lap would say, showing me his notes that included "needle in a haystack," "pop the champagne cork," and "benign demeanor." "Why do you say, 'I finished reading' instead of 'I finished to read'? Don't you use an infinitive after the verb?" No one could accuse these kids of asking for a free ride or blowing the opportunities the end of war had provided.

Lap's grandfather had spoken French as a second language, his father, Russian, and the twenty-two-year-old Lap, like multitudes of his contemporaries, was in the process of mastering English. Whether the Old Guard of the Party would ever reach out to Lap's generation and incorporate it into the tapestry of government and policy and national priorities was a moot question. Personally, I doubted it. Lap's age group represented the challenge of new ideas and new influences and new demands and was, I thought, going to have to muddle through a confusing transition on its own. But the generation after his will be born and reared in an era of *doi moi* liberalization. The grip of those shaped by war and sacrifice and ideology will have atrophied by then. And in a country where a whopping 80 percent of the population was under the age of forty, there was every reason to believe that once Vietnam tapped into the potential of its youth, the nation would find the treasures of freedom and prosperity that the revolutionaries had promised but been unable or unwilling to deliver.

Often I asked middle-aged Vietnamese what they thought of the postwar generation. Their response was about what I would have expected to hear had I raised a similar question in the United States: The twenty-somethings had it too easy; they hadn't known war; they were too materialistic, cared too much about money and themselves. There was no denying they wanted their cellular phones and Nike sneakers and Honda motor scooters, but that didn't make them unique. After lagging so far behind the rest of Southeast Asia for so long, they were just discovering what other kids in the region already knew: The only thing money won't buy is poverty.

I was delighted when the Vietnamese surprised me with an unpredictable response, which they did regularly. I asked my standard question about the young one day when I went to interview a Vietnamese businessman about the new economic order. Nguyen Tran Bat was fifty-five, a former North Vietnamese soldier who had started studying Marxism as a teenager. Given his credentials I was pretty sure I knew what he'd say. But he said:

"The young today love their country no less, I think, than my generation, but they love it in different ways. We wanted peace, unity, security. This generation wants Vietnam to be football [soccer] champion of South Asia. It wants its singers to perform like Michael Jackson. It's materialistic. It complains about the pace of reform. The kids are restless, impatient. If they live in the Highlands, they probably want to go to Hanoi for action and opportunity. If they live in Hanoi, they want to go to Ho Chi Minh City. And if they live in Ho Chi Minh, they want to go to California.

"And you know what? I don't blame them for complaining. It's the responsibility of the young to complain. How else do things improve? Crying for the past is an instinct but the reasons my generation gives for wanting back the beautiful past are not persuasive to the young. You can't prevent the young from doing their own thing. They have their own values and principles and whatever you think of them, those values are going to be the values of this nation ten years from now."

"How about twenty or thirty years instead of ten?" I suggested.

"No, ten," Bat said. "We've turned a corner. There's no going back. Things are moving fast in a lot of subtle ways, faster than people notice."

One of the things that surprised me about Vietnam's first postwar generation was how apolitical and accepting of tradition its members were. No one would think of talking back to his father or teacher. Young men still expected their brides to be virgins. They didn't get tattoos or dye their hair purple or wear their baseball caps backward. Attitude was not a problem in Vietnam's culture. Conformity was the norm.

A poll of Vietnamese in five cities, commissioned by the U.S. Information Service, found that more than 80 percent of respondents believed their living standards would improve in the year ahead. Nearly half said they were better off than they had been a year ago. Six in ten thought the economy was healthy. The younger Vietnamese were the most confident. Part of their optimism was easily explained: Life had been so terrible for so long, through the 1970s and most of the 1980s, that by comparison Vietnam really was enjoying a renaissance. The government walked a tightrope, trying to toss out enough amenities and incentives to keep young Vietnamese content, but not so many that they would get uppity or independent-minded.

The young bought into this, without apparently realizing that in doing so they and their countrymen had not yet truly won their freedom, at least from my Western perspective. No one called for multiparty democracy. Few seemed dismayed that the government decided what they should read and know or that it kept access to the Internet so prohibitively expensive most people couldn't surf, unless they went to an Internet café. I asked a young doctor who was headed to the United States for further medical study if he wasn't annoyed that a student in, say, Singapore—where the government promoted the Internet as a tool of national learning—had access to the latest medical information and advances that were denied him. Wouldn't that make him a lesser doctor? "No," he said. "we have all the information we need. When we need more, the government will make sure we get it."

The government had scored a lopsided triumph. It owned the minds of the young. But the victory was temporary. My friend, the doctor, had intended to stay in the United States only one year, but three years after he left Hanoi, he was still there. Like other Vietnamese who studied abroad, he would come home a changed person, less tolerant of being told not to ask "why" or "what if." It was fear of this attitude that explained why the government seldom allowed its young people to go to the West to study journalism. Such exposure could encourage inquiring minds to challenge the Party's legitimacy.

In its special Tet edition for the year 2000, the magazine *Tuoi Tre* (Youth) asked a sampling of the postwar generation what individuals it most admired. Former President Ho Chi Minh was the most popular (39 percent), followed by General Vo Nguyen Giap (35 percent). But one man had been dead for more than thirty years, and the other was nearly ninety. Only one nonretired Vietnamese made the list, Prime Minister Phan Van Khai (3 percent). Hillary Clinton received as many votes as Khai did; President Bill Clinton got twice as many. Bill Gates was seven times more popular than anyone in the politburo. The Party was appalled. State censors destroyed the print run of 120,000 copies within hours of the magazine appearing on the newsstands.

{{{   }}}

PHAM BA HUNG'S GRANDFATHER had been a shipping magnate during colonial times, running vessels out of Haiphong to Macao, Hong Kong, Jakarta. His father had studied in France and fought in the war against the United States. The Phams' big house in Hanoi and their privileges as members of the moneyed class disappeared as soon as the communists came to power, but the family thought that a small price to pay for independence. They had, in fact, paid a bigger one; at the family dinner table a place was set every evening for Hung's uncle, who had been listed as missing in action in the Central Highlands for more than thirty years.

Hung came as close to representing the face of the new generation as anyone I knew. He had studied Russian for seven years and now spoke flawless English. His eyes sparkled, and he had that wide, generous Vietnamese smile I found so enchanting. He bubbled with enthusiasm for everything: life, his girlfriend, the opportunities *doi moi* had provided, his job as a freelance photographer. He was twenty-five and like many Vietnamese his age looked no older than a teenager. He thought he had life figured out. "For my years, I think I understand many things," he said in a tone that did not sound cocky. He would continue to invest most of his income in Nikon cameras and lenses, he said. He would not get married until he was twenty-nine because he did not want his bride moving in with his parents, as most newlyweds did for financial reasons, and being bossed around by her new mother-in-law. He considered his father among his best friends. "I can tell him anything," he said. He was fascinated with my wife's work as a documentary film producer and peppered Sandy with questions about her Avid editing system. Sometimes he took her on the back of his motor scooter for rides through the paddies and would wax poetic about rice and the harvest and how they reflected the moods of the nation and the seasons.

"Hello, Mr. David," Hung would say when he bounced into my office, a Nikon around his neck, hand clutching a cellular phone. "Everything okay today with you?"

"Hi, Mr. Hung. Yeah, everything's fine. You?"

"Wonderful."

One day, after exchanging greetings, he stopped midway en route to Sandy's next-door office and came back to my desk. "We've known each other for three years, Mr. David," he said. "You don't need to call me *Mister* Hung any more, you know."

From then on he was Hung and I was David.

Hung had been trying to digitize the photo archives at a state-run magazine where he worked. I knew he had found the effort frustrating and I asked him over lunch one day how it was going.

"What I want to do," he said, "is digitize and cross-reference everything, so, for example, a researcher could put in the words corn and agriculture and Lam Dong Province and come up with a picture he needed. But I have to say, the old people who run things don't care about or know anything. They say, 'We've got the pictures in boxes. Why do we need to digitize them?' If I tell them I need a picture of a beautiful apple, they understand that. But I tell them I need a picture that evokes a particular mood, they have no idea what I'm talking about. They don't know what art is. That's old thinking. They're too proud as victors to admit that they don't know anything. They don't realize they're not of international standard."

We talked for a couple of hours that day. I said I could not understand why people his age didn't find the idea of democracy more appealing. "I have enough freedom to live," he said. "I understand what I can do and can't do." For now, a monoparty system was best for Vietnam, Hung said. So what did people want? "Just peace," he answered. "No more fighting, please."

"What do people of your generation think about communism, Hung?"

"A lot of my friends say communism is bad, stupid. But I say, careful. You were born a communist. You were taught under the communist system. Everything in your head is communist. You don't understand capitalism. I am a communist naturally, just like I am a Vietnamese naturally. That's how I was born. It's like you can only have one mother."

Hung's reason for embracing communism sounded no more radical than would that of an American explaining why he was a Republican or a Democrat. Hung wasn't talking about Marxism-Leninism. No one believed in that any more, except a handful of Communist Party hacks. If a young Vietnamese called a colleague "comrade," it was only to tease him and imply that he was out of step with the times. The fact was that Hung did not need the Party as people of his father's generation had. In his father's time, when there was no private enterprise, Vietnamese had to have Party support to get a career, a job, a promotion, a house. If an artist wanted to exhibit his paintings, he could do it only if he had a Party sponsor. Only members of the Communist Youth League could sit for university entrance examinations. But in the new Vietnam that was emerging, people only needed the Party to advance in jobs in government, the military, or the state-run business sector. Young men like Hung could get ahead on their ability, and when a sampling of young Vietnamese was asked by pollsters what quality they found most appealing in a person, more than half answered "talent." After that, the most respected qualities were "self-respect and high-mindedness," "altruism," and "decisiveness."

"By the time I joined the Party in 1984, it had changed," said Nguyen Khuyen, who was the editor of the English-language *Vietnam News* and showed courage pushing government censorship to its limits. "There was a time when it was doctrinaire, rigid, when intellectuals were looked down on with suspicion. Now the Party has people like me. What does it offer the young? A chance to move ahead. It's a strong link to my generation. It was the Party that won independence, not some alien body imported into our midst as in Eastern Europe. It was born from the people. A native Party.

"But things are changing. I'm sixty-three and you might say I'm quite conservative. Before, I couldn't dream of living away from my family. But one daughter is married to a German and lives in Germany. My second daughter is very vocal—liberal you might say—on everything. She stays out late, does what she likes. But I've managed to accept it so far. I've managed to make my children remember our family tradition for honesty, loyalty, respect for elders. So I'm reconciled to change. But I'm more comfortable with traditions being preserved."

Several of my younger friends were Party members who worked for the government, having passed up the risks and potential rewards of the private sector in favor of a job with lifetime security and poverty wages. Joining the Party was an arduous process that could take many years. Each prospective member had to find a sponsor, usually the chief of a neighborhood or village Party cell. The applicant's personal history was checked. Did he or she do well at work? How did he get along with others? Had he made a contribution to his community? Could he be critical of himself? Had he ever violated the law? If the candidate were considered worthy, he or she would be invited to begin political training within a cell and would serve an apprenticeship of six months to two years. I had many rational exchanges with friends who had joined. The discussions weren't about ideology. Rather they were about seeking change from within the system, about building the nation, about leading commendable lives, about finding a network of support. Some of my friends saw the possibility that the Vietnamese Communist Party would evolve one day into a socialist system such as Sweden's.

"There's a big difference between how the old and the present generations view the Party," Tran Le Tien told me after becoming a member. Tien, the son of Vietnam's former ambassador to Algeria, was studying to get an economics degree and hoped one day to be a diplomat himself. "In the past the Party dominated everything. It was sacred, like a religion. It was the ideal way of life. But a lot of the new generation wants to get out of the Party. They don't pay dues. They drop their membership. In the south, people don't want the Party to come into the workplace because it just means endless meetings. I think it's tragic they don't understand how much the Party has done for Vietnam. But the Party is facing a problem: How does it make itself suitable for the young?

"Even after *doi moi*, the Party still says a capitalist can't be a member. But informally in reality, it's okay. Some friends I know want to set up a small business, but according to the Party, that's exploitation. The Party's challenge is to offer reform and development without losing ideology. If it doesn't, young people won't believe in it. Those who join don't come seeking ideology. So yes, I think the Party's trying to be more practical. I think communism is still a good system for Vietnam and I think it will lead to the peaceful evolution of a more democratic Vietnam. It's just that after all the suffering of the war, people don't want anything to happen that will disturb us. They don't want fast changes. They just want to live with the peace."

I asked Tien if it were okay for me to quote him by name in a story I was writing for the *Los Angeles Times*. I heard nothing in his comments except an expression of hope that Vietnam would develop and prosper equitably. He was upbeat about his country's future. But I knew how sensitive the Party was regarding anything not read from a policy statement, and I didn't want to create problems for him. Tien said, sure, use his name. Not until several months later did I learn from other friends that the Party had raised holy hell over his comments and made him undergo self-criticism sessions. Tien himself never mentioned to me that my story had caused him problems.

{{{  }}}

EVERY YEAR I MILLION NEW STUDENTS enter Vietnam's school system. They are taught—even at university level—to memorize, not think;
to listen, not question. I can remember once getting a mediocre grade (I
actually got a lot of them) on a history essay at prep school. I complained
to the teacher: "But that's exactly what you said!" Mr. Broderick replied:
"That why I gave you a C-minus. I don't want you to just repeat what I
say. I want you to interpret what you hear." I was baffled. But it dawns on
me now that I would have made a terrific student in Vietnam's system.
Students are expected to listen politely, write down exactly what the
teacher says, and leave class quietly when the bell rings. In an exam, they
score well by reciting, as if by rote, what they have been told. Debating
the merits of a teacher's view of the world, challenging him, even asking
questions is considered the height of disrespectfulness. History was what
the teacher said—or more precisely, what the Communist Party said—it
was. It was not open to interpretation.

So you can imagine my surprise when I heard twenty-six-year-old Le
Nguyen Hung tell his architectural students at Van Lang University in
Ho Chi Minh City: "In this class, I want you to learn to think for your-
selves. I want you to examine the actions of others and make your own
decisions. Don't just listen to me. Decide if what I say is honest, if it
makes sense." I looked at the students to gauge their reaction. They
seemed confused. But no one raised a question.

After class I caught up with Hung, an accomplished artist, architect,
and composer, for coffee. He said he thought young Vietnamese had to
break away from the government-encouraged think-alike mind-set if
they were to realize their potential. The Vietnamese were good at accepting instructions but were generally afraid to take the initiative. Solving
unexpected problems gave them difficulty. They didn't think well on their
feet. Following was safer than leading. Conformity was an admirable goal
that got no one in trouble.

"If you are a nonconformist, if you're different, it is very hard to survive in this society," Hung said. "You are a cut above. In a job, if you have ideas, if you talk about different things than your colleagues, they say you are hard to get along with. To survive, you must conform, and that stifles creativity and keeps us from advancing."

He told me a joke the Vietnamese recite with a hundred variations. An American and a Vietnamese were fishing and each caught a large bucket of crabs. The American covered his bucket with a lid because the crabs were climbing its sides trying to escape, and one or two did manage to scale the top and scurry away. The Vietnamese left his bucket uncovered, and the American asked why he wasn't concerned about losing some crabs. "These are Vietnamese crabs," his friend said. "As soon as one gets to the top, the others will pull him back down."

Not long after my visit to Hung's class, the government decided to make an important break with the past. It chose English over French and Russian as the favored foreign language for students and said all bureaucrats under the age of fifty were expected to learn English. More important, it began to reform the education system under a new curriculum designed to move Vietnam away from its traditional methodology in which students were expected, in the words of one educator, "to sit down, shut up, and listen." The decision raised a few eyebrows because the program's goal—learning to think on one's feet, questioning authority, searching for independent, creative solutions—didn't exactly square with the Party's belief that decisions should be reached by consensus and that independent minds were dangerous.

One of the first steps was to start phasing out the English-language textbooks written by Russian advisers in the mid-1980s. They trumpeted *Sputnik* and the World Festival of Youth in Moscow and were full of "misspeak," such as "I am having a temperature" and "my car is running away." The books helped explain why many of Vietnam's 35,000 English instructors didn't speak understandable English themselves. The new textbooks were developed by American and Vietnamese educators in partnership with Vietnam's Ministry of Education. Right off the bat the ministry ordered a batch of the first printings destroyed so a reference to the South China Sea could be changed to the East Sea. The East Sea did not exist, except in the minds of Vietnamese officials who refused to use the proper name because Vietnam and China each claimed the Spratly Islands, located in the South China Sea.

The cost of redesigning the curriculum and supplying textbooks to millions of students were expected to reach $50 million—an expense underwritten by a U.S. nonprofit organization, the Business Alliance for Vietnamese Education, and twenty-four corporate sponsors. Some of the sponsors, such as Coca-Cola, were the same companies whose billboards Party officials had painted over in 1996 in an attempt to diminish the young's fascination with everything Western.

Putting together the new curriculum was a nice example of reconciliation between Vietnam and the United States. I made an appointment to see Tran Van Nhung, the education ministry official overseeing it, so I could include his comments in an article I planned to write. Nhung wasn't in his office when I arrived at the appointed hour, and it took some time to hunt him down. He seemed nervous to see me with notebook in hand.

"Are you the journalist?" he asked. When I replied yes, he said, "I only have a few minutes. We'll have to make this fast." He didn't offer tea, which was a sure sign we were off to a bad start. I said I only needed fifteen minutes of his time. He said he only had time for one question. His hands fidgeted and his face grew more ashen every time he saw me in the chair across from him, pen poised over paper. So I tossed him a nice easy slowball of a question: What impact would the new program have on the country's education system?

"I'm a mathematician and it's not for me to make personal judgments," Nhung said. "Now, you'll have to excuse me or I'll be late for my meeting." And he hurried down the corridor, evidently relieved to be distancing himself from a journalist.

Although such abruptness was unusual in Vietnam, a bureaucrat's unease at the thought of being quoted was not. There was no reward in saying the right thing and risk in saying the wrong thing. Accordingly, civil servants devoted most of their energy to ensuring that they didn't make a mistake or offend a superior. That meant saying nothing at all, making no decisions, deferring to authority, leaving no fingerprints on anything. It was not surprising that a Singapore research firm, Political and Economic Risk Consultancy, rated Vietnam's bureaucracy as the most obdurate in all Asia.

The education ministry deserved credit for raising the literacy rate—it was aiming for zero illiteracy under the new curriculum—and for making school compulsory through the fifth grade. But it was hard-pressed to keep up with the demands created by a growing population, a rural exodus to the cities, and the high expectations of parents for their children's future. The government could afford to spend only $41 per high school student each year (some affluent towns in western Connecticut spent $7,300 per student). Teachers had such a tough time making ends meet on salaries averaging $30 per month (some teachers' salaries in Connecticut topped $60,000 per year) that they commonly withheld critical components of instruction so they could get extra income tutoring their own students, who needed to know the missing information to pass examinations and advance to a higher education level. Also widespread were reports of buying degrees, selling grades, and principals supplementing their incomes with special fees assessed parents.

Educational reform, international development experts believed, was one of the three or four biggest challenges the government had to confront if Vietnam was to become more competitive, less corrupt, and more in tune with the aspirations of its people. There was a lot of ground to cover. In the World Economic Forum's ranking of global competitiveness among fifty-nine countries, Vietnam was in fifty-third place. In the Corruption Index for ninety countries published by Transparency International, Vietnam was the fourteenth most corrupt. The next year, 2001, a Hong Kong consultancy elevated Vietnam to the top spot as Asia's most corrupt country.

I knew that many of the bright young Vietnamese who were working so hard for an advanced education, who were so full of hope, had no idea the deck they were playing with was missing some cards. What they did know was that a, say, pharmaceutical representative for an international company in the private sector could make $500 per month—ten times what a doctor earned in the state sector—and they believed things were going to work out. But where in the world were the jobs? The 1.4 million jobs a year the government needed to create just to stay even? I knew electrical engineers who were working as waiters, computer scientists as cab drivers, liberal arts majors as chambermaids, English graduates as tour guides, and lots of educated kids who weren't working at all. I never heard one complain or indicate, when life got derailed, he or she believed anything was wrong that couldn't be fixed with more study, more work.

{{{  }}}

MIGRATION IN SEARCH OF OPPORTUNITY or safety is nothing new for the Vietnamese. When the country was divided in 1954 after the First Indochina War (against France), more than 1 million people crossed the DMZ, going both north and south, to relocate under new flags. During the Second Indochina War (against the United States), millions of Vietnamese fled from the Northern cities into the countryside to escape the U.S. bombing campaign, while in South Vietnam millions more moved *into* cities to seek protection from ground fighting in the rural areas. After the war, there was the flight of 1 million Vietnamese abroad and the involuntary resettlement of 2 million Vietnamese in the government's ill-conceived "economic zones" of the Central Highlands and Mekong Delta.

By the time I returned to Vietnam, another migration was under way, resulting in the most significant demographic change since the adoption of *doi moi*. This one involved mostly young, single, unskilled Vietnamese moving from the villages to the cities, in search of jobs, education, excitement. More than 5,000 every month were pouring into Hanoi, twice that

many to Ho Chi Minh City. A similar migration had fueled Europe's Industrial Revolution in the eighteenth and nineteenth centuries. In Southeast Asia the economic boom of the 1980s and 1990s had pushed the pop-
ulations of Jakarta, Manila, and Bangkok past 10 million each. The cities
filled up because that's where investors put their money and built their
factories—and thus created jobs. But not enough of them in Vietnam.

The tide of new residents strained Vietnam's urban social and housing
services, created environmental problems, disrupted the cohesion of the
family structure, led to increases in crime, prostitution, and the use of
drugs. Traffic clogged city streets: in Hanoi, 2 million bicycles, 1.5 million
motor scooters, and 60,000 four-wheel vehicles competed for space amid
a cacophony of blaring horns. But demographers agree that migration is a
rational act, that the search for opportunity and security is universal,
whether one is moving to a new neighborhood in New York City or
packing up his family in Los Angeles and resettling in Colorado. And in
Vietnam, the impact of the migration wasn't entirely negative. The un-
married city workers sent much of their income back to their families in
the rural provinces, and that helped reduce the disparity between Vietnam's rich and poor areas. I knew kids who had come to Hanoi to shine
shoes or sell postcards and who sent their money home to put a little
brother through the village school or buy their parents a water buffalo.

"There's no job I won't do," said twenty-eight-year-old Hoang Pham,
who hunkered with a group of former farmers on Hanoi's Giang Vo
Street, playing cards and hoping a passerby would offer him a day's work
as a casual laborer. He said his daily expenses for shelter and food were
about 5,000 dong, or thirty-five U.S. cents. For lugging bricks or digging
ditches dawn to dusk he might earn a dollar, maybe a little more. He sent
half to his parents in northern Phu Tho Province.

It is said in Vietnam that if your face is to the earth and your back to
the sun, your work is hard. I bicycled from Giang Ho Street to the far
bank of the Red River. The temperature hovered in the high nineties, and
heat bounced off the pavement in shimmering waves. Many of the

middle-class women I passed had donned white gloves that extended to their upper arms; they did not want their skin to darken, as had the skin of peasants who had spent a lifetime in the sun. There was a grimy factory at a bend in the river. Barefoot young men with rolled-up pants and soot-covered faces stood there in shin-deep muck, sweating, shirtless, molding mud and coal together to make the cooking bricks that fuel the crude stoves millions of Hanoians use on the sidewalks outside their homes. Each cylindrical brick sold for three cents and burned for up to two hours.

Tran Tien Dat, twenty-one years old and a high school graduate, said he had long dreamed about the wonders of Hanoi: the arousal of city life, the brightly lighted streets and late-night cafés, and, most important, a steady job. He could not shake the dream. A year earlier, despite his parents' reservations, he had left the rice paddies and made his way to Hanoi where he hired on at the factory and now toiled for $2 per day, sunup to sundown, seven days a week, in the shadow of the rebuilt Long Bien Bridge, which U.S. bombers had attacked repeatedly—and finally destroyed—during the American War.

"I came to Hanoi to establish myself," Dat said. "You know, save money, study some more, then get a really good job. I'm studying English two nights a week but I'm usually too tired when class starts to do well. This job is only temporary. It has no future. It's dirty and low-paid. Hanoi isn't as exciting as I thought and actually life is pretty lonely here for me. But my life in Hanoi is still better than what I had in the countryside, because between crops there's no work."

Among the sprawling peasant shantytowns that have sprung up on the outskirts of Hanoi and Ho Chi Minh City as a result of the rural exodus, one can hear the ticking time bomb of population growth. Vietnam's population doubled to 80 million between 1970 and 2000 and could reach 150 million within another generation, the head of the government's National Committee for Population and Family Planning told me.

North Vietnam was one of the world's first developing countries to formulate a family planning program, in 1961, but Government Decree 216 was quickly made irrelevant by the American War. Hanoi needed more young men, not less. On top of that, the casualties Vietnam suffered in the war left the country with a gender imbalance—fifty-one women for every forty-nine men. So many childless widows and never-wed young women had difficulty finding a husband in the early years of peace that the government said there was no shame in bearing children out of wedlock.

Since then Decree 216 has been resuscitated, and the government's family planning program has been one of the most successful in Southeast Asia. Its goal, for the sake of child welfare and national development, is the creation of "small, happy families," of two children each. Having three can result in a government employee losing his or her job or surrendering some perks. Sometimes there is a $12 one-time tax for a third child.

The government's plan worked. In 1989, the average woman gave birth to 3.8 children. By 2001, the figure was 2.3. In villages, the People's Committee loudspeakers boomed out the names of women who were to report to the clinic that morning to receive a fresh supply of pills and condoms. High schools began teaching courses on reproductive health and advising students where they could get condoms. A youth counseling center in Hanoi was set up. One of the questions teenage girls asked most often was whether kissing would make them pregnant. Condoms fell in such short supply that the government couldn't keep up with demand, and condoms replaced Johnnie Walker scotch as the most popular product smuggled across the border with China. The government plastered the cities with billboards and TV spots pushing condoms as a desirable alternative to abortion.

But Vietnam continued to have the world's highest abortion rate, according to the Alan Guttmacher Institute, a nonprofit New York research center, and abortion remained Vietnam's favored means of birth control. Nearly 50 percent of all pregnancies were aborted, the Vietnam Institute of Sociology reported, and on average women had 2.5 abortions in a lifetime. They were performed quickly and privately in government hospitals and private clinics for $3–8. They did not require parental permission, and the patient did not have to supply information about herself.

{{{   }}}

I COVERED THE STUDENT-LED RIOTS in Jakarta that ended President Suharto's long reign of power as well as the middle-class protests in Manila that pushed President Joseph Estrada from power. I wondered if anything like that could happen in Vietnam. Was there any scenario that would bring young people into the streets to challenge the government? I thought not. As much respect as I had for the postwar generation, its members seemed obedient to authority, almost passive in accepting the hand they had been dealt. But Western friends, who had been in Vietnam longer than I, said I had misread an important part of the culture: The Vietnamese will not be pushed around indefinitely, by foreigners or their rulers.

Emperors had come and gone over hundreds of years, and while I was in Hanoi peasant revolts had rocked Thai Binh and Pleiku Provinces, throwing the fear of God into the politburo. Thai Binh—where farmers protesting mismanagement and official corruption had stormed the Party headquarters, closed down the marketplace, and basically taken over the town of Quynh Hoa—was particularly worrisome to the government. The province was the very heartland of Ho Chi Minh's revolution, and the protesting peasants were mostly former veterans who had served their homeland dutifully. Thai Binh had a population of 1.8 million, and it had sent a half-million of its young men off to fight the Japanese, French, Americans, and South Vietnamese between 1940 and 1975. Forty-seven thousand were killed. More than 1,800 mothers lost two or more sons. One mother lost all seven. If it could happen in Thai Binh . . . well, that was a thought the politburo didn't want to think through in its worst nightmare.

I came to understand that Vietnam's society operated at extremes. It could be unruly and undisciplined or quiet and controlled. There was no middle road. In some respects it seemed the former. You could see it in the chaos on the motor scooter–jammed streets, where drivers careened the wrong way down one-way thoroughfares, roared through red stop signals, and drove on sidewalks when kids turned boulevards into soccer fields. Traffic cops were few and far between, and most could be bribed, so in the absence of legitimate authority, people did as they pleased. But beneath the surface, Vietnam was quiet and orderly, because the government kept a firm grip on the levers of control it deemed important in maintaining power.

One New Year's Eve, I stood on the third-floor balcony of a restaurant on Ly Thai To Street. In the streets below, tens of thousands of young Vietnamese were packed shoulder to shoulder. They seemed good-natured, festive, well-dressed, but when I had edged through the throng thirty minutes earlier to get to the restaurant, I had sensed—for the first and only time in peacetime Vietnam—the chill of tension. A cordon of policemen had blocked Ly Thai To and all the streets leading to the ninety-year-old French-built Opera House a block away. There huge spotlights lit up the night, and the echo of drums swept through the streets. A chorus of dancers and singers was already on the outdoor stage to welcome in the new year. The youths on the street thought this was to be a celebration for all Hanoi. They were wrong. The celebration was for the Party elite and invited guests. There was jostling as the students pushed against police barricades.

Then I heard a bottle shatter against the pavement. Stones bounced off or through the windows of the stately Metropole Hotel across the street. I saw a policeman clutch his bloodied face with both hands. A roar came up from the throats of the crowd. The police line broke, and the cops ran in disarray. The crowd surged down the street toward the Opera House, shouting triumphantly as it moved.

Seeing a confrontation between kids and cops in Vietnam amazed me.

I raced down the stairs from the restaurant to follow. Surely there would be big trouble at the Opera House as the momentum of disorder grew and the kids knew they had control. Then I saw something remarkable. As soon as they got to the Opera House, the kids dropped their stones. They stopped shouting. They slowed to a walk and melded quietly into the throng of invited guests, applauding the performers enthusiastically. They were spectators now, and that's all they had wanted. They had not come to cause trouble. Whether intended or not, their message was clear: The pleasures of the evening were not the exclusive domain of invited guests. The Party crashers, too, were participants—in the celebration and in all that would come with the new year.

The scene reminded me that the third phase of Vietnam's revolution had started. It could prove to be the toughest one of all. The first phase had been the wars against France and the United States. That had been won and relegated to the past. The second had been the transition into the global economy that had enabled Vietnam to rejoin the international community. And now the final phase was for the soul of Vietnam: Who would participate? Who would lead? Who would reap the benefits? Who held the right to decide what Vietnam would become?

# THE PAINFUL ART
# OF RECONCILIATION

THE DIRT ROAD TO PHO VINH was narrow and rutted and, in the monsoons, all but impassable. It jutted off Highway 1, south of Danang, and headed toward the hills, through lowland rice paddies and past little villages whose occupants had not seen a foreigner in nearly thirty years. People here moved by bicycle and on foot. They worked their crops by hand. Occasionally we would see a water buffalo in the fields, but that was rare. The sun was hard and steady and sweat came quickly. We humped, eleven out-of-shape, middle-aged former GIs and me. My companions were men on the mend. Behind me was Steve Lemire, and it had been seven years since he had slept with a loaded .44 on one side of the pillow and a bottle of whiskey on the other. Next to him was Buck Anderson. He was on his eighth marriage, and this one was working. Chuck Owens was in the pack, and he was 110 percent sober. Walt Bacak hadn't thought of suicide in a long time.

"I feel like I've been walking guard duty for thirty years," Mike Farquhar said to me, his eyes sweeping the road ahead. I knew we both had the same irrational thought: Did Charley plant any mines last night? "Up at night every two hours, smoke a couple of cigarettes, then try to sleep. Can't. If I get anything out of this trip, if there's something I'd pray for, it'd be to go home and get some sleep. The funny thing is, being back in 'Nam, I've slept really good every night."

Except for Bacak, this was the first time the men had set foot in Vietnam since the war, and returning had been very unnerving. Now they were headed toward a meeting with their former Viet Cong enemies— the very men some of the GIs had fought in this very spot—and what they hoped was that somewhere out here among the jungle-covered hills—or perhaps in the meeting itself—they would find the secret to finally come to grips with one simple fact: The war was over.

Bacak was nearly sixty, a three-tour, once-wounded vet. He was Airborne, an army lifer. He had first returned, alone, in 1997, bogged down in drugs, and he found the trip such a healthy antidote that he set up a nonprofit organization, A Quest for Healing, back home in Lakewood, Washington, and ran two trips a year for former veterans who wanted to return to Vietnam and lay the past to rest.

"I've never brought anyone back that didn't find the trip positive," said Bacak, who had spent a year fighting in the hills and paddies around Pho Vinh. "It doesn't eradicate all the problems, but it allows the vets to change the mental black-and-white photos. It lets them put a face on the men they fought. Over weeks, maybe months, they go home and find the nightmares diminish. They start sleeping better. They don't get angry so easily. Before my first trip back I was seriously into drugs. The only reason I didn't try suicide was because I'd spent so much time in 'Nam trying to stay alive. When I got back to Washington my wife, Joyce, says to me, 'Walter, this is like having a new husband come home.'"

This was Bacak's eighth trip to postwar Vietnam, and he had mastered the protocol. So at lunch in Quang Ngai earlier that day, he had tried to ease the Americans' apprehension about the meeting. "When you meet them," he said, "just keep it light at first. They won't speak English, but we've got a good translator. Be polite. Ask about their families. Don't ask, 'How many people did you kill?' or any shit like that. Then play it by ear. If they want to talk about the war, OK. Let them bring it up. You're going to find they're very gracious."

Pho Vinh wasn't much more than a cluster of shops and bamboo homes strung out on a dusty stretch of the road. In the small one-room building used by the Communist Party, three former Viet Cong guerrillas waited. The Americans entered warily, wearing baseball caps emblazoned with the words "Vietnam: I Came Back." An electric fan groaned overhead. A portrait of Ho Chi Minh hung on the blue wall. Outside, by the open door, villagers stood ten deep, trying to get a good look at these broad-shouldered strangers who towered over their hosts. The crowd kept growing until an old man in a frayed security guard's shirt arrived to shoo everyone away.

Doan Vinh Quay, who was sixty-two, spoke first. He wore a fedora, and over his best shirt he had pinned a black medal commemorating his parents, killed just up the road by U.S. artillery in 1967. He said he was honored to welcome the Americans as friends. He showed them scars where a bullet had shattered his hand. He asked what unit each had fought with and when each had served. A chorus came back: "First Mar Div, '65 . . . 1970, Eleventh Cav. . . . 101st Airborne, Second Brigade, '66. . . ."

"Ah, the 101st. They were good, very tough," Quay replied. He smiled when someone asked how long a tour of duty had been for the Viet Cong. For the duration, he replied. Quay had fought for fifteen years, some of his friends much longer.

Conversation did not come easily at first. What do you say when you meet a man whom thirty years ago you would have shot dead on the spot? But some of the men on both sides had brought scrapbooks and photos.

Everyone laughed that the Americans had grown hefty and the Vietnamese were still skinny. "That was your wife?" an American asked, pointing to one of the album photos. "Wow. Very beautiful. You lucky man." Tea was served, and the Vietnamese stood willingly among the Americans for group pictures. Before long, amid jokes and banter, the ice melted, the anxiety faded, and it was apparent to both sides that this was not a gathering of enemies. "I just want to say that, during the war, we had a lot of respect for the VC," Steve Lemire said. "You were good soldiers."

VC, or Viet Cong, was a contraction of Viet Nam Cong San, Vietnamese communists, used derogatorily by the Saigon regime but never by the insurgents themselves. They preferred National Liberation Front. Still, Quay nodded in appreciation, and one could hear him thinking, "I know."

Later, with Bacak walking point, the fourteen men—eleven Americans and three Vietnamese—set off for the old headquarters of the 101st's First Brigade, in the hills a mile away. It was, in a manner of speaking, a joint GI-VC patrol, a sight I never thought I'd live to see. During the war, I'd been just about everywhere in South Vietnam that U.S. units were based, including all three of the 101st's brigade camps. So I must have been in Pho Vinh before. But after a while the camps and fire support bases all looked pretty much alike, and any memory I might once have had of this place had faded with time. We reached the long, high empty plateau. Crumbling asphalt covered the chopper landing pads. Jungle scrub had reclaimed most of the hill. Not a trace remained of the sandbagged barracks where a thousand Americans once lived. One GI pointed to a head-high rock overlooking the valley and said a soldier nicknamed Wolfman used to howl at the moon there after coming back from long-range patrols.

"That's where we slept, right over there," one former grunt said. Former VC guerrilla Nguyen Minh Duc replied, "I know. And your command bunker was just over by the tree." He went on to recall exactly how many choppers were at the camp, where the mess hall was, what time patrols were likely to go out. "We were never far away," Duc said. He recalled how GIs used to search the villagers hired to do menial chores when they passed through the barbed-wire perimeter at the end of every workday. But what they stole wasn't some commodity hidden under skirts and shirts. It was intelligence.

So with darkness settling in on the abandoned hilltop base, the GIs and VC pulled up shirts and rolled up pant legs to show one another their wounds. They roasted seven chickens and drank beer. They shared more photographs and joked about building a veterans meeting hall for Americans and Vietnamese over by the old command post. One GI asked how much an acre of land would cost because this looked like a beautiful place for a retirement home, and the VC answered that in exchange for a visa to the United States he could provide an acre very reasonably. Everyone laughed.

"When I heard about this trip," Bob Garrison said, "I said, 'Man, I'd like to go, but we can't afford it.' And my wife says, 'Like hell we can't. You're going if I have to eat beans for a month.' She paid for me and Mike to come over. And you know, I'm feeling a little softer inside already."

One American swapped his sneakers for a Vietnamese's sandals. Two vets gave Duc their unit medals. He fingered them with interest and slipped them into his breast pocket. "Boom-boom," he laughed, his forefinger extended like a gun barrel. "I shoot you. You shoot me."

The Americans grew quiet after a while. When night came, they made a circle of rocks by the edge of the plateau, and one by one they entered it, sitting alone in the silent, peaceful darkness. The Americans had come of age as teenagers on hills like this. They remembered the adrenaline rush of combat, the dreamy calm of postbattle fatigue. Never had life been so terrible—or so exhilarating. Never had they known such camaraderie or had so much authority and responsibility. For many, all that lay ahead would be a mere footnote.

Don Harris left the rock circle. At first, until he drew close to the group by the flaming barbecue, he appeared as only a shadow, making its way out of the darkness. He had a rare heart disease, and his doctor in Tennessee had told him it was too risky to make the trip to Vietnam. But he had insisted on going, choosing to spend "some of my last days" with the people he truly cared about—Vietnam vets.

"Vietnam," he mused. "This is the one place I really felt like somebody."

{{{    }}}

MORE AND MORE AMERICAN VETS are making the journey back to Vietnam, though the total of those returning is only a small fraction of the 2.5 million who served. Clearly, Walt Bacak and his colleagues had led troubled lives; maybe they would have even if there had been no war. Of that I had no idea. But—and I don't think I was imagining this—I saw a change in them during the few days we spent together. After the Pho Vinh trip, they seemed less edgy. I saw Steve Lemire smile for the first time. One infantryman who had looked trampish when I saw him in Pho Vinh showed up for breakfast at the hotel in Danang bathed, shaved, and groomed, and I was surprised to see that he was quite handsome. Everyone was taken aback to discover that a people they had hated—Henry Kissinger had called North Vietnam's leaders "just a bunch of shits; tawdry, filthy shits"—were gracious, friendly, and decent. They had names. They had faces. They had families. They had their dreams and they had their sorrows.

As Bobby Muller, the paraplegic former Marine with whom I had toured the cemetery for North Vietnamese veterans, put it: "You could probably shut down a lot of VA psychiatric clinics in the States simply by bringing the vets back to Vietnam. It's better than any medication, and the angrier the veteran is, the more powerful the experience seems to be."

By the time I went to Pho Vinh with Bacak's group, I had been in Vietnam for more than three years. The country seemed so hospitable, felt so much like home, I could no longer quite fathom why so many Americans lived with its ghosts, why Vietnam kept playing games with our national psyche, opening wounds we thought had healed and forcing us to remember all that we had tried to forget. Perhaps it was that for my generation—including the 2.5 million Americans who went to Vietnam and the 13 million who were eligible but did not—Vietnam was not a country as much as a state of mind. It was where our childhood ended and the long, dark shadows of the Ashau Valley began.

Of the eleven wars the United States has fought on foreign soil, at the cost of 600,000 dead, none lasted as long. Only the Civil War was more divisive. And somewhere between Dong Ha near the DMZ and Ca Mau in the Mekong Delta, the character of an American era was defined. That era challenged the standards of World War II—the yardstick against which we had judged heroism and the rightness of battle—and turned society topsy-turvy in a social and political upheaval of drugs, free love, political scandals and assassinations, interracial strife, protest demonstrations, and the cry: "Hell, no! We won't go!"

Six U.S. presidents, from Harry Truman to Gerald Ford, felt the Vietnam War was worth fighting. Although revisionists believe John F. Kennedy would have extracted the United States from Vietnam, he said just weeks before his assassination: "I don't agree with those who say we should withdraw. That would be a great mistake. I know people don't like Americans to be engaged in this kind of an effort. Forty-seven Americans have been killed in combat with the enemy, but this is a very important struggle."

The problem was that Vietnam left Americans with nothing to celebrate. We didn't lose a battle, yet we remained emotionally stuck at a besieged fire base with no American flag to plant firmly in the ground. And if there is nothing to celebrate, what do you do? You continue to mourn. You go back to the Vietnam Veterans Memorial over and over again. But everything that helped heal, like the wall, also ensured that the wounds kept festering and denied us closure.

"We want a president to be commander in chief, not commander in chicken," U.S. Senator Bob Kerrey—one of 238 Americans who earned the Medal of Honor in Vietnam—said during Bill Clinton's presidential campaign in 1992. We were still trapped at the wall, grieving and groping, unable to move beyond it. Why were we still talking about Vietnam in our political campaigns, nearly twenty years after the war ended?

If the war was so widely regarded as a misadventure, why should Clinton have been penalized for deciding not to rush off to the jungles of Vietnam? After all, John Wayne—deferred from the World War II draft because of his age (thirty-four) and a football shoulder injury—and U.S. Army Captain Ronald Reagan—who spent the war making movies in Hollywood—were viewed as genuine patriots. Vice President Dick Cheney used his draft deferments to avoid Vietnam. Former Vice President Dan Quayle and President George W. Bush joined the National Guard, widely regarded as a dodge. Republican superhawk Newt Gingrich took a pass on Vietnam, too. Politician-journalist Patrick J. Buchanan, a fervent supporter of the war, stayed home with a bum knee. Twenty-seven million Americans came of age during the Vietnam War era, and the vast majority ducked the war through legal or illegal means. It was a huge voting bloc. Why didn't a candidate declare, "Hell, yes, I ducked it. I'm one of you." Because, I suppose, we still heard a voice whispering that all American wars are honorable and that one's duty, when called upon, is simply to go. It's part of punching the clock to adulthood, as every president from Truman to George Bush did.

We couldn't even decide in those days if the real Americans were Jane Fonda and Father Philip Berrigan or John Wayne and Cardinal Richard Cushing. There we were destroying a country in a distant war we chose not to win, being deceived by our leaders and given bloated body counts by our generals, so no wonder we were confused. "This used to be a hell of a good country," the drunken lawyer played by Jack Nicholson said in *Easy Rider*. "I can't understand what's gone wrong with it."

Kennedy's idealism, Johnson's Great Society—had they been just illusions? Most people in my wartime generation were keenly aware of what they *didn't* do, the road not taken. The grunt under fire in Tay Ninh was aware of the choice he didn't make—to go AWOL or dodge the draft. Those who fled to Canada or stayed in the United States, having found any one of a hundred ways to avoid Vietnam—straights became gay for a day at induction centers, old leg injuries started hurting again for the first time in years, feet suddenly went flat, colleges were swamped with applications—were aware of the innuendo of cowardice and knew there might be a price to pay for their decision down the road.

"Nothing seemed more absurd and horrible and went against everything you were taught in Sunday school and civics class [than the Vietnam War]," Doug Marlette, a Pulitzer Prize–winning political cartoonist with *New York Newsday,* told me some years ago. "But I couldn't find anything that felt right, that made me really feel comfortable personally. Even if you did object, you felt you should have gone to jail, that those who went to jail really had conviction."

Marlette had avoided the war as a conscientious objector. Applying for CO status in his small Southern town in 1970 was, Marlette once wrote, "a first in my family, my church, my town, my ZIP code, and [it felt like] my planet." His father, a retired Marine Corps officer, wrote the draft board and offered to serve in his son's place.

{{{　}}}

MY RECOLLECTION OF THE GIS I KNEW and saw in combat during the war bore little resemblance to what Hollywood producers would have us believe. They weren't a collective bunch of losers or a gang of psychopaths. They fought well and bravely and for the same reason soldiers fight in any war—to survive and go home. On operations I covered, most commanders went to extraordinary lengths to avoid civilian casualties. If there were shameful incidents for the Americans, such as the massacre of nearly 500 civilians at My Lai in 1968, there were just as many for the

North Vietnamese, such as the execution of as many as 3,000 civilians in Hue during the Tet Offensive. I was in Hue in 1969 when the victims' bodies were exhumed from mass graves. There were men and women, many of them teachers, merchants, low-level civil servants. Their hands had been bound behind their backs with wire. Neither in My Lai nor in Hue, I feel certain, was any official order given to kill civilians. In each case, an individual unit under bad leadership had run amok. The results were tragic but were not an accurate reflection of either nation's army as a whole.

Nearly 9 million men and women served in the U.S. armed forces during the Vietnam War era, including 2,594,000 men and 7,484 women in Vietnam and another 600,000 on the offshore fleet and at air bases in Thailand and Guam. As research by MIT professor Arnold Barnett and others, published in 1992, and the book *Stolen Valor*, written by B. G. Burkett and Glenna Whitley in 1998, have shown, they were neither undereducated and ill-disciplined nor disproportionately minority in racial makeup. Nor as a group were they unable to readjust to postwar life even though society gave them the cold shoulder instead of a warm welcome home and no particular benefits. By any criteria the negative image they had to bear as Vietnam vets was a bum rap.

Ninety-seven percent of Americans who served in Vietnam between 1965 and 1975 received honorable discharges—exactly the same percentage as for the ten-year period before the war. The use of drugs was no greater in Vietnam than it was among the same age group in the United States (and it was many joints less than in San Francisco's flower-child Haight-Ashbury neighborhood where I lived before heading off to the war). Only 249 men deserted in Vietnam. As Burkett and Whitley point out, no U.S. platoon ever surrendered as a unit to the NVA or VC; in World War II, several thousand Americans not only surrendered, they ended up fighting for Germany.

The average soldier in Vietnam was nineteen years old—seven years younger than his World War II counterpart. In Vietnam 80 percent of the

GIs had completed high school and 14 percent had attended college. In World War II, 35 percent had not gone beyond grammar school. Blacks made up 12.5 percent of the combat deaths in the Vietnam War at a time when blacks of draft age represented 13.5 percent of the U.S. population. Eighty-six percent of the men killed in action were Caucasian. After a statistical analysis of economic levels of ZIP codes where GIs had lived before entering the military, Barnett concluded that variations by income among Vietnam's casualties were minimal.

After the war, most Vietnam vets got on with their lives. Many became leaders in Congress, industry, and the media. In 1994, the unemployment rate for veterans was 3 percent, well below the national average of 4.9 percent. The Centers for Disease Control in Atlanta reported that suicide rates were within the normal range for the general population. In 1999, the *Vietnam Economic Times* reported that in an earlier U.S. poll 71 percent of vets said they were "glad to have served in Vietnam" and 74 percent said they "enjoyed" their tour of duty. A survey by the Veterans of Foreign Wars said 87 percent of the public held Vietnam veterans in high esteem.

{{{   }}}

A FEW DAYS AFTER SAIGON FELL IN 1975, communist cadres went from embassy to abandoned embassy, raising the National Liberation Front flag. The only embassy they bypassed was that of the United States. Nayan Chanda, the *Far Eastern Economic Review*'s Saigon bureau chief, one of a handful of journalists who stayed behind after the helicopter evacuation, asked a soldier guarding the U.S. Embassy why no Viet Cong flag was flying overhead. "We are not authorized to raise one," he told Chanda. "We do not want to humiliate the Americans. They will come back."

The response perhaps reflected more pragmatism than magnanimity. Indeed, the United States had economic and technological resources the Soviet Union lacked, and tapping into them would have provided a huge boost to Vietnam's development. But first Washington wanted to ensure Hanoi was punished for its victory: Washington froze Vietnam's assets in the United States ($260 million) and prohibited Americans from sending money to Vietnam; severed mail and telephone links between the two nations; refused to consider diplomatic relations with the newly reunited state; reneged on Nixon and Kissinger's promise to supply Vietnam with $3.3 billion in reconstruction aid; vetoed Vietnam's requests to join the United Nations; blocked credits and loans from the World Bank and the Asian Development Bank; and instituted a trade embargo that Japan and other allies were pressured into observing.

Washington's punitive policies pushed Vietnam toward the precipice of disaster. And Hanoi's doctrinaire rulers gave the country the final shove over the edge with an agenda that was both vindictive and ill-conceived. When Bui Tin of the North Vietnamese Army accepted South Vietnam's surrender on April 30, 1975—he was a journalist but, as a colonel, was the senior officer present—he told Saigon's nervous cabinet ministers: "You have nothing to fear. Between Vietnamese, there are no victors and no vanquished. Only the Americans have been beaten. If you are patriots, consider this a moment of joy. The war for our country is over."

But if the war was over, the Dark Years were just beginning: the reeducation camps and forced resettlement of peasants in so-called economic zones; the collectivization of farming and near famine; the confiscation of wealth and loss of civil liberties; the wars against Cambodia and China; paranoia, isolation, and deprivation. Never had anyone imagined peace could bring such deep suffering.

The anguish and misery of the people, however, did not stir much response from former antiwar protestors who had expressed such sympathy for the Vietnamese when they themselves had been in danger of going off to war. Tom Hayden had cheered the fall of Saigon, saying it would lead to the "rise of Indochina." Huh? A thousand University of California students had marched through Berkeley on April 30 in celebration. But in

celebration of themselves or the Vietnamese? Where was Jane Fonda after the war was over? There was silence, I suppose, because the protests
never had anything to do with the ultimate well-being of the Vietnamese
people. They were about self-interests and ending U.S. involvement.
Once those goals had been met, what the Vietnamese did to the Vietnamese didn't matter. Reconciliation could wait for another day.

{{{   }}}

JAPAN AND THE UNITED STATES normalized diplomatic relations six
years after the end of World War II. It took Vietnam and the United
States twenty years to take the same step. But if the war was character-
ized by missed opportunities for peace on both sides, so was the peace defined by lost chances to chart a new and constructive direction in U.S.-
Vietnamese relations. One of them came in 1977, two years after the fall
of Saigon, when President Jimmy Carter sent Leonard Woodcock, chief
of the U.S. liaison office in Beijing, to Hanoi to clear the path for normalized relations. "I understand President Carter's wish [is] to solve our
problems in a new spirit," Prime Minister Pham Van Dong told Woodcock. "And if so, I see no obstacle to our resolving the problems."

Sixteen months later, in September 1978, secret negotiations in New
York produced a breakthrough when Vietnam dropped its demand for
monetary reparations as a precondition for normalized relations. Both
sides were so sure they had a deal that the abandoned villa on Hai Ba
Trung Street in Hanoi, which had served as the U.S. Consulate in colonial times, was painted green in anticipation of the return of U.S. envoys.
Dennis Harter, a Vietnamese-speaking State Department officer in
Washington, checked out the shuttered Vietnamese embassy on R Street,
just off Massachusetts Avenue. The carpets were moldy, paint was peeling
off the walls. Three-year-old editions of *Time* and *Newsweek* detailing the
fall of Saigon were strewn about. Dirty plates from the last meal South
Vietnam's diplomats ate the day they walked out and locked the door

were still on the table. But the place, Harter concluded, could be cleaned up and made habitable for Hanoi's envoys.

In the end, both sides went home from the New York negotiations empty-handed. The State Department had been pressing for simultaneous recognition of Vietnam and China; Vietnam had been making plans to invade China-backed Cambodia. Zbigniew Brzezinski, Carter's National Security Advisor, decided that Vietnam was a "peripheral issue" and feared that the deal with Hanoi would kill all chances for a deal with Beijing. Within two months of the talks' breakdown, Vietnam had signed a twenty-five-year friendship treaty with the Soviet Union and invaded Cambodia. The stately old villa on Hai Ba Trung Street would stand empty for another sixteen years, until President Clinton lifted the trade embargo in 1994. By the time I returned to Vietnam it had been spiffed up and reborn as the American Club, a social facility that offered video rentals, five-star hamburgers, and an annual Fourth of July festival for the 300 or so Americans living in Hanoi.

Among the many strange twists along the rapprochement road Hanoi and Washington traveled was that the reconciliation process was started by the men who fought the war and concluded by a man, President Clinton, who avoided it. It began with the small group of vets Bobby Muller, the paraplegic Marine, had taken back to Hanoi in 1981. When he returned to Washington, he went to see then–U.S. Representative (and now Senator) John McCain, the former Navy pilot who had been shot down and taken prisoner within spitting distance of my Hanoi apartment. McCain shook with anger and pounded on his desk, "God damn it, Bobby! What are you going back and talking to the enemy for?" But McCain gradually softened. He came to believe the anger and hatred inside him only served to keep the past alive, and although he continued to refer to his torturers in Hoa Lo Prison as "gooks," he became a leading advocate of reconciliation. He was joined by other veterans, Republicans and Democrats, on Capitol Hill: Senators Bob Kerrey of Nebraska, John Kerry of Massachusetts, Max Cleland of Georgia, and Chuck Robb of

Do Muoi leaned close to Peterson and asked, "Were you ever tortured?" Such bluntness is unusual in Vietnam, and Peterson wasn't sure what to say. Had he wanted to, Peterson could have told him about his six years in Hoa Lo Prison—the Hanoi Hilton as American POWs called it—and other wartime prisons with nicknames like Heartbreak Hotel, the Zoo, the Pigsty, Dogpatch, and Camp Unity. He could have told him about the beatings that left him unconscious; about the leg irons and the elbows manacled so tightly behind the back that it felt his chest would explode at any moment; about solitary confinement and a diet of grass soup and pumpkin; about the ropes that curled his body into the shape of a rocking horse and the guards who sat on his contorted body and, smiling, bounced him up and down like a toy; about being forced to kneel for days, arms extended overhead, until swollen limbs went numb with pain and the mind went dead. He could have said all this, but he didn't. That chapter of his life was over. Peterson dismissed the question with a wave of the hand. "I'd rather talk about the future, about what we can do to move relations between the United States and Vietnam forward," he said.

But Do Muoi was insistent. "No, I want to know. Were you tortured?"

"Yes," Peterson said. He rolled back his shirtsleeves. Rope burns still scarred his elbows. He held up the hand that sometimes went so numb he momentarily wondered if it had fallen off his body. Do Muoi said nothing at first. Then he pulled up one trouser leg. The long scar he revealed was ugly and jagged. "I was tortured, too," Do Muoi said, "in the same prison as you, Hoa Lo. By the French, a good many years before you got there."

That exchange occurred in 1991, during Peterson's first trip to Vietnam since being released from Hoa Lo with other American POWs in 1973. He had come back to grapple with a question Americans were just beginning to ask: Was it time for the United States and Vietnam to exorcise the past and reconcile their differences? Peterson found the answer in the streets of Hanoi—in the faces of the students he passed, in the eyes of the street kids who hawked pirated reprints of Graham Greene's *The Quiet American* and Bao Ninh's *The Sorrow of War*, in the enthusiasm and graciousness of the young people with whom he stopped to chat—and the answer was a resounding yes.

"Only a small percentage of the people I saw had had any involvement with the war," Peterson said. "Most were born after we'd left. And I said to myself, 'Why should we disallow them the better life they want and deserve? Why should we disallow them the well-being of Vietnam?'"

Peterson was shot down by antiaircraft fire in 1966 on his sixty-seventh mission, a nighttime bombing run against the rail line just north of Hanoi. His arm and leg fractured, his plane in flames, Peterson para-chuted into the village of An Doai east of Hanoi. He heard the voices of angry villagers approaching through the rice paddies. He took his .38 re-volver from its holster and considered blowing his brains out. "Everyone mobilize," yelled militiaman Do The Dong, who was in charge of the vil-lage loudspeaker that day. "Find the American!" His eyes unfocused, squinting, Peterson could see the outline of a peasant mob pushing close, armed with rifles, sticks, knives. Enemies everywhere, not a friendly for a million miles. Never had he felt—or been—so alone. Many of the vil-lagers wanted to beat or kill the American, Dong later recalled, but did not because Ho Chi Minh had said many times that captured Americans were to be turned over to the authorities, not killed. After a night in An Doai, Peterson was dumped into a motorcycle sidecar and paraded through villages where peasants pelted him with rocks. It took several hours to get to Hanoi. There in the old French-built prison on Hai Ba Trung Street Peterson would begin the "most terrible, disgusting, sad event of my life"—six years as a POW.

Thirty-one years to the day of being shot down, Peterson returned to An Doai. I went to meet him, but I got lost on the ninety-minute drive from Hanoi. I stopped at villages along the way to ask directions, and smiling farmers would point this way and that, usually giving entirely contradictory instructions. Finally I happened upon a town where local officials had gathered in the dirt courtyard of the People's Committee headquarters, and I knew I'd arrived at the right place. The new U.S. ambassador pulled into An Doai an hour later, in a Toyota Land Cruiser that flew an American flag. He stepped from the vehicle, smiling, right hand extended, and greeted his former enemies in Vietnamese. If the event wasn't exactly a homecoming, it was at least a symbol of the reconciliation that would become Peterson's trademark as ambassador.

Peterson walked out along an earthen dike and stood by the mango tree where he and his copilot, Bernard Talley (who was captured, uninjured, the day after Peterson and now flew DC-10s for American Airlines), had landed by parachute. He didn't say much at first. Most of the village had gathered around him, and he asked if anyone had found the revolver he had ditched in the paddies as the militia approached. "I did," said seventy-year-old Nguyen Danh Xinh. "I found it and turned it over to the People's Committee. It had all six bullets in it."

"And my necklace. Did you find the necklace?" he asked, referring to the Christ medallion he had worn since he and Carlotta had purchased it at a church shop in Florida years earlier. That too had been found, Xinh said, but no one knew where it was any more. Peterson, clearly disappointed, let the matter drop.

One of the first militiamen to reach the downed Air Force captain, Nguyen Viet Chop (*chop* means "seize" in Vietnamese), had assembled his three daughters and four grandchildren for Peterson's return. Now seventy and a shopkeeper, Chop wrapped both his hands around the ambassador's right hand in greeting. He led him past a shed where a water buffalo was tethered and into his one-room home. Grapes and tea were on the table, and incense burned on the altar. The air was heavy with heat and humidity. Chop and Peterson came from such different worlds that there wasn't a great deal to talk about or many memories to share. But Chop said Peterson was the most important foreign visitor to ever come to An Doai; he would always welcome him in his home. Peterson spoke about progress toward reconciliation and told Chop to drop by the U.S. Embassy and say hello if he were ever in Hanoi. (One imagined Mr. Chop was not a man who left his village often. But a few months later, a puzzled U.S. Marine guard at the embassy called Peterson's secretary and said, "There's a Mr. Chop down here. He says he knows the ambassador and wants to say hello." Peterson came down to the lobby, and they chatted for fifteen minutes.)

During his more than four years in Vietnam, Peterson became a walking billboard for reconciliation. He could have harbored anger but didn't. He could have been a career POW but wasn't. He never apologized for the war or his involvement in it—Vietnamese officials never asked him to—but he never stopped thinking that a firm and lasting friendship was within Vietnam and the United States' reach.

Peterson became such a popular figure that ordinary Vietnamese would stop him on the streets and ask to have their picture taken with him. A popular expat restaurant, the Red Onion, located next to the Hanoi Hilton, printed a line on its menu stating that in deference to Ambassador Peterson it did not serve pumpkin soup. Peterson rode through Hanoi on weekends, unescorted, on his motor scooter, got his hair cut at a local barber shop for half a buck, and enjoyed slurping *pho*, the traditional noodle broth, in sidewalk cafés for lunch. At a diplomatic reception, he met a beautiful Vietnamese businesswoman, Vi Le, who had left Saigon as a child and become an Australian citizen, and in 1998 they were married in Hanoi's Catholic Cathedral. Their marriage, he said, wasn't about reconciliation—just love.

"I went back to Vietnam not because I had to," Peterson said. "I went back because I wanted to. I saw the Vietnamese at their very worst, and they saw me at my very worst as well. And it's a rare opportunity for someone to go back to a country like this in which there was so much pain, and to then focus on the future. I can't do anything about what happened yesterday, but I can help move forward positively and constructively on what happens tomorrow."

My time in Hanoi overlapped with Peterson's assignment as ambassador, and we became friends. I poked around, looking for a soft spot in his shield. He delivered his reconciliation message with the zeal of a warrior-turned-missionary, but surely he carried some animosity. He couldn't have laid all the demons to rest. Surely some monster images rattled around his head when he passed Hoa Lo Prison a couple of times a day en route to or from work. He denied it, and I came to believe him without understanding where he had found the capacity to separate past and present. Perhaps part of the explanation was that he was a religious man, which I assume gave him strength, but this was not something he talked about. He had known great personal loss with the deaths of his son and wife, and that probably reminded him of the value of filling Kipling's unforgiving minute with sixty seconds of distance run. The military had taught him discipline; prison, how to survive; war, that it was easier to destroy than to build.

My wife spent months shadowing Peterson for a documentary profile of him broadcast by PBS. Sandy and I both reached the same conclusion: He was who and what he said he was. Like the Vietnamese themselves, he had forgiven if not forgotten. He had channeled his pain into constructive energy. He did not let memories take control of him or what he did. "If I'd let them," he said, "I couldn't have functioned."

On Vietnam's National Day in 1997, his first in Hanoi as U.S. ambassador, Peterson walked in ceremonial procession up the red-carpeted stairs of Ho Chi Minh's mausoleum with other members of the diplomatic corps. At the open casket, each ambassador was to execute a left-face and make a respectful bow. Every eye was on Peterson. Would the former POW bow as he once had to do, in a sign of forced respect, before his sadistic prison torturers? Would the new ambassador show reverence to the man who had been his country's mortal enemy for a generation?

Inside the mausoleum the temperature was a controlled sixty-eight degrees. The light was dim, almost eerily so. At the coffin, Peterson did a smart left-face, paused with his arms extended at his side, and bent forward slightly from the waist. "I really had no trouble doing it," he later recalled. "Especially when I remembered Ho's policy that prisoners not be killed on the spot. If it wasn't for that, I might not be here today."

Even though the flag symbolizes all POW/MIAs, not just those in Vietnam, its popularity remains a trademark of the emotional grip that the POW/MIA issue—and, by extension, the Vietnam War—exerts on a nation's soul, a grip so firm that in 2000, twenty-five years after the war's end, Congress passed the Bring 'Em Home Alive Bill, offering resettlement in the United States to "any national of Vietnam, Cambodia, Laos, China or any of the independent states of the former Soviet Union who personally delivers into the custody of the USG [U.S. government] a living American MIA or POW from the Vietnam War." It was a cruel hoax that kept a flicker of hope alive among bereaved families. There were no living American MIAs or POWs from the Vietnam War.

The United States has spent more than $100 million searching for MIAs and has found the remains of several hundred. Not until I returned to Vietnam did it ever cross my mind that Vietnam might have MIAs as well. Did its people search, too? How many were there? Did mothers and widows still grieve?

{{{   }}}

PHAM KIM KY SAID THE WORDS IN A WHISPER: *mat tich*—"missing." She covered her mouth with a small, delicate hand, as though its mere mention brought a stab of pain too terrible to bear. She paused to regain her composure. "Look here," she said at last, opening her photo album to a grainy portrait of Ho Viet Dung, her son, fine-featured and bright-eyed, a seventeen-year-old headed off to a war from which he would not return. To all but Ky and her family, he was merely a statistic by the time I arrived in Hanoi—one of 300,000 Vietnamese MIAs.

Ky was a beautiful woman who carried her sixty-eight years well. Her gray hair was pulled back into a bun, her skin was as smooth as paper. She had tired, sad eyes. "How can I rest until I have found Dung?" she asked, as though I had an answer. "He was my eldest. Such a clever, kind boy. To think of him lying unknown, alone, in a distant field of killing is more than I can bear."

So Ky had joined Vietnam's wandering tribe of mourners—a collection of thousands of mothers, fathers, wives, brothers, and sisters whose lives were devoted, in whole or part, to crisscrossing the battlefields of what had been South Vietnam. They spent their time searching out witnesses, scouring military archives, digging up unmarked graves—all desperate for clues that would help them locate the remains of loved ones. Their search for closure was the final legacy of a war most other Vietnamese scarcely spoke of any more. As their numbers grew, along with the attendant publicity in the Vietnamese media, veterans groups throughout the country began asking: Why has so much been made of America's missing, and so little of Vietnam's? Is our grief any less? Are our sons somehow less cherished?

"My Beloved Family," Dung, then a twenty-year-old corporal, wrote his parents and younger brother, Thang, from the Central Highlands in January 1972:

> I am very well, and you don't have to be concerned about me. One and a half years on the front has made me strong, and I've gotten used to the hardships here. I suffered malaria, but my health is good now, maybe better than any time since I was in Hanoi. I carry with me every day your love. Thang, I want you to study hard so that you will be very smart when I come home.

Dung—his name translates as "brave" in Vietnamese—had been born into a family steeped in nationalistic struggle. His grandfather was a member of the resistance against the French in the 1930s and spent six years in France's notorious prison on Con Dao Island. His father had been wounded at Dien Bien Phu. His uncle served as an army doctor in the American War. "It seems we were at war forever," Dung's mother said.

In 1969, the year Richard Nixon was inaugurated as president and Ho Chi Minh died, Dung volunteered for the North Vietnamese Army. He was a high school senior. He had drunk only an occasional glass of beer in his lifetime and never had a real girlfriend. He had never seen a movie, ridden in a car, or been more than twenty miles from Hanoi. His first six months in the army were spent training in the mountains with his two best friends, who had joined up the same day.

"What kind of boy was Dung?" I asked.

"Well, one thing, he had such a lovely singing voice. I can still hear it so clearly." Ky spoke of Dung's good looks that caught the eye of every girl—he was too shy to ever ask for a date—and his kindness to Thang and his cousins. Her voice dropped again to a whisper. She pushed aside her teacup and reached into her purse.

First she withdrew a pair of baby shoes, wrapped in plastic. Then a tiny silk shirt and a child's pillow embroidered with the name "Viet Dung." She had carried them with her ever since her son joined the *mat tich* of Dak To. Twenty-five years, she sighed. "Dung has been dead longer than he lived."

The night before he was to leave for the Southern Front, Dung and his family gathered at their small home in Hanoi. They ate a dinner of rice and spinach, enhanced by a special treat in wartime North Vietnam— chicken. They gave Dung small presents they hoped would be useful: a needle to patch his uniform, cigarettes, candy, a towel, two pairs of warm socks. Later, his father sat with him and for the first time related his wartime experiences fighting the French at Dien Bien Phu.

"Dear Mother and Father and Thang," Dung wrote in March 1972 from Dak To, where five years earlier North Vietnamese and American troops had fought one of the war's bloodiest battles:

> I am preparing to go to the battlefield. Please, don't worry. My friends and comrades, we love each other. We are living together as a family, sharing our happiness and hardships, and that makes me feel better.

There were no more letters.

"I had a mother's feeling something terrible was about to happen," she said, and when she heard the news of a big battle around Dak To, she knew it had. Then for three years, there was only silence, broken at last, along with her heart, by a ritual repeated perhaps a million times in the North during the war. There was a knock at her door. On the steps stood a group from the local People's Committee, and the red-bordered document from the Socialist Republic of Vietnam they handed her began: "The Fatherland will never forget your son." Pham Kim Ky was now officially a "Vietnamese martyr in the struggle against America."

Ky wrote a lullaby to her son, and neighbors passing by her house would see her seated by the open window, singing softly:

> *I see you in the shadow of the Truong Son mountain,*
> *In the blooming of flowers and the singing of birds.*
> *This is my lullaby with all my love for you.*
> *I'm always with you until the end of my life.*

In the Vietnamese culture that combines Buddhism with local tradition, the dead are exhumed three years after burial. Their bones are washed, then reinterred, so that the soul may forever live in peace. Relatives tend the graves and pray over them often. They treat the dead as still-living members of the family, worshipping them in every home at altars on which fresh flowers and fruit are placed daily, talking with them through psychics, burning small paper replicas of clothes, TVs, electric fans, and beautiful homes so the dead may live comfortably in the afterlife. ("Our most difficult order was for a sewing machine," said a woman who makes the paper cutouts. "But what the living have, the dead also need. This isn't superstition. It's about faithfulness and showing serious feelings to your ancestors.") For those whose death date or grave is unknown, a special day of worship is set aside—the fifteenth day of the seventh month of the lunar calendar—but on other days their families carry a terrible burden. Since the souls of the missing cannot be taken care of properly, they are said to be destined to wander aimlessly, forever lost. "Pity . . . the souls of those lost thousands," the poet Nguyen Du wrote. "They are the ones for whom no incense burns."

Pham Kim Ky knew she must find her son's remains—but how? Where? Had he even been buried? Unlike the United States, Vietnam had no vast sums of money to assist a family's search and no computerized records. Casualty lists were sketchy. Countless thousands of nameless dead had been buried with just the words *liet sy*—"martyr"—on their headstones. Battlefields had been napalmed, incinerating the KIAs. Terrain had been transformed by Agent Orange and by B-52 strikes. Bodies had been stripped of wallets, identification, and family pictures by souvenir-hunting GIs. Many commanders and colleagues who might have remembered Ky's boy were dead.

With Dung's soul wandering somewhere in the Truong Son Mountains of Kontum Province, Ky began her quest in Hanoi and its outlying areas. For months, sitting behind her surviving son on the family motor scooter, she explored crowded alleyways and country roads, seeking out veterans of Dak To. She and Thang would get home at dusk each day. Her husband, Trinh, his right leg disabled by injuries suffered in the war against France, would hobble to the door and ask, "Any news? Anything at all?"

From her inquiries, Ky learned that Dung's unit, the Baza Brigade, had been the lead element in an attack on the Dak To airfield. Dung had been killed on April 21, 1972. She learned of no heroic deeds, no stirring last words—just vague details of one ordinary soldier's death. "It was a beginning," she said. "I knew I had to be patient."

The veterans she talked to described the terrain and drew maps. With her husband she set off one rainy February morning in 1976 for Dak To, nearly 1,000 miles south, on the first leg of four long trips to the southern battlefields. They traveled by train, bus, army truck, bicycle, and foot. Often she wept, knowing she was tracing the very steps her son had taken.

During those four treks, which spanned twenty-one years and often de-
pleted the family's $100 monthly pension, Ky and her husband questioned
army commanders and villagers. They scoured battlefields, climbed
mountains, struggled through jungle so dense that soldiers escorting
them had to hack a pathway with machetes.

Along the way they dug up forty-five unmarked graves, hoping one
would be Dung's or hold a clue to his fate. When Ky would declare, "We
must dig here!" the soldiers would ask: "Mother, how could you recognize
your son even if we find something? Bones are only bones." Ky would reply: "I will recognize Dung by his teeth. He had such beautiful teeth."

Ky never did find her boy. "Yes, I have been discouraged to search so
long and still not have the answer," she told me one day in Hanoi after returning from another journey to the distant Highlands. "There were
times I thought I could not climb another mountain or dig up another
grave. But I found the strength. Just as any mother would find the
strength."

At each battlefield she visited, Ky scooped up a handful of dirt and
pebbles and placed them in a plastic bag. Eventually she had many bags,
and one day she mixed all the dirt together and poured it into a ceramic
urn. She choose a handsome headstone and on it had the words cut HO
VIET DUNG, 1952–1972, LOVED ALWAYS. An engraved portrait of
Dung was mounted on the marker. Then, in a military cemetery in
Hanoi, she buried the urn and placed fruit and flowers and incense on the
grave. It was not what she had hoped for, but she comforted herself in
thinking that maybe in the dirt she had brought home were slivers of
Dung's bones, and in so believing, Dung's soul had been reclaimed from
the eternal wandering of the lost.

{{{  }}}

IN 1992 NGUYEN NGOC HUNG, a university English professor in
Hanoi, became the first former NVA soldier to go to the United States to

meet groups of U.S. Vietnam vets. Although Vietnam was still on Washington's enemy list at the time, Hung was allowed to travel freely throughout the country, and from his reconciliation mission grew a bond of kinship between veterans groups of former enemies. Two years later the Vietnam Veterans of America and other organizations began assisting the Vietnamese's search for MIAs—one of whom was Hung's brother, a twenty-year-old private who died fighting U.S. troops near Danang. Since 1994, thousands of GIs have turned over to the Vietnamese embassy in Washington and to their local service organizations souvenirs and photographs and letters and wallets taken from dead soldiers. They have passed on scores of maps showing unexplored battle sites and places where bulldozers dug trenches for mass graves. Their efforts have helped locate thousands of Vietnamese MIAs.

But for innumerable families, the search goes on. The army provides soldiers to escort families to battlefields and to help dig up unmarked graves. Local People's Committees provide financial assistance—$1.75 per day for guides and 80 cents per day, for no more than four days, to cover a family's food costs. The state-run TV network broadcasts a thirty-minute show each week showing pictures of MIAs and reporting what information is known about their final days; it is the most-watched program in Vietnam.

Like most Asians, Vietnamese are superstitious. They would not consider making an important decision or picking a date to start construction on a home or getting married without consulting an astrologer. They won't pose as a trio for a photograph because the person in the middle is apt to be struck by ill fortune. The communist government frowns on superstition and mysticism; in the 1970s and 1980s it banned fortune-telling and even ordered a village in Vinh Phu Province to stop worshipping Ho Chi Minh as the eighteenth king in the Hung Dynasty. But as Vietnam began lightening up in the 1990s, the ban on fortune-tellers was lifted, and psychics and seers returned in strength. Some have become specialists in locating MIAs.

I climbed the stairs to the second-story Hanoi home of Nguyen Van Lien, an MIA psychic whose fame had spread throughout Vietnam. Thirty or more pairs of shoes were arranged neatly on his doorstep. In the sparsely furnished living room there was a gold bust of Ho Chi Minh, a Vietnamese flag, and an altar overflowing with red and white flowers, rice, fruits, small amounts of money, burning incense, several roasted chickens, and a bowl of candy. Lien's visitors sat barefoot on the tile floor, packed shoulder to shoulder, each hoping that he or she would be summoned by the great seer to unlock the mystery of a relative long listed as missing in action. Lien was a thin, wiry man of thirty-seven. He had a soft, high-pitched voice and a steady, steely stare. Like some other clairvoyants who had had success in locating unmarked graves, his work was sanctioned by the government's Science Technology Union. Lien could not explain his gift, other than to say, "I had two serious fevers as a young man, and when I survived I found I had the ability of a fortune-teller."

An elderly man and his wife were called forward. They pulled up chairs in front of the wooden table where Lien sat. On the table were a desk phone, a portable phone, a tape recorder, a large pad of white paper, and five colored felt-tip markers. Lien only wanted a single piece of information from his visitors: their family name (it was Tran). Wordlessly Lien began to sketch. The old man leaned forward to watch. His wife began to pray. Lien's fingers swept over the blank sheet of paper as though propelled by exotic forces. Rivers took form. Then from the green marker, mountains. Towns were filled in as series of short vertical lines. Bit by bit a detailed map emerged: roads, forests, paddies, a cemetery, then black dashes for individual graves. His pen stopped in midstroke. He fixed the Trans with a smile. The room was hushed. Lien took a drag on his waterpipe and slapped at a mosquito.

"Here," Lien said, tapping a black dash with his pen. "This is where you must dig. You must leave as soon as you have money from the harvest to travel. Your son died May fifth of the moon calendar. His grave is in the fifth zone, Quang Nam Province, Que Phong district, Que Son com-

each other to get information about those military personnel and foreign civilians of the parties missing in action, to determine the location and take care of the graves of the dead so as to facilitate the exhumation and repatriation of the remains."

North Vietnam released 591 American POWs (South Vietnam held about 40,000 communist prisoners at the time), and in March President Richard Nixon announced that "all our American POWs are on their way home." Skeptics had their doubts. Hanoi was believed to have held about 1,325 POWs in 1969. The number Nixon accepted seemed low. Had hundreds of POWs been murdered? Had Hanoi held back POWs as bargaining chips? On the first question, there has never been a satisfactory answer. On the second, various congressional studies concluded in 1977 there was no credible evidence any American MIAs were still alive. President Jimmy Carter reclassified more than 1,000 POW/MIAs to KIA/BNR (killed in action, body not recovered), or definitely dead. But for reasons motivated by genuine concern, self-promotion, anticommunism, and sometimes greed, a lot of people didn't want the issue to go away. Under pressure from the National League of Families of American Prisoners and Missing in Southeast Asia and some veterans groups, the KIA/BNR classification was changed back to POW/MIA. That raised the false hopes of families that some MIAs were still alive and ensured that the controversy would not die, sidetracking moves toward reconciliation—just as anti-Vietnam groups in the United States wanted. It led to the most extensive and expensive search for MIAs in military history.

"To a large extent, the whole MIA issue was manufactured," said Michael Leaveck, associate director of the Vietnam Veterans of America Foundation in Washington, D.C. "The Reagan administration used it for political purposes; the Bush administration perpetuated it; a cottage industry profited from it; some political forces used it as leverage for a broader agenda. I would never deny the importance of putting a family's pain to rest, and I know there are a lot of unresolved feelings, but at some point you have to say there is nothing left we can do that will produce—

alive—returned Americans. You have to accept a certain number of unre-solved missing cases whenever you go to war."

I caught up with Pete Peterson in Danang. The U.S. ambassador boarded a Russian-made helicopter piloted by a Vietnamese major. We headed for an unnamed hill where two American pilots—a captain and a lieutenant—had been shot down in 1969 while on a bombing run in sup-port of U.S. Marines battling North Vietnamese regulars. Witnesses saw the napalm drop that August morning, saw the F-4 Phantom shudder as the pilots tried to pull the jet out of its dive, saw the fiery crash. For two days Marines swept the hill-laced branches of the Ho Chi Minh Trail but in the end withdrew empty-handed, with neither the airmen's bodies nor confirmation of their deaths. For thirty years the crash site had lain as undisturbed as a ghost town's cemetery.

The ambassador stared silently out of the chopper's porthole windows, chin in the palm of his left hand. Triple-canopy jungle and an occasional isolated village whisked by below us. Had life taken a different twist, he knew, he could have been the one that the task force was excavating for on this day. His helicopter circled twice and landed in a whirl of dust on what was a replica of the fire support bases I had seen so often in the war—a small clearing in the jungle, cut by hand, on the slopes of a hill a million miles from nowhere.

Peterson stepped out. On the ground a company-sized unit of Ameri-cans and Vietnamese—some civilian, some military—had been at work for three weeks, eight hours a day, trying to find clues that would confirm the pilots' fate. They had torn up the hillside, digging long, narrow trenches, sifting dirt through screens, in their search for a tooth or bone or belt buckle. They used tape measures and pegs to stake off sections of the site. Not a trace remained of the jet bomber, which probably had been disassembled by villagers decades ago and carted off piece by piece to be sold as scrap. The joint task force included a U.S. anthropologist, a mor-tuary technician, and a photographer. So far they hadn't found much—a small patch of a flightsuit, a pocket knife, a chunk of a pilot's helmet, a boot sole. It was not enough to bring closure to Case No. 1474. By the time the evacuation site would be abandoned in a week or two, the bill for the mission would total $1 million.

"How can you put a value on an effort like this that is unprecedented in history?" Peterson asked the men who gathered around him. "You know, sometimes people ask how many dollars it cost to look for our MIAs. Well, I think we should tell them proudly how much money we're spending."

"Were you ever in Vietnam during the war, sir?" asked a GI, who had been born a year or two after it ended. "Yes, for quite a while," the former pilot replied, without adding that his entire six-year tour on the ground had been spent in a prison.

Through excavations like the one for the Air Force captain and lieutenant, 435 U.S. servicemen have been accounted for and confirmed dead in Vietnam. Just under 1,500 men (including 21 civilians) remain officially unaccounted for, although in all but a handful of cases the details and whereabouts of their deaths were known. I had no doubt that the search for the missing was an honorable mission of which the United States should be proud. It brought closure to bereaved families and reminded serving military personnel that their commanders would spare no effort on their behalf if they were ever among the missing. But I had no idea what a hornet's nest the MIA issue was until I returned to Hanoi and wrote an article for the *Los Angeles Times* about my trip with Peterson.

In the article I mentioned that 78,000 GIs from World War II and 8,000 from the Korean War were still listed as MIA and wrote that in Vietnam nature had set a deadline: Bones disappear in thirty years or less in acidic soil. Of all the body parts that can be used for identification, only teeth have an indefinite life span—and, in the new-growth tangle of thick jungle where MIA sites are located, teeth were increasingly impossible to find. Then I included two paragraphs:

Some U.S. officials and veterans groups are privately raising a question no politician would dare ask publicly: At what point should the United States say it has done everything possible to account for its missing and start winding down a campaign that is costing millions of dollars?

Although the MIAs are a mantra for every member of Congress visiting Vietnam—the issue, each is quick to point out in news conferences, is the first topic raised with Vietnamese officials—the fact is that MIA groups no longer have the access they once did on Capitol Hill. And, U.S. diplomats say, the issue is gradually being relegated to a less prominent position on the agenda of foreign affairs.

Normally newspaper articles I wrote didn't get much reader response, maybe an e-mail or two at most. This time I was inundated with e-mails, letters, faxes, even a few long-distance phone calls. Among the readers' complaints: I was un-American, ignorant, misinformed, inaccurate, pro-communist, insensitive, a "chicken-shit coward" who had never heard a shot fired in anger, unprofessional, antimilitary, or, as one reader put it, "a god damn lying son of a bitch of a journalist, 'cause all you bastards have your own agenda." So many telephone calls flooded the *Times*'s headquarters in Los Angeles, from the managing editor's office down to the foreign desk, that I received a message from one editor, asking: "This is out of control. Isn't there something you can do to call these guys off?" There wasn't.

I had particularly incensed the group of readers mentally trapped in the distant past with a reference to Senator John McCain. After being released as a POW, McCain had written of his captors: "You get to hate them so bad that it gives you strength." Like other POWs, McCain had broken under torture and supplied more than his name, rank, and serial number, as stipulated in the military Code of Conduct. (After the war, the code was rewritten to reflect the reality that every man has a breaking point.) But McCain had been a lot more courageous than I—and possibly some of my readers—might have been in similar circumstances. Several times his captors offered to release him. Each time he refused, because under military tradition those who had been imprisoned longer than he deserved to be released first. Each time he refused, he was tortured more.

To the people who contacted me, McCain was a collaborator with the enemy, the Manchurian Candidate. The reason for the vehemence, I suspected, had little to do with his conduct as a prisoner. It had everything to do with the fact that he had abandoned "the cause," introducing legislation in 1987 to open a U.S.-interests section in Hanoi. He was at the forefront of the movement to reconcile differences between the United States and Vietnam and thought the MIA issue, although important, was not the top priority facing the two countries.

Every U.S. administration after the war tied improved diplomatic relations with Vietnam to increased cooperation on MIAs. It was never a Democrat-Republican issue or a conservative-liberal wedge—it was an American problem. Hanoi was perplexed and slow to cooperate. It didn't take linkage seriously and didn't understand the emotional depth of Americans' commitment to bringing home their sons and husbands: "We've fought wars before, and, when they were over, we exchanged prisoners and that was it," said Le Van Bang, Vietnam's ambassador to the United States. "The unaccounted-for issue wasn't even raised. So this was an issue many Vietnamese had a hard time understanding."

Nguyen Ngoc Hung, the university professor and former NVA soldier who toured the United States in 1992, encountered protests and hostile questions when he appeared on U.S. college campuses and talk-radio shows and in town forums. But Hung was a moderate man, sensible and articulate, who spoke perfect English in a soft voice, and the people he won over were veterans. He would tell their groups, "I was drafted, too. I didn't want to go to war." He'd mention that the war had devastated his life—and his country's—and that his brother was an MIA. Usually the meetings ended with hugs and handshakes.

"I was amazed how the MIA issue had galvanized the United States," Hung said. "I'd pull into a gas station in Georgia, and every car seemed to have an American flag and one of those POW/MIA stickers. I got back to Hanoi and was debriefed at the foreign affairs and interior ministries. They said, 'Well, it looks like just a matter of a short time before Washington normalizes relations, right?' And I said, 'Dead wrong. Relations aren't going anywhere until the MIA issue is resolved.'"

Yet some in the United States who could never accept a Vietnam lost to communism seized on the MIA issue as the wedge to keep Hanoi and Washington apart, convinced Vietnam would never be a partner in the search for missing GIs. It was a way, they believed, of keeping Vietnam isolated indefinitely. But they had it wrong. Vietnam started cooperating. Instead of a being a wedge, the MIA issue became the bridge that led to full diplomatic relations. The Vietnamese secretly let U.S. searchers into Ho Chi Minh's mausoleum to check out the wild rumor that American prisoners were being held in underground caves. It let U.S. teams into Buddhist cemeteries under the cover of darkness to exhume bodies, which reports had indicated might be those of Americans. It allowed U.S.-Vietnamese teams to fly off to remote villages on an hour's notice to check accounts that remains had been found or an American had been seen. The teams investigated 21,000 reported sightings of live Americans. None held up. More than 30,000 pages of archival material was handed over to the Americans.

"Although questions remain about archival access," McCain said when I met him in his Washington office, "the Vietnamese military has let us do things the American military would never allow a foreign country to do. We've gone into their prisons, gone into their defense headquarters. Can you imagine us letting a bunch of Vietnamese into the Pentagon to run around under similar circumstances?"

I called Delores Alfond in Bellevue, Washington, who ran the National Alliance of Families and whose brother is an MIA. I said to her that everything I had seen and learned didn't square with statements from some POW/MIA groups that live Americans were still in captivity and that the Vietnamese government was more a hindrance than a help to the U.S. effort to obtain "the fullest possible accounting."

"Definitely I believe Americans are left alive there," she said. "Specifically they're probably moved around and moved out of the way. American investigators come into a location and they're not allowed to speak with any Vietnamese . . . until they've been rehearsed and checked. The statements you hear in the media and from the JTF [the joint U.S.-Vietnamese MIA task force] are basically lies, misrepresentations. Americans cannot go into a village without having a Vietnamese with them. So if you're a Vietnamese peasant, are you going to tell the truth?"

Would the search ever be called off? Probably not in my lifetime. The MIA issue had become institutionalized. It had created military career paths and civilian livelihoods. Dozens of independent researchers had devoted years to tracking down leads and developing theories. Lobbying groups had been formed, with offices in Washington and access to key figures on Capitol Hill. But as McCain said, "We're spending a lot on this effort, and at some point we have to decide priorities. Would, for instance, the money be better spent on veterans hospitals?"

I wondered, had an MIA been able to share his thoughts, how would he have chosen to be remembered a generation after his death? By a $1 million excavation of a Vietnam hillside that might or might not produce a tooth or a bone? Or by the construction of, say, a hospital wing or school named in his honor? I called an economist at the World Bank in Hanoi and asked how much it would cost to build a rural school in Vietnam. He said $30,000 for a quality six-classroom school with a cement foundation and a life expectancy of thirty years. So the $1 million would build about thirty-five schools, and each, the economist said, could handle an enrollment of 300–400 students. Maybe it would have been a tough call. But educating more than 300,000 students over three decades would have been an achievement to last a lifetime—and beyond.

{{{ }}}

FOG ROLLED IN OFF THE SOUTH CHINA SEA EARLY, and when I got to Hanoi's Noi Bai Airport, just before lunch, a soft drizzle had dampened the grass and shrouded the runway in mist. Parked off to one side, away from the passenger terminal, was a U.S. Air Force C-141 Starlifter, its jawlike rear cargo door open. Seven empty aluminum caskets—the same type that took home so many thousands of Americans from the war—rested on wooden supports nearby.

When the first remains of Americans were repatriated, Vietnamese officials would not allow their caskets to be draped with the American flag. So, until 1993, a folded flag was placed on each casket. (In neighboring Laos, where Americans from the Vietnam War were also listed as missing, the communist government initially insisted remains be carried away in ordinary suitcases, the occasion accompanied by neither ceremony nor publicity.)

The seven Americans who were to leave Vietnam this day at the end of a thirty-year journey were publicly unidentified, but their families had been notified the remains were presumably those of their loved ones. Had they lived, most would have been about my age. What would they have made of their lives had they been lucky and survived? The men's names had been engraved on the black marble Vietnam Veterans Memorial in Washington long ago, each marked by a cross to signify missing in action. Once the Army's Central Identification Laboratory in Hawaii had positively ID'd them—a process that could take from a few months to years— the cross by their names would be changed to a star.

An unfurled American flag covered each of the caskets, and an eleven-person honor guard, newly arrived on the C-141 from Hawaii, stood at parade rest. A handful of journalists, both American and Vietnamese, milled about. Off to one side, the official U.S. delegation had gathered: Ambassador Peterson, the former POW, with several top diplomats from the embassy; Senator John Kerry, a naval officer in the Mekong Delta during the war; members of the Vietnam Veterans of America, led by Tom Cory, confined to a wheelchair as a result of being shot in the neck in Quang Tri Province, who had returned to Vietnam with old maps, videotapes, and photographs he hoped would help Vietnamese families find their MIAs. "We've been talking with the Vietnamese from the beginning about building trust, and this builds trust," Cory said. "As American vets who are committed to families of MIAs, if we didn't follow through on this and bring the families the information we have, we wouldn't be fulfilling our duties as vets."

On the tarmac, the remains of the seven Americans rested in numbered wooden containers, each hardly bigger than a shoe box. A Vietnamese customs official pried loose each top with a screwdriver and inspected the contents—mostly bones and teeth—before signing the papers that gave Lieutenant Colonel John Kelly, commander of the MIA task force, possession of the "shipment for export." The honor guard placed each of the wooden boxes in one of the caskets, which, one by one, were carried into the plane's cargo hold, accompanied by military members of the guard and the civilian Vietnam vets.

The plane's cargo door swung shut, and moments later the giant C-141 thundered down the runway on the outskirts of a city the repatriated Americans had known only as the enemy capital. It lifted off and soon disappeared in the cloud-covered skies of Hanoi's winter morning. John Kerry said quietly to no one in particular: "Thirty years and home at last."

# THE VIET KIEU

*Strong Brains, Deep Pockets*

W AR, NEAR FAMINE, ECONOMIC HARDSHIP, and rigid
communist policies scattered the Vietnamese people. Geo-
graphically if not spiritually, one people became two: those
who stayed and those who left. The emigrants were called Viet Kieu, or
"overseas Vietnamese," and for a long time the Hanoi leadership viewed
them as an enemy and potential political threat—a disgruntled, dispos-
sessed throng who had sought refuge in seventy countries, dreaming of
the day the communist government would fall and the Vietnam of their
memories would be reborn. By the time I returned to Vietnam, the Viet
Kieu population had swollen to nearly 3 million—a community half the
size of Ho Chi Minh City—and if its members had a common denomi-

nator, it was that they were achievers. Everywhere they went, they did well, even though many landed in the United States, Canada, Australia, and France penniless, not speaking the local language, not knowing a soul, and not having ever been outside Vietnam before. More than 300,000 overseas Vietnamese have been awarded university and postgraduate degrees in their adopted countries. More Vietnamese medical doctors work abroad than in Vietnam. In the United States, Vietnamese hold important positions in research institutions, universities, hospitals, the computer industry, and on Capitol Hill. More than a dozen are CEOs of high-tech Silicon Valley firms. Forty thousand in France are top-end professionals—doctors, lawyers, professors, business leaders. In Australia top-of-the-class honors go to Vietnamese Australian students with striking regularity.

Almost everyone who had a close wartime relationship with the United States left Vietnam. A few disenchanted revolutionaries, like Bui Tin, the North Vietnamese journalist who had accepted the surrender of the South Vietnamese government in 1975, also left. Bui Tin settled into a communist-voting suburb of Paris. Better educated and more prosperous than those who stayed, the Viet Kieu were a potential national asset for Vietnam. Hanoi estimated that the "Viet Kieu economy" generated $20 billion a year.

Even during the war, Hanoi worried about losing its best and brightest to other lands. Students sent to East Germany to study had to sign pledges they would not have "contact"—read: sex—with locals because of the fear they would fall in love, marry, and not return home. North Vietnam's prettiest young women were often denied permission to travel to the Eastern bloc on the assumption they'd be the first to tumble. As Vietnam struggled through the postwar Dark Years, 12,000 young Vietnamese managed to ignore the call home and remained in, or returned to, Eastern Europe; 80,000 stayed in the Soviet Union.

When the Dark Years passed, to be replaced by the *doi moi* liberalization of the late 1980s, Hanoi looked for ways to tap Viet Kieu resources. It established the National Committee for Overseas Vietnamese and said that to rebuild the country Vietnam needed the Viet Kieu, or at least those who accepted a communist Vietnam and understood that the old days weren't coming back. Perhaps the government's intent was sincere, but it did little to make Viet Kieu feel welcome. Hanoi required them to get visas, even if they had dual citizenship and held a Vietnamese passport. It charged them the foreigners' rate for hotels, transportation, and communications, not the greatly discounted rates non–Viet Kieu Vietnamese paid, and it slapped a 5 percent tax on remittances they sent to their families in Vietnam. Every step returning Vietnamese took in their homeland was tracked by Hanoi's pervasive internal security agents; everyone they visited became suspect. They had to stay at hotels and could make only daytime visits to their families. When Party officials spoke of "dark forces" trying to sabotage Vietnam, it was the Viet Kieu they were referring to.

But a Vietnamese never loses his or her Vietnameseness. "No matter where you go, you always have that feeling of longing to come back because you're Vietnamese," said Binh Nguyen, an American Viet Kieu who runs Vietnam's FedEx operation. In the late 1980s and early 1990s, the Viet Kieu started trickling back to check out the new Vietnam. Soon the trickle became a flood. They came—300,000 strong a year—to study, to do business, to visit families, and, if they were young, perhaps to search for their cultural identity. They added style, sophistication, and worldliness to a country not keenly attuned to life beyond its own borders. And as more and more came, the government's suspicions diminished a notch or two, and tax incentives, liberalized business codes, and the right to buy property were introduced in an attempt to entice them to invest in Vietnam.

"I know we made some mistakes in the past, and we are correcting them," Pham Khac Lam, vice president of the National Committee for Overseas Vietnamese, said. "Our policy is now open. It is up to them to decide. If they think it is better to stay where they are, and just come back once or twice a year to visit, that is all right. If they want to come back and stay and participate in the reconstruction of Vietnam, then we welcome them as an integral part of the Vietnamese population. The overseas Vietnamese have an important role to play in our development. Theirs is a community that is strong in gray matter and deep in the pockets."

It was noteworthy, I thought, that those who had opened this path through the minefield of reconciliation were the younger Viet Kieu—the first generation of thoroughly Westernized Vietnamese. The product of two worlds, most spoke English as a first language, hadn't seen a rice paddy since childhood, and probably knew more about the history of the United States or Australia than of Vietnam. They were, initially, strangers in their parents' land. In the end, they became a bridge in helping the United States and Vietnam overcome the animosities of a devastating war.

"To be honest, I felt a lot of apprehension coming back," said David Thai, a twenty-five-year-old Californian who at six-foot-one towered over every native Vietnamese. "I expected to see a lot of guns and cops. I didn't know how people would react to me. I mean, I grew up with so many conceptions of Vietnam, of communism, of the war. But they were my parents' conceptions, not mine, because we left when I was two."

Many parents of Viet Kieu were aghast at their children's decision to return. The parents had risked their lives to escape communism. Sometimes it took them ten or twelve attempts to get out. When their plans were foiled by police, they went to prison. When they did manage to scramble onto an overcrowded fishing boat, they had to give the captain the gold and money they had brought to start a new life. Thailand and Hong Kong lay two weeks away, through seas roiled by killer storms and patrolled by savage Thai pirates. Thousands died. And now the survivors' children wanted to return voluntarily? The young Viet Kieu who had settled into Hanoi or Ho Chi Minh City—temporarily, if not for a lifetime—would write home and try to explain that the communism the government practiced was mellower and more flexible than the system from which their parents fled. They would say that the disastrous policies of the 1970s and 1980s had been reversed, that the government was stable, and that dreams of a reborn South Vietnam were gone forever. Their message did not always span the generation gap.

"I tell my family how taken I am with Vietnam and its culture," one returnee said, "and someone always says, 'Ah, so you've fallen in love with communism.'" Another told me he sent his younger brother in California a T-shirt imprinted with the Vietnamese flag—a flag that in his father's time had flown over only North Vietnam. The boy wore it to dinner and was sent away from the table with his father's warning: "Don't ever show that flag in this house again!"

I never could distinguish a Viet Kieu from any other Vietnamese. But native Vietnamese could in a snap. Viet Kieu were apt to speak Vietnamese with a Southern accent. In fact, if they had left as children, they might not even speak the language fluently. Viet Kieu males were taller and heavier as a result of not being raised on a rice diet. They were more comfortable using a knife and fork than chopsticks, and sometimes they forgot to take off their shoes when entering a home. They would get funny looks when they suggested that friends divvy up a restaurant or bar bill—the concept of Dutch treat doesn't exist in Vietnam, where someone is always designated as host—and they were likely to be more interested in the fortunes of the Los Angeles Lakers than those of Vietnam's national soccer team. But it was more than that. There was something in their bearing that gave them away. They were, compared with native Vietnamese who didn't belong to the Communist Party, a privileged class. Their deportment carried hints of confidence, sometimes superiority or arrogance.

David Thai, who had left Vietnam with his family in 1972, grew up in Orange County, California, believing that if one wanted to be part of the American dream the first step was to bury everything Asian. "I was truly an American kid," he said, as we drank Vietnamese coffee at the café he owned across the street from the Italian ambassador's residence. "My friends were predominantly white. I preferred speaking English to Vietnamese. I hated it when my father brought us to the Buddhist temple; I wanted to go bowling. You could say I completely denied my heritage. I'd never dated an Asian girl. I didn't even know if I could get aroused by an Asian girl. I went to college and saw other Asians and I'd say to myself, 'I'm better assimilated than they are.' I didn't even have an accent."

At the University of Washington in Seattle, Thai took a course in Asian affairs and made friends with a few Asians. An interest in Vietnam took root. He wondered, *What part of me still belongs to a homeland I don't even remember?* In 1995, he came back for the first time with a group of Vietnamese American students to study at the University of Hanoi for a semester. On the bus from the airport, the students threw high-fives, and someone shouted, "Wow, we're in 'Nam, man!" The bus rolled by glistening rice paddies—the greenest green Thai had ever seen—and passed through dusty villages and followed the Red River down Yen Phu Street to a city his parents had never been in and one that was far more beautiful than he had dared expect. It took Thai about an hour to fall in love with the country of his birth.

After graduating from the University of Washington, Thai returned to Vietnam with $700 to look for an opportunity. He opened an outdoor coffee shop on Hoan Kiem Lake. When business started going gangbusters, his Vietnamese partners elbowed him out and kept the place for themselves—a fate that befalls many foreign entrepreneurs in a country where the legal structure is primitive and written contracts are not enforceable. "Part of it was my fault," Thai said. "I was naive, too demanding. It was the American way or no way. Once you think you're Mr. Big, the Vietnamese are going to take it out on you."

It was Culture Lesson No. 1. Culture Lesson No. 2 was that Vietnamese will tell you only what they want you to know. They always hold something back; nothing is ever completely up front. Westerners tend to associate this trait with deception, but I think that misses the mark. Vietnamese simply don't unload intimate personal details and what they're really thinking on quasi strangers the way Americans are apt to do. They are skilled negotiators who drive Westerners bonkers because they never go in the front door. They will bicker over meaningless points for months—as they did in Paris in the early 1970s over the size of the table to be used for peace talks—in order to slip in a side door and win concessions on something that counts. Relationships are built on trust and confidence, not on written documents.

Thai was down to his last 50,000-dong note (about $3.50) and on a noodle diet after being shortchanged by his Vietnamese partners. His mother came to visit and cried. Her son had lost fifteen pounds and was living in an apartment furnished with only a chair and a mattress. But his wretched living conditions didn't bother Thai. He was a workaholic who oozed confidence—not necessarily an attribute in Vietnam—and used words like "synergy" to explain his business plans. He was sure the can-do American attitude had applications, even in a business environment where entrepreneurs operated by the seat of their pants and where having well-placed contacts was more important than how much capital one had to invest.

Within days, he had leased the patio of a faded downtown villa owned by the wartime mayor of Hanoi and opened a new coffee shop that he called Au Lac Café. It proved a bigger success than the first place. I adopted it as my unofficial morning office. It was a hangout where I could learn all kinds of useful information about what was going on in Vietnam by hopping from table to table, and if my bosses in Los Angeles couldn't reach me on the telephone at home, they knew they could find me at Au Lac. Thai brought Western concepts to an Eastern setting to make the café work. He talked to his young employees—most of whom were college students—about teamwork and focus and long-term goals. He set up "smiling workshops" and role-playing sessions to teach them customer service. He ran a two-week "academy" for new workers and established a school to teach local kids math and English. All his workers shared in profits, even the ragged street urchins he recruited to shine customers' shoes and do odd jobs. After a while I noticed that the street kids started looking cleaner and neater. They dressed better, and their English improved. I asked one of them what his job was, and he said, "Businessman."

Thai, who went on to invest in a coffee plantation and a coffee-export business, shared something with most of the young Viet Kieu I met in Hanoi and Ho Chi Minh City: They wanted to contribute and make Vietnam a better country. They had come back for personal reasons as much as for business reasons. When they arrived many asked themselves, *Am I American or Vietnamese?* They usually decided they were both. They were at an advantage over native Vietnamese because they had foreign passports and could leave if the Vietnam experience turned sour. They were at a disadvantage because they didn't have a political safety net; if problems arose, there was no uncle or cousin at one of the ministries to sort things out. But in returning, whether it was to visit or stay, the Viet Kieu had become an important stepping-stone between two worlds.

"Two years ago, I went back to the village [in what had been North Vietnam] where my parents were born," said Vic Duong, a forty-year-old San Franciscan. "Some of my family is still there. They were curious to see what their cousin from America looked like, but our worlds were so different. It made me realize how far we'd traveled from the little village. They were still farming, tending the rice paddies. I guess that would have been me if we'd stayed. They couldn't even imagine what my life was like in the United States.

"I'll admit," Duong went on, "that when I first decided to come back and get into business, my parents said, 'Why? Why in the world would you want to do that? You've got everything you could possibly want in America.' But, you know, my father returned to Vietnam for his first visit a little while back, and when I was taking him to the airport, he said I'd made the right decision. That made me feel good."

Like virtually every overseas Vietnamese family, Duong's had been sending money to relatives in Vietnam for years. It was an important source of hard currency for Vietnam: $1.2 billion in Viet Kieu remittances flowed into Vietnam annually through banks; another $2 billion came back in suitcases and through unofficial channels. Now the government hoped the Viet Kieu would invest in and help develop the country's fledgling high-tech industry, which ranged from software development to website design. Vietnam's young information-technology workers were so capable that the World Bank office in Hanoi used them not only to deal with local IT issues but also to fix problems emanating from the United States.

Returning Viet Kieu walked a fine line and arrived with two strikes against them. Many Vietnamese resented them—on first meeting at least—because they or their parents had deserted their country in a moment of hardship and had not shared the suffering of the Dark Years. Others complained Viet Kieu had an air of superiority, like city dudes come to visit their country cousins. The government was suspicious of them. Jealousy fitted into the equation as well: A native Vietnamese who toiled on pauper wages and might not have finished high school envied an emigrant with a college education, a good job, and money in his pocket. A natural thought crossed his or her mind: *If I'd done what you did twenty-five years ago, what would my life be like today?*

Lan Ai Trinh, who was twenty-seven, had given up a successful career as a TV producer in Hong Kong to return to Vietnam. I met her in Ho Chi Minh City, where she was holed up in a $250-a-month studio apartment over a food shop. Trinh had left in the 1978 purge against Vietnamese of Chinese origin; her return, to research a book on the family's saga, stirred bittersweet memories: There was the transformation of her family from prosperous to impoverished, the imprisonment, and the escape—her father by boat to Thailand, her mother on foot to China, where she and scores of others were held hostage to their ethnicity, forced to camp out for weeks in cardboard cartons on a bridge that spanned the border. At the north end of the bridge, Chinese authorities denied them entry because they were Vietnamese; at the south end Vietnam blocked their return because it considered them Chinese. Then, there was starting a new life. It seemed to Trinh the family was always starting over. In Houston. New York. Australia. Hong Kong. And now, for Trinh, Vietnam. Again.

"I'm determined not to be plagued by the past," she said as we sat in her small apartment. We had to speak in loud voices to be heard over the din of honking car and motor-scooter horns in the street below. "I keep saying I want Vietnam to be my last stop. I've made so many stops. But I'm not sure exactly what will happen. All I can say for sure is that for now, this is home. I feel comfortable. As far as the Vietnamese reaction to me goes, well, I think I'm seen as just a foreigner coming back with U.S. dollars. I don't mean that to sound cynical, because I have cultivated some very good and real associations with local Vietnamese. I eat at food stalls on the street. I fit in. Yesterday I tried on an *ao dai* [the traditional flowing pants suit] for the first time and it felt pretty natural.

"My initial feeling when I arrived at the airport was, I've gone too far to come back now. I'd moved on, put Vietnam behind me. But, although it took me a while to realize it, the me who left is not the same me who is returning. The same goes for Vietnam. It's changed too."

{{{  }}}

I KNEW WHAT SHE MEANT. I had celebrated my twenty-eighth and twenty-ninth birthdays in wartime Vietnam and don't remember either day. But I do remember that I felt immortal in those days, that I would survive the risks I took, that life felt endless. It was a comforting thought. Now my sixtieth birthday was approaching. I went to Bangkok for laser surgery to remove potentially cancerous spots on my face. Happily, the procedure took away some facial wrinkles as well. I hadn't quit smoking, despite my promises to the contrary, but I was in good health and, I think, aging fairly gracefully. The enthusiasm to sniff out a good story, to

was: In many cases, to the United States. In California, Florida, and Arkansas, where authorities were making plans to resettle Vietnamese refugees, protestors gathered to deliver a message to the people the United States had gone to war to help: Stay out. One wire-service photo prominently displayed in many U.S. newspapers showed a factory worker holding a placard that said: "Only [President] Ford Wants Them."

Everyone said it was about jobs. They were tough to find in the United States in those days. Of course, employment was also something of a problem in Vietnam at the time, because leveling villages and cities with American and Russian ordnance hadn't created many jobs except in funeral parlors and the army. While following the refugees, I struck up a conversation with an amiably drunk American expat at the bar of a Manila hotel. I asked him what he thought about the United States airlifting Vietnamese out of Saigon and rescuing them from their boats in the South China Sea. He said he didn't really have an opinion one way or the other. Another drink later, he volunteered, "If you ask me, the whole thing stinks. We just don't need another minority." After some uncomfortably silent moments, he added, "I'm sorry. That's just how I feel."

In the half-dozen or so tented refugee camps I visited, I met engineers, doctors, university professors, architects, intelligence analysts, poets, generals who had commanded thousands of men in battle. It was clear the United States was to be the beneficiary of one of the greatest brain drains in modern history. Many of these people asked me about the picture they had seen of the factory worker with the placard and said, "Do most Americans feel this way?" I understood that the Vietnamese had as many apprehensions about going to America as Americans had misgivings about receiving them, but I don't remember precisely how I replied. I think I said something about the United States opening its doors to 46 million immigrants since 1803 and believing we could find room for a few more. I might have said that a 105mm artillery round cost $75, and given the fact that we could afford to fire hundreds of thousands of them during the war, Washington could probably find some money in its budget to help the refugees. I found in my files the other day an article I had written for the *Los Angeles Times* on May 12, 1975, after spending time in a camp on Guam. It said, in part:

> For too long we have had the option of turning off Vietnam with a twist of the TV dial. The war, we have come to say, was a mistake, so let's forget it. If we can learn from that mistake, then fine, let's do so. But let us not forget the people who believed what we told them about America being a land that cared about others besides herself.
>
> If the time ever arrives that America becomes so preoccupied with her own problems that she turns Hungarians and Cubans and Vietnamese away from her ports, that she forgets that an individual's tears and laughter are the same in every language, then surely that is the time to accept mediocrity as a national destiny.

Hundreds of thousands of boat people—the lucky ones who survived rough seas, pirate attacks, a lack of potable water—made landfall in Thailand, Malaysia, Hong Kong, Indonesia, and the Philippines. They weren't wanted there either. Some languished for years in detention centers that resembled wartime POW camps. But newcomers kept arriving because until 1989 anyone escaping Vietnam was automatically classified as a political refugee and eligible for resettlement, usually in North America, Australia, or France. In an effort to end the crisis, the international community, under the auspices of the United Nations, offered $360 to every Vietnamese in the Hong Kong camps who agreed to return to Vietnam. That made the problem worse. Entire villages near Haiphong on Vietnam's northern coast emptied, with everyone getting on boats for Hong Kong to claim refugee status. They collected their reward and were put on charter flights back to Vietnam. A family of four returned with enough money to build a comfortable house in the countryside.

In 1996, the UN began the forced repatriation of Vietnamese refugees from the Southeast Asian camps. Some rioted and were dragged onto planes kicking and screaming. Others left voluntarily. Human-rights groups expressed concern that the Hanoi government would punish the returnees, as it had the Southern supporters of the Saigon regime after the war, and the office of the UN High Commissioner for Refugees (UNHCR) monitored the lives of those resettling in Vietnam. It found no persecution or intimidation.

"We even had access to returnees imprisoned for criminal offenses after they came back, and we found zero incidents of mistreatment," Keisuke Murata, the deputy director of UNHCR's Hanoi office, told me. "The government understands their reintegration into society is important, and it has worked hard to close this chapter of the war. Given the industrious nature of the Vietnamese and their basic instinct to seek better lives, I can safely say that although many returnees were disoriented at first, the great majority managed to regain their livelihoods within a few years."

In the course of the Diaspora, the United States accepted enough Vietnamese refugees, including more than 90,000 young Amerasians fathered by American servicemen, to fill a city the size of Baltimore. Australia—whose restrictive and racist immigration policies through the 1960s had been based on fear of the "yellow peril" to the north—became the home of 200,000 Vietnamese. Another 200,000 went to Canada, where Vancouver took on the trappings of a distinctly Asian city. Slowly the Asian detention centers emptied, and in August 1997, twenty-two years after the end of the war, the UN High Commissioner for Refugees said in Hanoi: "The saga of the Vietnamese boat people, one of the most tragic examples of human suffering in the region's recent history, has finally come to an end."

{{{ }}}

"It's over?" Nguyen Van Y asked, incredulous. "Then what am I doing still here? When the French ship picked us up, we thought three, maybe six months in the Philippines, then the United States. That was nine years ago."

I was sitting with Van Y in the noodle shop he ran in Puerto Princesa, on the Philippine island of Palawan. "Mr. Bojangles" blasted out of a boombox on the stove. His two friends pulled their stools closer to our table to hear what Van Y was saying and to examine the photograph he held, of himself as a twenty-one-year-old soldier in the Mekong Delta, wearing a South Vietnamese uniform. They too had served with the army of the South, and they nodded when Van Y said he could never return to a communist homeland. One of them, Tran Nhu Ban, added: "Nine years is a long time to wait. We hope the Americans will recognize our plight, but I'm not sure anyone knows about us any more."

Indeed, a year after the United Nations had cut off resettlement funds and declared the refugee crisis over, few people did. The three former soldiers were part of a lost, forgotten fraternity whose scattered members, perhaps 3,000 in all, were never resettled because of a variety of circumstances. They lived in a twilight zone of statelessness—unwilling, in most cases, to return to Vietnam and unwanted by any new homeland. They had either failed to convince screeners in the Philippines or Hong Kong that they were political refugees, or they had been deemed by U.S. interviewers to have medical problems or character flaws. They had invested a decade in making the dangerous escape from Vietnam to get, really, nowhere.

The last best hope the twilight people had was a twenty-eight-year-old Vietnamese Australian lawyer, Hoi Trinh, who had abandoned a conventional legal practice in Melbourne, and the high salary that went with it, to work for a subsistence stipend trying to resettle the last of the boat people. Trinh lived in a dumpy Manila flat crawling with Vietnamese refugees, whom he fed and let camp out for free. He had become a surrogate dad to a four-year-old boy named Minh whose father, an Amerasian, had committed suicide after being denied entry to the United States. He drove consular officers at the U.S. and Australian embassies nuts because he came up with the damnedest arguments to show why so-and-so had been denied justice and was entitled to immigrate. But he was often successful, and every couple of weeks he put someone else on the plane to start a new life in Orange County or Perth.

Trinh was the same age as I when I went off to cover the war. At that age I thought little about anyone but myself; he thought mostly about others. I never met a Vietnamese quite like him. First, the notion of helping strangers is as alien in Vietnam as the concept of volunteerism. Second, anyone who turned his back on a high-salaried job to work basically for free would be dismissed in Vietnam as retarded, and Hoi really didn't care if he had two pesos to rub together as long as he was winning his legal battles, one by one, to find homes for the asylum-seekers. And third, whereas Trinh trusted everyone, the Vietnamese were largely distrustful of and unconcerned with anyone outside their immediate circle of family and friends. It was a distrust born in centuries of wars between regional dynasties and, more recently, in the xenophobia of a communist system that encourages watchfulness and makes undercover security spooks an essential apparatus of state control.

Trinh and I had met in Manila, and he took the flight to Palawan with me so I could meet some of the people he was trying to help. I asked him how he had ended up in Australia. Trinh said his father—a high school principal when Saigon fell—had been sent off to a reeducation camp in the Mekong Delta in 1975. "We got to visit him once there for two days," Trinh said. "I didn't understand why my dad was there. I was seven. I asked my mom and she said, 'He has to be here. There has been a change.'"

Chinh Trinh was released in 1977 and dispatched, with his family, to Phu Quoc Island. The authorities told him he could never teach again. He was to be a farmer. Phu Quoc had no electricity, no running water, no doctors. Hoi Trinh's baby brother died there of an unknown disease and an absence of medical care. Trinh sold cigarettes and watermelons on the beach. "My mom and dad were terrible farmers," Trinh said. "What did they know about farming? They were educated city people. The soil was awful on Phu Quoc. Nothing grew. My parents tried potatoes, but they didn't get any bigger than my thumb." After ten failed attempts, Chinh Trinh escaped Vietnam in 1980. He spent twelve days adrift in an eighteen-foot boat and made landfall in Thailand. The family was reunited in Australia five years later.

"A lot of people, including my dad, wanted to stay in Vietnam and make a difference," Trinh said. "But it was impossible. How could you stay in a place where you were treated as a third-class citizen? It's so sad. The government was scared of intellectuals. It was scared of my father even though he was only a bloody teacher."

When Trinh started high school in Melbourne, he spoke no English. He ate mostly rice. Shoes hurt his feet because he had only worn sandals. By the time I got to know him, he had his law degree, had clerked for a federal court judge in Melbourne, and been chosen the Young Vietnamese Australian of the Year for his work with the refugees. He had been accepted at Oxford to study for a master's degree in law. His father, after ten years as a bus driver in Melbourne, was teaching again.

{{{   }}}

So now Trinh and I were sitting at the noodle shop on Rizal Avenue, in the tropical city of Puerto Princesa, listening to Nguyen Van Y and his friends talk about how they had risked everything for democracy and freedom. Van Y held a scrapbook with photos from Vietnam; he turned each page slowly. "Seriously, if Vietnam wasn't communist, I'd go back," he said. And another former soldier, Nguyen Van Vui, added, "Escaping was dangerous, but we did it for liberty. Just by being here in the Philippines I am making a statement how much that liberty means to me."

But the memories they clung to were a myth. The wartime South Vietnam I had known had been neither democratic nor free. Thousands were imprisoned. Torture was common. Newspapers were censored. Elections were fraudulent. Religion was suppressed. Antigovernment protests were brutally crushed. Corruption reached scandalous levels. The United States ran "independent" South Vietnam just as France had run colonial Vietnam. I did not volunteer any of these observations. My hosts were good people, and they had precious little to hold on to. If rewriting history gave them some comfort, so be it.

"We've got to get going," Trinh said after a couple of hours at the noodle shop. "I want you to see the camp." Van Y lent us his motor scooter, and we headed out of Puerto Princesa along narrow roads that cut through the jungle to the sea and a pristine white beach where a sun-baked refugee camp had once stood. The camp was emptied and leveled when the United Nations declared the crisis over, but several slumlike barracks remained, inhabited by twenty or so Amerasians. Some of them bore no physical Vietnamese characteristics and looked as American as the GIs who had fought the war. It seemed odd to hear them speaking Vietnamese instead of English. They lived in squat crumbling buildings, drinking contaminated water, sleeping on concrete floors, and covering themselves with cardboard when it rained. Trinh introduced me to Pham Thi Nga, the twenty-six-year-old daughter of a U.S. serviceman she had never met.

"We're the leftovers of the war," Nga said. "But what I'd like to know is this: In the United States, you do a crime and go to prison, and one day the sentence ends. For us, this is a sentence. Just tell us how long it will last."

Of all the war's leftovers, the Amerasians were surely the most hapless. In Vietnam, they had been taunted and bullied by their schoolmates. In the United States, they had a tough time adjusting. In refugee camps they kept to themselves and did not mix with the pure-blooded Vietnamese. Carrying U.S. visas, the Amerasians left Vietnam in the early 1990s not by boat but in planes chartered by Washington to resettle Amerasians in the United States. The Philippines was to be only a brief transit point.

The vast majority of Amerasians made it the rest of the way, to a new home in the United States. What this last group didn't understand was that a visa doesn't guarantee a person entry to a country; it only gets him on an airplane, giving him the right to seek permission to enter upon arrival. Because the Amerasians left Vietnam legally, they were required to meet the same standards as, say, an Australian or a Mexican applying for U.S. immigrant residency.

For various reasons, visas issued for the people still stuck in the Palawan ghost camp had been revoked. In some cases, U.S. officials said, their behavior was "antisocial," which usually meant drinking and fighting; others had medical problems or, like Nga, had committed fraud by providing false information on their applications, often claiming friends and distant cousins as part of their immediate family to make them eligible for resettlement. The officials wrote "Canceled" across the visas. Case closed.

Unlike Van Y, who could have returned to Vietnam if he wanted, Nga and her friends had nowhere to go. Hanoi would not take them back because they left under a bilateral agreement with Washington—which wouldn't accept them because they had been judged unfit for resettlement. The Manila government considered them illegal immigrants because their now-expired transit visas had been valid for only days, not years. It wanted to deport them—but to where?

I asked one young man his name, and he said, "I am Nguyen Van Diem, No. BV-867523." He had spent so long as a refugee that, in his mind, his name and camp number had become one. Diem said, "I go to the U.S. Embassy and they say, 'Go home to Vietnam,' and I tell them, 'I've been trying to do that for four years, and Vietnam won't take me.'"

Diem lived in a corner room in one of the abandoned barracks. The room had burlap rice bags for a ceiling and Marlboro posters on the walls for decoration. A small battery-powered radio rested on a cardboard box that served as a bedside table. He said it was broken but thought maybe it only needed batteries, which he couldn't afford. On one wall he had written in Vietnamese, "God, I don't know what to do. Life has been too hard." Unless Hoi Trinh could put together one of his miracles, there was no easy way out. With the U.S. Amerasian resettlement program now ended, chances were good Diem would never get his own copy of the letter the Joint Voluntary Agency at the U.S. Embassy in Manila had sent to other children of unknown American servicemen. It read:

> Congratulations. You soon will depart to the United States. If you have any problems upon arrival, please give this letter to a policeman and he or she will assist you.
>
> The third page of this letter is a map of the United States to help you familiarize yourself with your new home. Have a safe trip and good luck.

Everyone knew Hoi Trinh in the camp, and people appeared out of nowhere to ask his counsel. They tugged at his sleeve. They showered him with questions and handed him files stuffed with papers documenting their attempts to immigrate.

They were desperate for someone who cared and listened. Trinh did both. He scribbled notes, translated letters, heard a score of stories. Sometimes he said, "To be blunt, you just don't qualify for immigration." And sometimes, "I'll see what I can do." By 10 P.M. I had grown weary and told Trinh I was going to take a taxi back to the hotel in Puerto Princesa. He said he'd be along in thirty minutes. When we met for breakfast the next morning I asked him what time he had returned to the hotel. He said he had spent the night at the camp.

We flew back to Manila together that afternoon. The pockets of Trinh's Bermuda shorts were stuffed with notes and papers, and he fell asleep reading a document he had prepared for one of the refugees. We took a motorcycle taxi to his one-bedroom apartment, tucked in a teeming alleyway. It had no air-conditioning, and the place dripped with a sauna's heat. A pot of tea and a kettle of noodles simmered on the stove. I counted fifteen Vietnamese refugees. One of them was playing a ukulele at the kitchen table. Two children were asleep in Trinh's bed. Trinh could never remember the flat being empty.

Trinh became a treasured friend. Several years after our trip he said something that helped explain the turn his life had taken. "I see these Vietnamese kids shining shoes on the streets or stuck in a refugee camp or whatever and you know what? I see me. That could have been me selling cigarettes and watermelons on Phu Quoc." Trinh would e-mail me when he had managed to find a new home for people I had met in Palawan—"Mr. Tran Nhu Ban and his wife and seven families left for Australia three weeks ago," he said in one message—and whenever I was in Manila, I'd take him to dinner at a restaurant called New Orleans. He always ordered seafood thermidor and chocolate cake with ice cream and ate as though he hadn't seen food in a month. I drank whiskey. He drank Cokes. I talked about the places I'd been in Southeast Asia for the *Times*. He talked about mustering funds and support in the Viet Kieu communities for the stranded refugees. Back in Hanoi, I e-mailed Trinh, asking how many Vietnamese he had succeeded in resettling. Here is what he e-mailed in reply:

> About two hundred. But it's not just about the numbers or me. It's about giving them legal advice, accurate, accessible, and free. It's about "educating" our communities in the United States and Australia. It's about working together, young and old. It's about self-discovery.

# THE ROAD SOUTH

F EBRUARY BROUGHT THE RAINS. It was my fourth winter in peacetime Vietnam, and Hanoi lay under a blanket of thick mist. The days were gray, and long stretches passed without a trace of sunshine. Everything felt damp and cold. I wore a sweater under my rain gear for the daily fifteen-minute bicycle ride to Au Lac Café and, farther down the street, my office. Motor scooters barreled through puddles in the Old Quarter, drenching me with sheets of water. Had that happened in the States, I would have given drivers the finger. But in Hanoi it didn't bother me. The whole city got wet on these winter commutes, and it was a small price to pay for the privilege of not owning a car and being able to bike everywhere.

I'd take refuge en route to work under an umbrella on Au Lac's patio, and my waiter-friend Dai—a former boat person who had spent six years in the refugee camps of Hong Kong—would pour me a cup of Vietnamese coffee and bring me that day's edition of *Vietnam News*, which contained little news but devoted many columns to the accomplishments of the Party. Two or three times a week Dai would ask me if I was going to leave Hanoi for Tet, assuming that, like many expatriates, I'd use the lunar new year holiday for a trip to Bangkok or beach resorts in Danang or Nha Trang. I'd tell him no, I was staying put. Tet was my favorite time in Vietnam. I liked the quiet streets, the festive mood as families gathered to share sumptuous feasts and to honor departed ancestors. Tet marked the communion of man with nature, the coming of spring, when heaven and earth were in harmony. It was like New Year's Eve, everyone's birthday, and Christmas Day wrapped into a single three-day festival. It recharged the people's spiritual energies, and all Vietnamese carried to the grave memories of their happiest Tet.

"Why would I get out of town?" I asked Dai. "Tet is everything I like about Vietnam. Sandy's even got a kumquat tree." (It was the local equivalent of a Christmas tree.) This pleased Dai, and he said to me one day, "Careful. You're beginning to sound like a Vietnamese."

For a good many years after the American War, Hanoi's dour communist cadre frowned on Tet. They considered it bourgeois. Its religious overtones made them uneasy. They criticized the spending on gifts and preparations as more in keeping with the excesses of capitalism than the frugality of socialism. The tradition-bound Vietnamese paid no heed—asking them to give up Tet was like telling them to stop watching TV or drinking beer—and the government eventually had to make an abrupt about-face, embracing the holiday with enthusiasm. As the first Tet of the new millennium approached, Dai told me the prime minister had given every government worker a $7 bonus. Over coffee one morning he translated an editorial in *Nhan Dan* for me.

"Bid farewell to *Canh Thin*, the Year of the Dragon," the paper said. "Vietnam is proud of its achieved landmarks. . . . [Tet] brightens the intellect and strong will of the Vietnamese people. . . . The first decades of the twentieth century saw . . . the oppressed nation stuck in a dead alley. Fortunately the foundation of the Communist Party of Vietnam in 1930 cast aside the dark clouds of oppression and slavery."

Now Vietnam was midway between the winter solstice and the spring equinox. The Year of the Snake was a day away. Astrologers spoke optimistically of the future; the stars, they said, were properly aligned. In millions of homes, families took their last baths of the year, to wash off the dirt of past misfortune. They held send-off ceremonies for Ong Tao, the kitchen god, who ascends to heaven on the eve of each new year to give his report to the Jade Emperor on the moral conduct of household members. More than 150,000 Vietnamese who lived abroad had come home to spend Tet with family. Planes and trains between Hanoi and Ho Chi Minh City were booked solid for a week. Hanoi merchants had stocked up 700 tons of pork and beef, more than 2 million bottles of rice wine, and 26,000 gallons of peanut and other cooking oils. The only Tet delicacy missing from the markets was rat, whose population had been ravaged by recent floods in the Mekong Delta and Vietnam's antirat campaign.

On the first morning of Tet, the Vietnamese awoke to a seemingly abandoned land. City streets were deserted. Every shop was closed. No farmers or water buffalo worked the rice paddies. In a country where shopkeepers routinely work twelve or fourteen hours a day, seven days a week, and farmers labor sunrise to sunset for months on end, it was an odd sight to see Vietnam devoid of bustle and honking horns and crowded sidewalk cafés. In home after home, families dressed in their best clothes and gathered around small altars where incense burned and flowers, fresh water, pears, plums, and a hand of unripe bananas had been placed for dead ancestors. The families ate *banh chung*—sticky steamed rice stuffed with pork and egg and wrapped in a banana leaf—and were exceedingly careful to be polite and never show anger. Even bossy mothers-in-law made peace with their daughters-in-law. Any transgression from civil behavior could bring bad luck in the year ahead.

My assistant at work seemed agitated in the days leading up to Tet, and I couldn't figure out why. It turned out he was having difficulty determining who the first visitor to cross his doorstep should be in the new year. The matter was one of grave importance: If that visitor were someone who had known misfortune in the old year—such as losing a job, suffering ill health, or experiencing a death in the family—my assistant's family could be cursed with bad luck throughout the Year of the Snake. Mr. Hung overcame his dilemma by stationing his wife at the door to keep away unwanted visitors. Then at the stroke of midnight, he crossed his threshold upon returning from a short walk. He was his own first visitor, and there was nothing in the mix of mythology, tradition, and religion that constitutes Tet to suggest his choice wasn't perfectly sensible. My waiter-friend Dai gave me *li xi*, lucky money—a 10,000-dong note (about sixty-six cents) in a small red envelope—and asked me to be his first visitor. He prepared a Tet meal for me in his one-room apartment, and although I had trouble getting down the chunks of pig fat, I was honored.

I wrote a story about Tet and its traditions for the *Times*. An acquaintance in Los Angeles sent back a note, saying she enjoyed learning about Vietnamese culture and hadn't realized Tet was a holiday. "I always thought it referred to a Viet Cong offensive," she said.

{{{   }}}

TET HAD BEEN TWICE SHATTERED by significant battles in Vietnam's history. In 1789, Vietnamese forces launched a surprise offensive under Emperor Quang Trung to drive China's occupying forces out of Hanoi. And in 1968, communist forces struck South Vietnam in a series of coordinated attacks that changed the course of the American War. The magnitude of the offensive became clear with five simple words spoken by the U.S. Marine guard who awoke Ambassador Ellsworth Bunker in his residence at 3 A.M.: "Sir," he said, "Saigon is under attack."

The Viet Cong had begun infiltrating Saigon in threes and fours during the days just before the Year of the Monkey. Their first stops were the graveyards, where weapons had been buried in coffins, thus explaining the large number of funerals that had been held in Saigon in recent days. Not until several hours after Ambassador Bunker had been awakened and hustled off in an armored carrier to a safehouse, still wearing only his bathrobe and pajamas, did intelligence analysts learn the full extent of the offensive: Heavy fighting had engulfed 100 South Vietnamese provincial and district capitals.

In Saigon, nineteen barefoot commandos breached the U.S. Embassy before being killed. In Hue, the Viet Cong flag flew atop the Citadel and would remain there for twenty-six days until U.S. Marines retook the city, inch by inch. In a Danang hospital, three doctors performed more than 100 operations a day for two weeks. Communist troops roamed through Pleiku, Nha Trang, Dalat, Dong Ha, and Can To. In North Vietnam's port of Haiphong, Bob Eaton, an American Quaker who had arrived with a shipment of medicine for civilians, found the city abuzz. Residents who could understand English walked the streets with transistor radios pressed to their ears, listening to news of the offensive from the U.S. Armed Forces Radio—an American-run military network that the North Vietnamese found more trustworthy in its accounts of the war than their own state-run broadcasts. "The Americans aren't going to have a sense of humor about this," Eaton remembered someone telling him in Haiphong. "They'll level the city. You better get out." He did.

Militarily, Hanoi suffered a profound setback in the Tet Offensive. U.S. and South Vietnamese forces took back every town, usually in a matter of days. The popular uprising in the South that the communists envisioned never materialized. Viet Cong guerrillas suffered as many dead (about 58,000) in one month as the United States did in its eight years of direct combat involvement in Vietnam. The offensive left the Viet Cong's infrastructure so shattered that North Vietnamese regulars had to take over the brunt of the fighting.

"The Tet objectives were beyond our strength," General Tran Van Tra, the commander of the Viet Cong's attack on Saigon, wrote in 1982—an assessment that ran counter to Hanoi's official line and led to his being purged from the Party. "They were based on subjective desires of the people who made the plan. Hence our losses were large, in materiel and manpower, and we were not able to retain the gains we had already made. Instead we faced myriad difficulties in 1969 and 1970."

One of those difficulties was growing tension between the Southern indigenous Viet Cong guerrillas and their communist allies from the North, who, after the military debacle of Tet, began playing an increasingly influential role in the affairs of the National Liberation Front (Viet Cong) and its Provisional Revolutionary Government. Hanoi's men were a testy group, weaned on unyielding Marxist ideology and disdainful of the bourgeoisie; their love affair was with the proletariat. Before long they began treating non-Party Viet Cong officials like second-class citizens. "This was a new attitude and an unsettling one," wrote Truong Nhu Tang, a founder of the liberation front.

The reaction of the NLF's senior leaders, Tang wrote in *A Viet Cong Memoir*,

was especially resentful. Many of us were from well-to-do families and had been used to the good life before we enlisted in the revolution. Our reasons for joining were perhaps varied, but we all regarded ourselves as people who had already sacrificed a great deal for the nation and were quite ready to sacrifice everything. Many of us had struggled in one way or another against the French, and in moving to the jungle all of us were decisively committed against the Americans. Whatever comforts we might previously have enjoyed were part of history. We were not touched by guilt about our class background, and we felt that our motives were every bit as pure as those of our ideologically minded colleagues. The idea that some of the cadres regarded our previous, citified life-styles as a subject for mockery and contempt was insupportable. After the prisons, B-52s, diseases, and malnutrition, it was outrageous to suggest that we were somehow second-class revolutionaries.

Despite the military losses and the resultant tensions, the political dividends Hanoi gained from the Tet Offensive were huge. "In all honesty, we didn't achieve our main objective," North Vietnamese General Tran Do said. "As for making an impact on the United States, it had not been our intention—but it turned out to be a fortunate result." Suddenly, Americans were thinking, If the Viet Cong can pull off a coordinated, nationwide offensive, surely the light at the end of the tunnel has been an illusion.

U.S. public sentiment against the war grew, support in Congress waned, protests spread. Backing for President Lyndon B. Johnson's handling of the war fell from 40 percent before Tet to 26 percent. Three weeks after shocked U.S. TV audiences watched Marines battle Viet Cong guerrillas inside the fortress U.S. Embassy, CBS-TV anchor Walter Cronkite, one of the most influential American journalist of our time, said on the evening news: "It seems now more certain than ever that the bloody experience of Vietnam is to end in a stalemate. . . . To say that we are close to victory today is to believe, in the face of the evidence, the optimists who have been wrong in the past. To suggest that we are on the edge of defeat is to yield to unreasonable pessimism. To say that we are mired in stalemate seems the only realistic, yet unsatisfactory, conclusion." He went on to say, "The only rational way out . . . will be to negotiate, not as victors, but as honorable people."

A month later, on March 31, 1968, President Johnson made his historic announcement: "I shall not seek, and I will not accept, the nomination of my Party for another term as your president." The United States would spend the next seven years trying to extricate itself from Vietnam.

{{{  }}}

THE VIETNAMESE PRESS made scant mention of the Tet Offensive during the holiday when Dai and I shared *banh chung* in his apartment. Dai, in fact, who was twenty-four, had never heard of the offensive, and as far as I could tell older Vietnamese didn't even speak of it. Why spoil the sweetness of a peaceful Tet with dark memories? There was peace. Families were together again. There was ample food on the table. The isolation and deprivation were over. That is precisely what the Vietnamese had prayed for during the wartime Tets. Having achieved it, they were more than willing to let the past slip away.

I carried Truong Nhu Tang's memoir with me when I headed for Quang Tri Province a few days after Tet to see what had happened to the 1st Corps battlefields I remembered from the war. The Vietnamese had not yet gotten back into high gear from the Tet holiday, and the flight to Hue was half-empty. I had not heard of Truong Nhu Tang before I found his book in a Bangkok shop—it wasn't available in Vietnam—and I was struck by the grace of his prose and his nationalistic, reasonable tone. He had been a revolutionary for thirty years, serving as a high-level economics official in the South Vietnamese government while secretly organizing the Viet Cong resistance. He had served as minister of justice in the Provisional Revolutionary Government and helped design the policy of national reconciliation intended to reunite Northerners and Southerners after the war.

But for Tang the war's end brought deep disillusionment. The political prisons of the South were empty yet the reeducation camps were full. The Americans had gone yet the Russians had arrived. The guns had fallen silent in the DMZ yet the shooting had begun on the Cambodian border. Now there were new enemies: hunger, poverty, isolation, and ideological arrogance. Tang fled to Paris where a generation earlier he had been a student and first been smitten with the romance of revolution.

"The national democratic revolution itself became a casualty, choked by the arrogance of power among those who were responsible for the nation's fate," he wrote in 1985.

Instead of national reconciliation and independence, Ho Chi Minh's successors have given us a country devouring its own and beholden once again to foreigners, though now it is the Soviets rather than the Americans. In the process, the lives that so many gave to create a new nation are now no more than ashes cast aside. That betrayal of faith will burden the souls of Vietnam's revolutionary leaders—even as surely as their rigid ideology and bellicose foreign policies have mortgaged the country's future.

I hired a driver in Hue and headed north on Highway 1, a once-bloodied stretch of road the French had called the Street Without Joy. An hour out of Hue, we crossed into Quang Tri. It is one of Vietnam's poorest provinces and one of the few still laced with the reminders of war. French pillboxes, dark with age, stand silent vigil at road junctions, and half the land is unsafe for farming because of landmines and unexploded ordnance. Wellwater remains poisoned by defoliants sprayed from U.S. planes. The same chemicals reduced the province's forest cover from 85 percent to 20 percent and stripped away the jungle canopy over vast expanses of the Ho Chi Minh Trail. Young soldiers from the North who had humped down the trail arrived in Quang Tri carrying farewell gifts from their girlfriends—white handkerchiefs with her initials embroidered in one corner. So many of the boys never returned that handkerchiefs became a symbol of grieving and parting throughout Vietnam.

At the visitors' center in Dong Ha, Truong Van Tam, a young guide with DMZ Tours, the government's tour agency, said Quang Tri Province attracted 12,000 tourists a year. The majority were Japanese. "Why the Japanese come, I don't know," he noted. "Most don't speak much English and don't understand much about the war." But they dutifully made the rounds: They walked the Hien Luong Bridge that spanned the Ben Hai River on ten piers, linking the two former Vietnams, and they asked their guides to translate Ho Chi Minh's words on a towering monument on the southern bank: "The Vietnamese are one. The rivers can dry up and the mountains can fall down, but this idea will never change." They peered without apparent comprehension at the remnants of the McNamara Line, an electronic barrier designed to stop infiltration of men and materiel into South Vietnam, and they visited the forgotten sites that once had been part of the world's vocabulary: the Rockpile, Con Thien, Cam Lo, Hamburger Hill, Khe Sanh.

These places had once been part of my vocabulary, too, part of my life. But I felt no particular sweep of nostalgia on coming back to them, no surge of emotion. I felt detached, as though those days had been lived by a different person. I could no longer imagine the high-pitched whistle of an incoming mortar round or the rush of fear that builds in the stomach and leaves you short of breath. The names, but not the faces, of the soldiers and Marines whose lives I briefly shared in these now-abandoned outposts had been lost to time. So had the pledge to myself, made a generation ago when I first left Indochina, that Vietnam would be my last war. It turned out there would be others—Somalia, Zaire, Uganda, Iraq, Rhodesia, Beirut, the Persian Gulf, and Afghanistan, as well as violent upheavals in Iran, Liberia, Indonesia, East Timor, and Rwanda. Though none aroused the same intensity of passion and intimacy that Vietnam had, each in its own moment seemed the most compelling and significant story of my life. Today I couldn't remember what some of those wars had even been about. Neither could I remember any more what it was like to be young.

Outside Dong Ha my driver—with the government guide, Mr. Tam, now aboard—turned west, and we bumped along Highway 9—Ambush Alley as GIs had called the road to Khe Sanh. The two-lane road was being widened and repaved with World Bank financing to open a trade route from Laos to central Vietnam. But until construction was completed and surveillance increased, this road belonged to smugglers. Almost every motor scooter approaching us from Laos was loaded down with Johnnie Walker scotch, Marlboro cigarettes, TV sets, soap and toothpaste, electric fans, even motor scooters, disassembled and packed in kits. The land we traversed was barren and unpopulated, and it seemed odd that so many men had fought and died for real estate worth so little.

We drove for two hours, almost to the doorstep of Laos. Off to the right, down a dirt road, was the deserted base at Khe Sanh where U.S. Marines had withstood a seventy-six-day siege in 1968. It sits in a long, low valley, surrounded by 3,000-foot mountains, and except for the outline of a weed-clogged airstrip, there is little to distinguish it from the rest of the countryside; you could drive right by never knowing anything of consequence ever happened there. Everything of value—concrete from the bunkers, sheet metal from the latrines, spent bullets and artillery shells—had been lugged away years ago by local villagers and either sold or used to repair nearby homes. The trenches where Americans lived like tunnel rats were filled in, and over them farmers had planted coffee trees. The sky was heavy with the threat of rain, and a wind murmured out of the jungle-covered hills. A dog barked, then silence. No village was within sight. No cars passed on the road. No sound except the wind. My driver and Mr. Tam stayed in the car while I walked the perimeter of the airstrip, feeling as alone as the last survivor of a lost platoon.

I jumped at the touch of a hand on my shoulder. I turned and behind me was a young man in sandals and a thick sweater. *Was he an apparition? There wasn't anyone here a minute ago.* Nguyen Van Tran had come up the road on foot at the sight of my car. He held out a small display case with U.S. dogtags, Viet Cong medals, North Vietnamese Army insignia, Zippo lighters engraved with slogans like, "WHEN I DIE I'M GOING TO HEAVEN BECAUSE I'VE SPENT MY TIME IN HELL." Tran tugged at my sleeve. "Look," he said. "Good souvenir. Real souvenir. You buy?" I found his presence as a salesman offensive to the memory of the brave men—on both sides—who had fought and died at Khe Sanh. I told him so, but I don't think he understood. At least I hadn't been hustled. Stuff like his was available throughout Vietnam, and I knew it was all fake, produced by industrious Vietnamese capitalizing on tourists' lingering fascination with the war.

The siege of Khe Sanh took the lives of 205 Americans, more than 1,000 South Vietnamese, and as many as 15,000 North Vietnamese. The Americans had occupied the valley to anchor the western defense of the

DMZ and to use it as an eventual jumpoff for interdicting the Ho Chi Minh Trail. The North Vietnamese had besieged it as a distraction, hoping to camouflage their buildup for the nationwide Tet Offensive. In the end, no one won the battle for Khe Sanh. North Vietnamese resistance eventually melted away in March, and the 1st Cavalry Division reopened Highway 9 in April, relieving the battered Leatherneck garrison. In July the Marines blew up the bunkers, rolled up the metal sheets covering the airstrip, and withdrew. Khe Sanh went back to what it had been and what it is today—a forgotten valley at the end of the earth.

{{{  }}}

KHE SANH—LIKE IA DRANG, Hamburger Hill, and many other battles during the American War—was fought, indirectly at least, for control of the Ho Chi Minh Trail, a meandering track and logistical marvel that started in a gorge that North Vietnam's troops called Heaven's Gate. It cut through five provinces in Vietnam, three in Laos, and two in Cambodia before reaching its terminus in Tay Ninh Province, a ninety-minute drive from Saigon. Without the Ho Chi Minh Trail, Hanoi's dream of uniting the two Vietnams might have remained only a dream, especially in light of the heavy Tet losses in 1968. It made the difference between victory and defeat. Without it, the United States might never have learned one of the important lessons of the war—that airpower alone doesn't guarantee victory and that military might is often no match for nationalism. As many as 2 million men walked to war over the Ho Chi Minh Trail between 1959 and 1975.

"We march all day bent under the weight of our packs," one of Hanoi's first soldiers on the route wrote in his diary. "In the heat and humidity we are forced to stop often for rest and to get our breath back. In the evening, utterly exhausted, we hang our hammocks and mosquito nets from the trees, and sleep under the stars. At times we have to search far from the trail for a waterfall or spring where we can drink and fill our canteens. There are tigers and leopards in the jungle, and we knew about attacks on stragglers and people who have become separated. We climb mountain faces of over a thousand meters, pulling our headbands down over our eyes to filter the sun's rays. From the summit a spectacle of splendor and magnificence offers itself to us. It is like a countryside of fairy tales. Those who get sick we leave at the next way post. The group continues to march. We must have faith in our struggle, in our leaders and in our country to endure these tests of suffering and pain, when we can no longer distinguish the line between life and death."

The trail confounded America's top military strategists for a decade and was as much a logistical nemesis to them as the B-52s were a deadly nightmare to the North Vietnamese. Then the war ended and the Ho Chi Minh Trail—which wasn't really a trail at all but an intertwined network of roads, dirt paths, and arteries covering 10,000 miles—was abandoned, to be reclaimed by the jungle, the leeches, and the ghosts of hard times. For a generation, this place belonged to history.

Now, as I crossed Quang Tri Province in the first days of the Year of the Snake, along a washed-out mountain road near Khe Sanh, a remarkable transformation was under way. The long-silent jungle stirred again with voices and movement and, at last, the dividends of peace. In the largest state-financed public works program since the war, the Ho Chi Minh Trail was being reborn and rebuilt, this time as a national highway that would link Hanoi to Ho Chi Minh City, 1,050 miles south. The twenty-year project would cost $400 million, a staggering sum for one of Southeast Asia's poorest countries. Three hundred bridges needed to be built, hills razed, tunnels burrowed. Narrow dirt roads would be widened, raised for flood control, and paved. Unexploded mines and bombs had to be located and defused. The conversion of the Ho Chi Minh Trail to the Ho Chi Minh National Highway was, I thought, the perfect metaphor for Vietnam's own journey from wartime deprivation to peacetime development.

Before leaving Hanoi, I had met with government officials who dismissed the concerns many voiced about the project. Environmentalists said the highway would disturb ecologically sensitive areas, including Vietnam's first national park in the North. Culturists worried that the lives of minority tribes would be disrupted. Economists questioned the feasibility of the project, suggesting it would have been far less costly to upgrade the existing national road, Highway 1, which runs down the eastern seaboard, or improve the North-South rail line.

"No, we can make this work," Ha Dinh Can, the project's general director, told me. "The highway will have a big economic impact. There will be a huge boost to employment. Timber and coffee producers will have easier access to markets. Tourists will be able to get to remote areas that were unreachable before. A whole new section of the country will be opened up to development. Driving times between major cities will be shortened." He neglected to add that the highway would also strengthen Vietnam's military capabilities and make it easier for soldiers to reach the homeland of minority tribes, whose loyalty to the state was frequently questioned.

But whatever its peacetime evolution, the Ho Chi Minh Trail will forever remain entangled in the myths and realities of war—in the U.S. bombing, as relentless as it was, that managed to shut the artery for only two days in a decade's time, in the deaths of 20,000 North Vietnamese soldiers, in the kinship that bonded people who lived and worked on the trail, sometimes for years at a stretch, and found in their communal hardship an inexplicable romanticism and contentment.

"I loved everyone with a passionate love," wrote Le Minh Khue, a Hanoi novelist who lied about her age and joined the army at fifteen. She worked for five years repairing bomb damage on the trail. Of her feelings for her fellow workers and the southbound boy-soldiers everyone called the "Hanoi men," she wrote in her book *The Stars, The Earth, The River* that hers was a love "only someone who had stood on that hill in those moments could understand fully. That was the love of the people in smoke and fire, the people of war."

The project officials in Hanoi told me the initial survey work on the new highway had begun two weeks earlier and, if I wanted to take a look, that I should locate the 11th Engineer Brigade. That proved difficult. The washed-out road that ran off Highway 9 crossed a bridge built by the Cubans and followed a jungle-covered ridge into the interior. There was no sign of an encampment, no indication that anyone else had passed this way in years. After a few miles we happened upon three barefoot Montagnard women collecting firewood. Mr. Tam rolled down his window and asked if they'd seen any soldiers. But he spoke Vietnamese; the women spoke only their tribal language. They shrugged and smiled, their betel nut–stained teeth black as coal. We went on. I was about to give up the hunt and suggest we turn back when our driver spotted a cluster of bamboo huts and tents off to our right, at the base of a steep ravine. "That's got to be them," Mr. Tam said. "Who else would be living out here?" We parked and made our way down the muddy hill, half-walking, half-sliding on our heels.

It was lunchtime. The thirty members of the 11th Engineer Brigade showed no surprise at finding an American poking around the Ho Chi Minh Trail. One of them poured me a bowl of chicken and rice broth from a charcoal-warmed caldron. Freshly washed fatigues were laid to dry across the bushes. No one carried a weapon. I lit a Marlboro and passed around the rest of the pack, which was received enthusiastically. We went inside a bamboo barracks to get out of the sun. There was a poster of Ho Chi Minh on one wall but no amenities such as toilets, electricity, or running water. I asked how many of the soldiers had been on the trail during the war. Three hands went up. I asked how many of their fathers had been on the trail, and almost every one raised his hand. Unlike the U.S. military, enlisted men and officers were social equals in the 11th Brigade, as they were in all North Vietnamese Army units during the war. They bunked side by side in the barracks, hunkered together around the same campfire at mealtime, and shared all the same hardships. Privates and sergeants addressed their officers as *Anh*—"Big Brother"—not "sir" or "lieutenant."

One of the young soldiers, Lieutenant Dam Trong Nam, was eager to engage me in conversation. He was, I think, the only one who spoke English. How long had I lived in Vietnam? What did I think of Vietnam? Did I like the Vietnamese? How old was I? How many children did I have? Did I think Vietnam was making progress economically? What was the future of relations between Vietnam and the United States? He would translate each of my answers for his men. They looked at me with compassion upon hearing I had no children and murmured approval when I said I thought relations were improving and that the two nations were moving toward a position of lasting friendship.

Lieutenant Nam gave me his address and asked me to write. I handed him my business card and said I'd be happy to take him to lunch any time he was in Hanoi. But he said he wasn't likely to get home for a year or two. "We're in the middle of nowhere here," he said. "We don't get leaves or weekend passes. Where would you go if you got a pass? On a jungle walk? But when you think of what the people went through during the war on the road, you don't complain. We're building our country just like they did, only in a different way. We're helping develop the economy. I really hope the Americans understand how important the highway is and help us more and more to develop our economy."

The Ho Chi Minh Trail was born on May 19, 1955, Ho Chi Minh's sixty-fifth birthday, when, with the French colonial army defeated and gone for a year, Hanoi began laying plans to bring South Vietnam under its control. Major Vo Bam, a logistics specialist who had fought the French in the Central Highlands, was put in charge of forging a supply route to the South. The mission was so secret no written records were kept. Hacking through triple-canopy jungle, avoiding villages, enduring biting cold and suffocating heat, hunger, exhaustion, and disease, Bam and 500 volunteers from the 559th Engineer Brigade—the unit's motto: "Blood May Flow but the Road Will Not Stop"—skirted the Truong Son Mountains, crossing Route 9 just east of Khe Sanh, and plodded south. The rudimentary track they carved out would fuel the American War.

Using elephants, horses, sweat, brawn, Chinese-made Phoenix bicycles (the same brand of bike I now rode in Hanoi) that could carry 300 pounds of supplies, and, later, trucks, Hanoi's volunteer Shock Youth Brigades Against U.S. Aggression for National Salvation eventually turned Bam's old footpath into a vast labyrinth of hundreds of hidden paths, bypasses, parallel tracks, and access roads onto which traffic could be rerouted, as in a railroad switching yard. By 1968 buried communications cables and a pipeline ran alongside Truong Son Road—only the Americans called it the Ho Chi Minh Trail—and by 1974 it carried convoys of trucks, speeding along a modern paved highway with rest and service areas and comfortable bungalows for VIP visitors.

"We got our orders to move south in 1966," Nguyen Duc Bao, a retired colonel, recalled. "The trail was very secret then. When we had to cross a dirt highway near a village, we'd lay a canvas sheet over it, and the last man across would roll it up so there'd be no footprints. We carried our own weight in weapons, supplies, medicine. We set up storehouses for rice. Usually, it was a twenty-day walk from one storehouse to the next. In between, we ate roots.

"At first, the American bombing wasn't so bad. But malaria, snakes, starvation, drowning, accidents were very deadly. In the four months it took us to reach the South, a hundred men from my regiment died. I counted twenty-four different ways you could die on the road."

The United States dropped 1.7 million tons of bombs on the Ho Chi Minh Trail and made Laos the most heavily bombed country in history in an unsuccessful effort to cut off supplies and infiltration. It used rain-inducing techniques to flood the trail, Agent Orange to strip away the jungle awning, chemicals that broke down the soil into mud. It gave anti-personnel cluster bombs their first significant test on the trail and dropped "invisible" parachutes—sensor devices that burrowed into the ground like bamboo sprouts and relayed data back to Nakkon Phanom in Thailand for evaluation. The U.S. aerial campaign set the forests ablaze, triggered landslides, left the trail littered with scorched vehicles; bits of corpses were collected piece by piece and buried in pots. But month after month, year after year, the soldiers and supplies reaching the South increased. The CIA estimated that it took 300 bombs to kill one North Vietnamese soldier.

"My unit shot down thirty-two U.S. planes," Nguyen Thanh Son, a fifty-year-old former antiaircraft gunner, told me. We were in his modest Hanoi home, where he leafed through an album with grainy black-and-white photos of his war days and kept refilling my teacup. I asked him what he thought of the Americans who had rained terror on the trail. "I used to think of your pilots as savages when they were in the planes," he said. "Then I saw three or four who'd been shot down, and they were like little children. They cried. They were afraid of the bombs—the *American* bombs—like we were.

"Our trenches were only large enough for Vietnamese, not the Americans, who were very big. So, when we'd get a warning that American planes were headed our way, we gave them shovels and said, 'Dig your own trench.' They dug very quickly. They were frightened. In short, up close they were human beings like us."

Son said it was funny, but despite the death and destruction he witnessed, he still clung to memories from those years that were warm and reassuring. The best friends he ever made were along the road. There was beauty in the sounds of soft rain tapping on an overhead jungle canopy and in the sight of cloud-shrouded mountains. Solitude and companionship were strangely intertwined. There was comfort knowing the achievement of one was the accomplishment of all. Son remembered almost every detail from those years, even the names of the photographers such as Trong Thang, who had spent time with his unit and who developed his film in glazed clay pots by candlelight and helped bury the dead by day.

Trong Thang was one of North Vietnam's most celebrated wartime photographers, and with Son's introduction I went to see him. Thang had spent four years documenting daily life on the Ho Chi Minh Trail and in 1991 toured fifteen U.S. cities with his photographs. The images were haunting, focused more on the emotions of war than the chaos of war: a rare moment of tenderness between a teenage soldier and a girl volunteer; a North Vietnamese soldier named Dien sharing his water canteen with a wounded South Vietnamese infantryman; three adolescent privates with uncertain smiles and arms over one another's shoulders headed off for a commando mission from which they knew they would not return. "After taking their picture, I had to turn away and weep," Thang said.

We went through several cartons of black-and-white photos. I was fixated by the faces—the clear, steady eyes, the smooth, acne-free complexions, the expressions that radiated determination and devotion but still held something back. I knew these same faces from the streets of Hanoi. I passed them a hundred times a day. And they were all so young.

"Our happiest times on Truong Son were when we got mail from home," Thang said. "We'd read the letters aloud to each other. Pretty soon one soldier would laugh over something in a letter, then everyone would laugh until the forest shook with laughter. Then you'd feel so guilty for being happy, you'd cry, and the whole forest would cry.

"We hungered for love. I remember watching, from behind a bush, three girls take off their clothes and bathe in a stream. When they emerged, they looked like fairy princesses. They were so young, so beautiful. I wanted to shoot their picture, but I didn't because they were nude, and it wouldn't have been appropriate. An hour later, they were killed in a B-52 strike. I still ask myself, 'Why didn't I take their picture nude to keep their memory alive for history?'"

{{{ }}}

To the Vietnamese, at least those of the North, the Ho Chi Minh Trail remains the symbol of the war. Most of the men, and many of the women, I knew in Hanoi who were over forty-five had been on the trail, and they spoke of it with reverence. They had survived the world's deadliest road, and over the course of sixteen years they had built a legend.

Many had left home as teenagers who had never shaved or held a girl's hand and returned to their parents as thirty-year-old veterans, aged beyond their years. Strange, but I never found anyone who had gone back to see what the abandoned trail looked like in peacetime—or even wanted to. Some, like Son, the antiaircraft gunner, didn't even like the idea of turning the trail into a highway, preferring that it be left untouched—a monument, however inaccessible, to a generation's rite of passage.

"The most important memory of life is time on Truong Son Road," Son said. "When we vets get together, we often say, 'We have nothing now. We are very poor. We have only the memory of Truong Son Road.' It was a time of hardship, of sacrifice, but in a way it was also a time of happiness because we were young and still romantic then."

## { 14

# CLOSURE

THE HO CHI MINH TRAIL STOLE THE ADOLESCENCE of North Vietnam's young, as surely as the war itself robbed America of its innocence. For Americans, the words "Vietnam War" came to refer to an era, not just a conflict. It was an era of distrust, divisiveness, disconcertion, of long hair, drugs, rock music, and free love. It changed the relationship between generations, between media and government, people and politicians, those who served and those who did not. Those who went returned home to hear World War II vets in the VFW halls tell them they hadn't fought in a real war. Those who chose to stay at home had to grapple with the consequences of their decision and would never know the answer to a question every American male has asked himself at one time or another: *Would I have the balls to be brave in combat?*

But undeniably antiwar activists had scored a brilliant strategic victory: Not only had they been smart enough to duck the threat of death in combat, as Tom Wolfe wrote, "they had also managed to shift the onus onto those who fought. Never mind Ho Chi Minh and socialism and napalmed babies and the rest of it. The unspeakable . . . goal of the New Left on the campuses had been to transform the shame of the fearful into the guilt of the courageous." Then, ten or fifteen years after the war ended, a funny thing happened. Thousands of people who had avoided the draft became Vietnam wannabes. They began identifying themselves as veterans, sometimes weaving elaborate tales about their lives in the jungles of Indochina. Vietnam was such a defining moment for their generation that even though these people had never set foot in Vietnam they had been there in their heads. Some probably believed their self-deluding fantasy; others apparently fabricated service histories because they carried some emptiness in a culture that finds heroes and defines honor through war and the call to serve.

Before long "Vietnam" became an adjective, usually with a negative connotation. We spoke of the "Vietnam era" and lumped it together with Watergate, the resignation of Nixon, political assassinations, and urban race riots. We were insistent that the 1991 Gulf War would not mire us in "another Vietnam"—that it would not be prolonged, fought without popular support, or marked by high casualties. And yes, of course, we would give our men and women a rousing welcome when they came home from the 100-hour Gulf War, so rousing we might forget that we never embraced those who came home from Vietnam.

Never before had the United States committed so much in battle and ended up with so little. Korea wasn't a victory either, but at least we had something to remind us we had not sacrificed in vain—an independent South Korea that eventually became democratic and prosperous. But Vietnam? We had endured what was, after the U.S. Civil War, among the most traumatic events in our nation's history, and there was nothing to justify the costs. We had been outfoxed at the negotiating table and outmaneuvered, though not outfought, on the battlefield. We had fled for our lives, abandoned an ally, seen the enemy flag fly over a now-communist land we had paid dearly to save. We weren't who we thought we were. We were not invincible. Perhaps we weren't even morally superior.

We couldn't figure out whom to blame or how things had gone so wrong. What were we to think when an architect of the war, former Defense Secretary Robert McNamara, told us in his 1995 memoir, "Yet we were wrong, terribly wrong. We owe it to future generations to explain why." There wasn't much to do but grieve. At the Vietnam Veterans Memorial wall. In confessionals when haunted GIs got together. Over our POWs and MIAs, even though no POWs remained and there was nothing left of our MIAs except scattered teeth and bone fragments. We were shocked when former U.S. Senator Bob Kerrey said that, on a moonless night thirty-two years earlier, he led a Navy Seal mission to eliminate several prominent Viet Cong in a Mekong Delta village. When the confusion of combat lifted, he realized he and his men had killed twenty civilians, he said. The U.S. media geared up to fight the war all over again. (One reporter asked Kerrey what he thought about setting up a war-crimes tribunal to bring "people like you" to trial. To reporters who grilled him, Kerrey responded: "You wouldn't be asking me those questions if I had been in World War II.")

What was it that shocked us about Kerrey's admission and the related story that appeared in the *New York Times Magazine*? That innocents die in war? That a Medal of Honor winner could be a wartime assassin? Not likely. What should have surprised us was that the pain and guilt of Vietnam kept popping up every time we thought we had buried them. We had admitted the war was a tragic mistake, so why wouldn't it just go away? Part of the reason, I think, is that when confronted with Vietnam, time-frayed black-and-white images and Hollywood stereotypes of Vietnamese and American combatants spring to mind. To update those images, to humanize today's face of Vietnam in order to understand postwar Vietnamese, is, for many, to lay the pain and guilt to rest.

We may have entered Vietnam naively—but not without warnings. In the early 1960s, Undersecretary of State George Ball told President John F. Kennedy if he went ahead with plans to up the U.S. ante from a commitment of "assistance" to South Vietnam to one of "limited partnership," it would mean "within five years, we'll have 300,000 men in the paddies and jungles and never find them again." Mike Mansfield, the Senate majority leader, warned Kennedy, "South Vietnam . . . could become quicksand for us. . . . It is not an American war." Not exactly words to warm the hearts of Cold Warriors. The position that prevailed was articulated by McNamara in January 1964 during testimony before the House Armed Services Committee: "The survival of an independent Government in South Vietnam is so important to the security of all of Southeast Asia and to the Free World that I can conceive of no alternative other than to take all necessary measures within our capability to prevent a Communist victory." Having taken those military measures, and then some, McNamara would later say, "I never thought it would go on like this. I didn't think these people had the capacity to fight this way . . . to take this punishment."

"Communist" was the operative word in McNamara's testimony to the House committee. Had Ho Chi Minh been a Buddhist dictator, a Catholic warlord, an imperial soldier of fortune—*anything* but a communist—I suspect the United States would have been content to track the war from afar. What the United States went to war against was communism. It just happened to be North Vietnam's misfortune to be standing in the way. To dismiss Ho as a communist puppet, as administration after U.S. administration did, was a grave miscalculation. It ignored the depth of Ho's nationalistic passions, and it misrepresented Vietnam as a tool of international communism, which it never was.

Ironically, despite misreading all the signs in Vietnam, the United States ended up achieving the objectives it set out to fulfill by going to war in Indochina. Communist insurgencies in Southeast Asia sputtered and failed. With stability, most of the region—with the notable exceptions of communist Vietnam and Laos, military-ruled Myanmar (Burma), and a Cambodia ravaged by Pol Pot's Maoist-inspired genocide—enjoyed an era of development and prosperity unparalleled in the Third World. The Berlin Wall came down. The Soviet Union collapsed. The achievement of these goals was, to some degree at least, an unplanned byproduct of the war and was, to a large degree, a result of forces the United States had unleashed on the world: globalization, democratization, and the opening of free-market economies. In country after country—from Africa to Asia to Latin America—military governments were retired, political futures were decided by ballot boxes instead of guns, and state-run economies gave way to private enterprise. What brought about Vietnam's transformation in the 1990s from a rigid, repressive country to one offering increasing personal liberty and economic opportunity had nothing to do with the government's desire to democratize and everything to do with the forces of globalization.

{{{  }}}

WHEN I WORKED IN SUB-SAHARAN AFRICA during the 1970s, we used to joke that you couldn't buy an African government—you could only rent one for a day. Ethiopia, for example, had been a longtime U.S. ally; its next-door enemy, Somalia, was a Soviet satellite state. Then overnight Ethiopia kicked out the Americans and turned to Moscow for military advisers and millions of rubles in aid. Almost simultaneously Somalia expelled the Soviets, tore down the anti-American posters in Mogadishu, and threw open its arms to the Americans. The flip-flop had less to do with ideology than with who was offering the best deal. In the Central Africa empire, President Jean-Bédel Bokassa, a Christian, pocketed $2 million from Libyan leader Muammar Qaddafi and adopted the Islamic faith and the name Salah Eddine Ammed. No sooner had Qaddafi gotten on his plane for the flight home to Tripoli than Bokassa said, oops, he'd made a mistake. Ammed the Muslim became Bokassa the reborn Christian.

Vietnam was different. It didn't beg, and it wasn't for sale. Sure, it accepted aid money, sought foreign investment, cultivated friends—but all that bought precious little influence. The World Bank put together an annual package of $3 billion for developmental assistance every year I was in Hanoi. It sweetened the pot with millions more in incentives if Vietnam took certain steps toward achieving a free-market economy. Vietnam never cashed in on a penny of the incentive money because it never adopted the extra reforms Western donors wanted. "You can't pressure these guys," said Andrew Steer, head of the World Bank's Hanoi office. "They do things their own way, at their own pace. If they thought we were interfering, I have no doubt they'd say, 'Thanks for your help in the past and now it's time for you to go home.'"

This attitude perplexed many Americans. They came bearing gifts. They had lots of advice and an abundance of good intentions. They'd put motorcycle helmets on the kids to make the roads safer and condoms on the men to make families smaller. They'd teach Vietnam about democracy and free enterprise. They'd save the wildlife, protect human rights, wire the country for broadband. Admirable goals all. The problem was that their agenda was often not Vietnam's agenda. One day a group of two dozen high-tech U.S. executives who had fought in the war flew in. Many, returning to Vietnam for the first time, were millionaires. Two arrived aboard their own planes. They made the rounds for high-level meetings at various ministries.

"If you're going to catch up with the rest of Southeast Asia, you need high-speed Internet access," one executive said. "My company can do that. We'll wire Vietnam for broadband. The entire country. For free." Government officials listened politely, thanked their guests, and said they'd consider the offer. And so it went with each offer. The businessmen went home, mumbling that the Vietnamese were ingrates, arrogant, out of touch. *They just don't get it. They've got their heads in the sand.* There were moments when I agreed. But the bottom line was that it was about priorities, not money. And broadband wasn't high on their list of immediate priorities. Political stability was. Education was. And better roads, more plentiful rice harvests, increased employment opportunities, a higher standard of living. Everything, though, was undertaken with caution and much deliberation. They looked around at their neighbors who had embraced democracy and Western models of development: Indonesia was a political shambles, the Philippines an economic wreck, Thailand a social disgrace with its flourishing sex industry. Even the most liberal Vietnamese didn't want that. Most were content to move with vigilance and patience, characteristics that had served Vietnam well in the past.

I asked a thirty-year-old Viet Kieu who had returned to Vietnam for his first visit since fleeing as a child of war what three adjectives he would use to describe his homeland. He said "nostalgic," "sad," "inspiring." Strangely, it is all those things. It is nostalgic, for me anyway, because my generation—even those who never set foot in Vietnam—came of age in this faraway land and lost an innocence here that can never be reclaimed. It is sad because Vietnam could have been much more prosperous and healthy if its entrenched, aging leadership had sought reconciliation between North and South and understood that nationalism can mean challenging the failures of one's government as well as applauding its accomplishments. Given the dangers of challenging, most Vietnamese opted for safe passage. Trinh Cong Son—the antiwar balladeer known as the Bob Dylan of Vietnam—forsook social protest and turned to writing love songs before he died of cancer in the spring of 2001. Bao Ninh—whose internationally acclaimed book *The Sorrow of War* had been criticized by Vietnam's generals as insufficiently celebratory of the communist victory—took to writing short stories for newspapers. They had surrendered their creative voices. And Vietnam is inspiring because a proud, industrious people endured terrible times, both during and after the war, and were strong enough to bury the past, to capitalize on the peace, and to reach out to people like me who were once their enemy.

Perhaps the graciousness and warmth Americans receive in Vietnam reflect a universal mentality that is not unique to the Vietnamese: Those who have suffered—even if they have brought the suffering upon each other—share a bond. "You have your pain," said economist Ngo Duc Ngo, who served in North Vietnam's army and lost two brothers in the American War. "We have our pain. So we understand you." The irony is that the Vietnamese understand us better than we understand them. We became so self-obsessed with our pain that we never thought much about theirs. Theirs was a pain rooted in a stunning statistic: One of every ten Vietnamese was killed or wounded in the war. If the United States had suffered as many casualties as Vietnam did, our dead, on a per capita basis, would have numbered 27 million.

An hour's drive northwest of Hanoi lies the Thuan Thanh Rehabilitation Center for military veterans. One hundred thirty-six men live there. All are paralyzed; most were soldiers of the American War. Sometimes in the night Be Van Nhop hears a voice that calls out from the next room, "Rush forward, comrades! The enemy's everywhere," and Nhop will answer softly, "Be still, Tran. You are having a bad dream. Be still."

Tran falls silent, and the next morning he has forgotten his nightmare. By lunchtime he has joined Nhop to watch a pickup badminton match among the staff. Nhop moves the wheelchair, which he calls a "flying dragon," through the center's paved yard with dexterity, his forearms muscled, his hands callused from years of self-propulsion.

"In a way we are lucky because we live as a family here," Nhop said. "We have sympathy for each other and love each other—and anyone who knows what it is to suffer in war. Some time ago an American soldier from the war came to visit us. He had lost both legs. When we saw his condition we cried and hugged him. We considered him one of us. The fact we were enemies on the battlefield didn't matter. Here at Thuan Thanh we were friends."

One of the doctors, Dinh Van San, showed me around the center. It didn't remind me at all of the cheerless, antiseptic VA hospitals I'd seen in the United States. Thuan Thanh was just a cluster of one-story buildings constructed around the yard. It looked more like a school or a rural hotel than a hospital. Around the facility a village had grown. Families had moved into the village to be near crippled loved ones. Village children adopted uncles from among the vets who were without families. The vets were free to come and go as they pleased, and you'd pass them cruising down the road in their flying dragons or hanging out at the shop near the front gate, drinking Coke and smoking 555s.

The integration of the veterans into the community reflected Vietnam's belief that the best rehabilitation was not to isolate war invalids. Most of the vets, if they didn't need continuing medical attention, were reabsorbed into families and villages, where the local populace granted them a large measure of lifetime respect in recognition of their sacrifice.

"Sometimes you see psychological scars of wartime experiences," Dr. San said, "but most of the veterans have dealt with their injuries in an amazingly optimistic manner. One man has learned how to repair radios. Another is writing short stories. Several are learning English. You'll find surprisingly little self-pity or bitterness."

Dr. San introduced me to Nguyen Van Hoi, a lieutenant wounded in Quang Tri Province after a three-month trek down the Ho Chi Minh Trail. I told him I had spent a lot of time in the province in the late 1960s. We looked at each other for a moment in silent acknowledgment of a shared past. What passed between us is what the nineteenth-century Vietnamese poet Nguyen Trai must have had in mind when he wrote: "After war the people you meet differ so from former times." I asked Hoi if he didn't sometimes ask himself, what if?

"Sure I wonder what my life would have been like if no war had happened," he said. "But if I am angry, it is mostly with myself. I need help to do anything. Eat. Dress. Piss. And that makes me angry. I see my friends feeding themselves, using the toilet, and I say, 'If they can do that, why can't I learn to take care of myself, too?'"

The center at Thuan Thanh was established in 1965, the year the

United States began its sustained bombing of North Vietnam. Today all sixty-one provinces have similar facilities, and in principle soldiers from the defeated South were entitled to the same care Hoi and Nhop received. In reality it didn't work out that way. Priority went to the Northern victors. The Southerners, for the most part, were left to fend for themselves.

{{{  }}}

FIVE YEARS AFTER THUAN THANH RECEIVED ITS FIRST PATIENT, Bill Clinton, who had written, spoken, and marched against the war, sent a letter to the head of a local Arkansas ROTC, thanking him for "saving me from the draft," which he called "illegitimate" for forcing men to fight a war they might oppose. It was a decision that would color his relationship with GIs, past and present, when he became commander in chief of U.S. forces. But now, as my assignment in Hanoi was drawing to a close, Clinton, serving as president of the United States, was flying across the Pacific, headed for Vietnam. His state visit would symbolize all that was ironic and inexplicable about the war: The most prominent American to dodge the jungles of Vietnam was the one who would make reconciliation and closure a hallmark of his presidency.

"He has a lot of nerve [to go to Vietnam] after he dodged the draft and failed to do his part," retired Admiral Thomas H. Moorer, a wartime chairman of the Joint Chiefs of Staff, told my *Times* colleague Robin Wright before she left Washington to travel with Clinton to Vietnam. "I wrote to the mothers of the men who were killed, and I know how they feel. I don't see how he has the nerve to go. It's totally inappropriate."

I couldn't follow his reasoning. If Clinton didn't move the relationship between the United States and Vietnam out of the past, who would? His successor, George W. Bush, who also had taken a pass on Vietnam and hardly ever left the shores of North America? Or were we to grieve and wrestle with guilt and redemption for another generation, as Robert Mc-Namara had done in his books and his trips back to Hanoi to discuss "missed opportunities for peace" with former North Vietnamese commanders? (McNamara had expected a frank exchange of views. That's not the Vietnamese's style; they insisted the only ones who missed opportunities were the Americans by not going home earlier.) Yet Admiral Moorer was right in that Clinton did have nerve to make the trip, even if he had widespread bipartisan support at home for the trip. A lot was at stake: If Vietnam's communist leadership decided to play hardball, Clinton stood to look like a fool; if he made one small misstep—if, for example, he paid tribute to Ho Chi Minh or laid a wreath at Hanoi's memorial to its fallen soldiers or acknowledged that Agent Orange had caused birth deformities—he would anger millions in the United States.

Hanoi's leadership was ambivalent about the visit. On one hand, senior officials very much wanted good relations with Washington, and they realized the visit represented a kind of final triumph—an acceptance by Washington of Vietnam's war-won unification and independence. On the other hand, they were nervous. If Clinton was confrontational on human rights and religious freedom, it would be embarrassing. If he was bombastic on the strengths of democracy and the weaknesses of communism, his visit could be a catalyst for political change, particularly among the postwar generation. What the leadership did not want was a free exchange of ideas that might get people wondering if communism really was the best route for economic development and individual fulfillment. So the Old Guard opted to downplay the visit.

The news that Clinton was coming to Vietnam in four days was limited in the Vietnamese press to a thirty-four-word announcement. In *Vietnam News*, it appeared next to a long article in which a senior official urged journalists to have "firm political convictions" in order to "firmly defend socialist Vietnam." No details of the visit were provided the rest of the week. The time of Clinton's arrival wasn't mentioned. Neither were the name of his hotel, the route his cavalcade would travel, his schedule, and whom he would meet. But the lapel buttons Coca-Cola executives passed out by the thousands—American and Vietnamese flags sprouting out of a Coke bottle—confirmed something big was afoot.

When Fidel Castro visited Hanoi a few years earlier, officials had to bus kids in from the countryside and give them Cuban flags to make a crowd. Russian President Vladimir Putin attracted nothing more than yawns and a score or so of curious onlookers outside his hotel when he visited in 2001. But for Clinton, the Vietnamese went nuts. They started lining up on the road from Noi Bai Airport at 4 P.M. By the time Clinton arrived at midnight, young Vietnamese by the tens of thousands stood six-deep along the airport road, and as his limousine sped by a throaty roar of excitement filled the night. Another huge crowd gathered outside the Daewoo Hotel to cheer his arrival. The police had never seen a spontaneous display of public enthusiasm before and didn't know what to do. So they threw up rope barriers and pushed at the throng of twenty-somethings with electric cattle prods, to no avail. Everywhere Clinton went for three days there were multitudes of cheering young people.

What they cheered wasn't Clinton the man. It was what he represented: prosperity, opportunity, freedom—attributes in short supply in Vietnam. This was the voice of the postwar baby boomers, and it underscored the vast generation gap between the young who wanted change and the old-time conservatives who liked things as they were. Clinton's reception unnerved the leadership. For days afterward the press banged away on the need for young people to hold fast to Vietnam's socialist traditions and nationalistic values.

Despite their misgivings, Vietnam's leaders were good hosts. Ho Chi Minh (who would have been 110 years old) was conveniently off in Moscow when Clinton arrived, his corpse being pumped up and touched up. And the memorial to Vietnam's war dead near his mausoleum was closed for "renovation," thus sparing Clinton an uncomfortable visit, as every foreign dignitary was expected to make. The politburo also let Clinton deliver his major speech—to college students—on live national television, a concession Hanoi had never made before to any head of state. An estimated 20 million people—one of every four Vietnamese—watched it.

A gaggle of 300 foreign journalists—the likes of which Vietnam had not seen since the war—descended on Hanoi for the visit, and most of us traipsed out to the university for Clinton's speech, which would be delivered in a lecture hall, with a bust of Ho Chi Minh off Clinton's right shoulder, the American and Vietnamese flags, side by side, to his left. His speech struck a tone that reflected remarkable sensitivity toward Vietnam and the Vietnamese. He did not lecture or tell Vietnam how it should run its affairs. Instead he spoke of a history of shared suffering that had bound former enemies with different cultures, religions, and languages in some sort of common destiny.

Two centuries ago, during the early days of the United States, we reached across the seas for partners in trade and one of the first nations we encountered was Vietnam. In fact, one of our founding fathers, Thomas Jefferson, tried to obtain rice seed from Vietnam to grow on his farm in Virginia two hundred years ago. By the time World War II arrived the United States had become a significant consumer of exports from Vietnam. In 1945, at the moment of your country's birth, the words of Thomas Jefferson were chosen to be echoed in your own Declaration of Independence: "All men are created equal. The Creator has given us certain inviolable rights—the right to life, the right to be free, the right to achieve happiness."

Of course, all of this common history, two hundred years of it, has been obscured in the last few decades by the conflict we call the Vietnam War and you call the American War. You may know that in Washington, D.C., on our National Mall, there is a stark black granite wall engraved with the name of every single American who died in Vietnam. At this solemn memorial, some American veterans also refer to the "other side of the wall," the staggering sacrifices of the Vietnamese people on both sides of that conflict—more than three million brave soldiers and civilians.

This shared suffering has given our countries a relationship unlike any other. Because of the conflict, America is now home to one million Americans of Vietnamese ancestry. Because of the conflict, three million American veterans served in Vietnam, as did many journalists, embassy personnel, aid workers and others who are forever connected to your country.

Almost twenty years ago now, a group of American servicemen took the first step to reestablish contacts between the United States and Vietnam. They traveled back to Vietnam for the first time since the war, and as they walked through the streets of Hanoi, they were approached by Vietnamese citizens who had heard of their visit. Are you the American soldiers, they asked? Not sure what to expect, our veterans answered, yes, we are. And to their immense relief their hosts simply said, "Welcome to Vietnam."

More veterans followed. . . . When they came here, they were determined to honor those who fought without refighting the battles; to remember our history, but not to perpetuate it; to give young people like you in both our countries the chance to live in your tomorrows, not in our yesterdays. As Ambassador Pete Peterson has said so eloquently, "We cannot change the past. What we can change is the future."

Two nights after Clinton's university speech, I dined with several Vietnamese officials in Ho Chi Minh City. Clinton had clearly been a hit, with the young as well as with the Old Guard, but the officials said politburo members had been so unsettled about Clinton's speech they had agreed to the live broadcast only on the condition that the government receive a copy of the speech three hours before its delivery. If there were any surprises, they would simply pull the plug and blame the blackout on technical difficulties. No objections were raised. "We are closer today than we were yesterday because of Clinton," one of my guests said. "He played by the rules. He showed an understanding of our culture and respected our dignity. That's all we ask, but that has not always been the case with American presidents."

Clinton's trip to Vietnam represented a significant step toward reconciliation. For everyone, except those who would never accept the notion of a communist Vietnam, there was every reason to believe that now, more than twenty-five years after the shooting stopped, there was light at the end of the tunnel. It was the light of closure.

{{{  }}}

DURING THE WAR we all had a short-timer's calendar, and we'd cross off the days one by one as our return to The World—home—drew closer. The plane that would take us there was known as a Freedom Bird. "How long you been in-country?" a GI would ask. "Eleven months, two weeks, three days," would come the reply. "Oh, man, you're *short*! You'll be back in the Big PX in the Sky like in no time." The day my short-timer's calendar ran out in 1970, I was drunk by 2 P.M. and walked unsteadily up the ramp to my Freedom Bird. It took me to Bali, where I lay alone on a beach for four days to wash away the imprint of Vietnam and the war.

This time, in the late spring of 2001, I felt no elation at the thought of leaving. I e-mailed a friend in London and said, "Four years in Hanoi gone in a flash. The gig is up." It was about as long as a correspondent stayed in one of our bureaus, and the time had come to move on, in this case back to Washington, D.C. My friend e-mailed back, "The gig may be up but the game's not over. You'll find new adventures." I hoped he was right. But discovering peacetime Vietnam would be hard to beat. Sandy and I had seen a country emerging from years of isolation. We had seen a country taking the first fitful steps from a state-run to a free-market economy. We had seen Americans as well as Vietnamese wrestling with ghosts from the past, and we had encountered a postwar generation for whom names like Khe Sanh and Hamburger Hill rang no bell of recognition.

Taking potshots at Vietnam's Old Guard and criticizing its leadership were not difficult. But it was easy to forget how far Vietnam had come. Fifteen years ago the Vietnamese wore homemade raincoats of palm leaves, didn't have enough to eat, and traveled by foot (or bicycle if they were middle-class). They had no individual liberties except those sanctioned by the state. Vietnam still had a long way to go before it met internationally acceptable standards on human rights and religious freedom. But the winds of change were stirring, and today the Vietnamese have more personal freedom than they have ever known—and arguably have as much as the South Vietnamese did in the era of U.S. sponsorship.

The question never was, Can Vietnam make it? It can. The book on how to turn an economic backwater into a developed nation has already been written—in Korea, Taiwan, Singapore, and elsewhere. With its literate, entrepreneurial, proud people, all Vietnam had to do was follow the instructions. The real question is, *Will* it? In time, I suspect it will. But the unimaginative elderly leaders who don't appear to know much except how to follow the rules have wasted so many years with their dithering that the goalposts—compared to the progress enjoyed among Vietnam's regional neighbors—have grown more distant. While Singapore's leaders wire their country for broadband, Vietnam's grapple with how much information they can safely dish out without letting people get so well informed they might challenge the government's legitimacy or the wisdom of Marx's doctrines. In many ways, though, Vietnam has been the victim of the West's unrealistically high expectations. When the country opened up to foreign investors and tourists in the late 1980s, we proclaimed the birth of a new Asian economic tiger. That was our aspiration, not the government's. It wanted to move as Vietnam always has: cautiously and deliberately. As a result of that caution, Vietnam remains closer to impoverished Laos than it does to developing Thailand. Yet the Vietnamese have always had staying power and been good at capitalizing on opportunity; their country brims with potential.

{{{  }}}

THE MOVERS CAME ON A THURSDAY. It was a springlike day, and you could see the western mountains from our ninth-floor balcony. In the nearby lake where Senator John McCain had crashed after being shot down in 1967, a lone fisherman was at work, propelling a tiny rowboat by his feet, which were placed in stirrups attached to the oars. In less than six hours the movers had packed up our memories and left our apartment empty. The place had looked warm and welcoming before. Now the bookcases were empty, and the barren walls had been stripped of the Vietnamese paintings Sandy had bought. It was no longer home.

Once again I was about to be rootless, which is both the curse and the blessing of a wandering life. Counting the war, I had spent nearly six years in Vietnam. I was comfortable with what I had learned about the country and intrigued with all that still mystified me. I had first arrived in Vietnam in 1968 to cover the war lugging only a suitcase and a cold-water Thermos that a friend in the United States had given me as a farewell gift. I left behind my parents, two brothers, and a sister. My parents were now long gone, and my three siblings had died while I was far off in Vietnam. My brother Ernie had been killed in an automobile accident while I was surviving the war. My surviving brother and my sister died of cancer during my last two years in peacetime Vietnam. The fact that the years had slipped by so quickly—that I, the youngest, was now the last of my family—distressed me. Vietnam had both given to and taken from my life.

Sandy and I checked into the Metropole, with our two cats, for the final weekend in Hanoi to await the Ministry of Culture's clearance of my books and the tapes of a documentary Sandy was producing. I don't know how people found out where we were, but the man who drove the motorcycle taxi Sandy regularly rode knocked on our door with a huge bouquet of flowers. Pham Kim Ky, the woman who had searched for years for her MIA son, arrived with a set of lacquer plates. My waiter-friend at Au Lac Café gave me small statues of three old Vietnamese men. One represented wisdom, one love, and one luck, he said. So many gifts piled up in our hotel room that we had to buy an extra suitcase.

Son Khanh Nguyen called to say goodbye. I had met him when he was a ten-year-old on the streets selling postcards and pirated copies of *The*

*Sorrow of War.* I had helped him go to English-language classes and get a job at a restaurant that an Australian Viet Kieu had set up to get street kids into a secure environment where they could be trained as waiters and cooks. Now a French attorney had taken a liking to Son and enrolled him in the French International School. "This school is very good. But it is sooooo difficult," Son said. "I don't know if I can do it." I reminded him how far he had traveled since he had first hustled me four years earlier into buying a stack of postcards I did not want. "Just keep trying, Son," I said. "There's no turning back." He said he would write and let me know how he was doing.

Finally it was time to go, to leave Indochina as I had done twice before in the bad days of war. This time my Freedom Bird was Vietnam Airlines Flight 833, Hanoi to Bangkok. I was sober. I had just turned sixty-one. I was ending my career as a foreign correspondent where it had begun more than thirty years earlier. Vietnam had been my bookends. Our French-made Airbus lifted off the runway at Noi Bai and banked westward toward Laos, over a sea of rice paddies, then jungle, and finally the Truong Son Mountains and the Ho Chi Minh Trail. I remembered the apprehension I felt when I had first seen Vietnam from the window of a Pan Am jet as we descended into Saigon in 1968, and I thought about the war. But only for a moment.

It seemed so long ago.

# ACKNOWLEDGMENTS

I OWE MANY THANKS, especially to the countless Vietnamese who shared their confidences, trust, and hospitality without ever asking for anything in return. They made Vietnam feel like home. They brightened my days and many became friends. To them I offer apologies for knowing so little about contemporary Vietnam when I arrived and hope they give me a passing grade for the knowledge I accumulated over four years. I also hope they one day will own the same freedoms I do— the freedom to choose their leaders, to speak their mind without fear of reprisal, to gain unfettered access to information.

My wife, Sandy Northrop, shared every day of the Vietnam experience with me, and I couldn't imagine having spent those four years without her. Her enthusiasm for Southeast Asia was infectious, her intellectual curiousity a stimulant for me. We made a good team, and of that, we are both proud. She produced and directed two moving documentaries on Vietnam—*Pete Peterson: Assignment Hanoi* and *Vietnam Passages: Journeys from War to Peace*—that were broadcast on PBS to wide acclaim. The latter closely follows the themes and tone of this book and in many ways represents the visual interpretation of *Vietnam, Now.*

Shelby Coffey, the former *Los Angeles Times* editor, gets the credit for putting a bureau in Hanoi at a time Western newspapers were paying little attention to Vietnam. I thank him for a good decision and for letting me have a shot at the assignment. Thanks also to Simon Li, the *Times* foreign editor, and his colleagues on the foreign desk who offered unwavering support and wise editing that saved me from a thousand blunders. I am indebted as well to the Pew Foundation and the director of its journalist-in-residence program, John Schidlovsky, for the fellowship that enabled me to complete the writing of this book.

Anil Malhotra, a World Bank developmental economist, was my ace in the hole when I couldn't make sense of Vietnam as well as a wonderful companion with whom to explore the pleasures of Hanoi. Others who shared guidance, friendship, and a caring for the future of Vietnam include Chuck Searcy, a former GI now coordinating demining projects in Vietnam; Lady Borton, a Quaker aid worker who has devoted nearly thirty years to Vietnam and wasn't even chased away by the war; Bob Schiffer at the U.S. Embassy; Mark McDonald of the *San Jose Mercury News*; Peter Ryder, president of the American Chamber of Commerce in Hanoi; Ambassadors Pete Peterson of the United States, Michael Mann of Australia, Aftab Seth of India, and Ryu Yamazaki of Japan; Dennis de Tray of the International Monetary Fund; and Andrew Steer of the World Bank.

Irwin Rosten massaged the manuscript into shape and made many suggestions that were incorporated into the text, and Katherine Reese found scores of misspeaks and misplaced punctuation marks in what I thought was an error-free manuscript. My agent, Carl D. Brandt, who shepherded me through five previous books, once again provided sage counsel and unflagging enthusiasm. At PublicAffairs, publisher Peter Osnos and editor Kate Darnton were my last, best defense and a great team to have on my side.

# PHOTO CREDITS

*Bicyclists cross the Red River into Hanoi,* Pham Ba Hung; *Can Tho's floating market in the Mekong Delta,* David Lamb; *The French bombed Vinh from 1931 to 1952,* David Lamb; *Le Van Vang and his wife, both tailors, hold their wedding picture from 1963,* David Lamb; *When Senator John McCain returned to peacetime Hanoi,* Vietnam News Agency; *Nguyen Duc Bao, a retired North Vietnamese Army colonel, spent nine years fighting the French, ten the Americans, and six Pol Pot's Khmer Rouge guerrillas in Cambodia,* David Lamb; *East Germany helped Vinh rebuild after the war,* David Lamb; *For eight years during the war, Trinh Thi Ngo was the voice of the communist North Vietnam,* David Lamb; *The most respected South Vietnamese journalist to work for the Americans during the war, Pham Xuan An,* David Lamb; *Like four hundred thousand southerners, Duong Cu, a former South Vietnamese Supreme Court justice, was sent to reeducation camp when Saigon fell in 1975 and was later denied meaningful employment,* David Lamb; *Nguyen Thi Le holds a picture of her husband, a South Vietnamese*

*Army artilleryman,* David Lamb; *Nguyen Van Tran on the airstrip at Khe San, where U.S. Marines withstood a bloody seventy-six-day siege in 1968,* David Lamb; *A group of U.S. veterans mingles with former Viet Cong guerrillas,* David Lamb; *Three college professors—all former North Vietnamese soldiers—with the author in Hanoi,* David Lamb; *Returning GI Chuck Owens meets an elderly village woman in Pho Vinh, once a Viet Cong stronghold,* David Lamb; *With nowhere to go, a handful of Amerasians remain stranded at a ramshackle refugee camp in the Philippines,* David Lamb; *Hoi Trinh with Amerasian children in the Philippines,* David Lamb; *For the first time in decades, soldiers are back on the Ho Chi Minh trail—this time as unarmed engineers who are turning the legendary route into a national highway,* David Lamb; *Life has improved dramatically for the post-war generation and young Vietnamese like photographer Pham Ba Hung have opportunities their parents dared not imagine,* David Lamb; *A boom in coffee production has made Vietnam the world's third largest coffee exporter and brought prosperity to parts of the Central Highlands,* David Lamb; *Vietnam's government worries that the move toward a free-market economy could lead to moral decay and the importation of "social evils" from the West,* Sandy Northrop.

PUBLICAFFAIRS is a publishing house founded in 1997. It is a tribute to the standards, values, and flair of three persons who have served as mentors to countless reporters, writers, editors, and book people of all kinds, including me.

I. F. STONE, proprietor of *I. F. Stone's Weekly*, combined a commitment to the First Amendment with entrepreneurial zeal and reporting skill and became one of the great independent journalists in American history. At the age of eighty, Izzy published *The Trial of Socrates*, which was a national bestseller. He wrote the book after he taught himself ancient Greek.

BENJAMIN C. BRADLEE was for nearly thirty years the charismatic editorial leader of *The Washington Post*. It was Ben who gave the *Post* the range and courage to pursue such historic issues as Watergate. He supported his reporters with a tenacity that made them fearless, and it is no accident that so many became authors of influential, best-selling books.

ROBERT L. BERNSTEIN, the chief executive of Random House for more than a quarter century, guided one of the nation's premier publishing houses. Bob was personally responsible for many books of political dissent and argument that challenged tyranny around the globe. He is also the founder and was the longtime chair of Human Rights Watch, one of the most respected human rights organizations in the world.

.    .    .

For fifty years, the banner of Public Affairs Press was carried by its owner, Morris B. Schnapper, who published Gandhi, Nasser, Toynbee, Truman, and about 1,500 other authors. In 1983 Schnapper was described by *The Washington Post* as "a redoubtable gadfly." His legacy will endure in the books to come.

Peter Osnos, *Publisher*